THE APPRENTICE
OF SPLIT CROW LANE

The Story of the Carr's Hill Murder

Jane Housham

riverrun

First published in Great Britain in 2016 by riverrun
This paperback edition published in 2017 by

riverrun

An imprint of
Quercus Editions Ltd
Carmelite House
50 Victoria Embankment
London EC4Y 0DZ

An Hachette UK company

A CIP catalogue record for this book is available
from the British Library

PB ISBN 978 1 78648 1 603
EBOOK ISBN 978 1 78648 1 597

10 9 8 7 6 5 4 3 2 1

Typeset by CC Book Production
Printed and bound in Great Britain by Clays Ltd, St Ives plc

THE APPRENTICE OF SPLIT CROW LANE

ripping – reveals a society in moral turmoil'   William Shaw

Vell-written and excellently researched, this chilling tale of a
ictorian sex murder opens out into an investigation into the
orkings of the lunatic mind and the asylums which treat it'
                                                        Julie Peakman

his was a fascinating read, particularly for those who are interested
 Victorian provision of the criminally insane ... She also gives us
 lavour of the population of the time, of the haves and the have-
 ts and really conjures up details of the place where the crime was
 mmitted in astonishing detail ... enlightening and clear-sighted'
                                                Cleopatra Loves Books

ousham is a dogged researcher and evocative writer. She sheds
 owerful light on the era, skilfully describing the febrile, lawless
 osphere of 1860s Gateshead'   Jenny McCartney, *Mail on Sunday*

 lls, for the first time, the gruesome tale of an 1866 child murder
 lding modern insight to the murderer's motives and the system
 t incarcerated them'   *History Revealed*

Contents

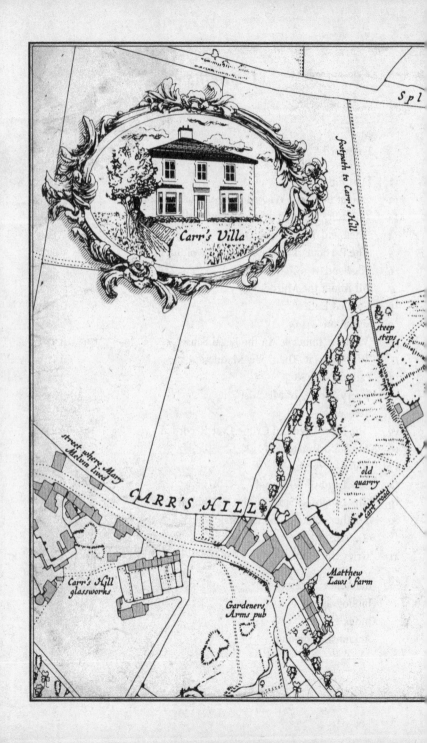

Carr's Villa

Spl

footpath to Carr's Hill

steep steps

old quarry

Carr road

CARR'S HILL

street where Mary
Melvin lived

Carr's Hill
glassworks

Gardeners
Arms pub

Matthew
Laws' farm

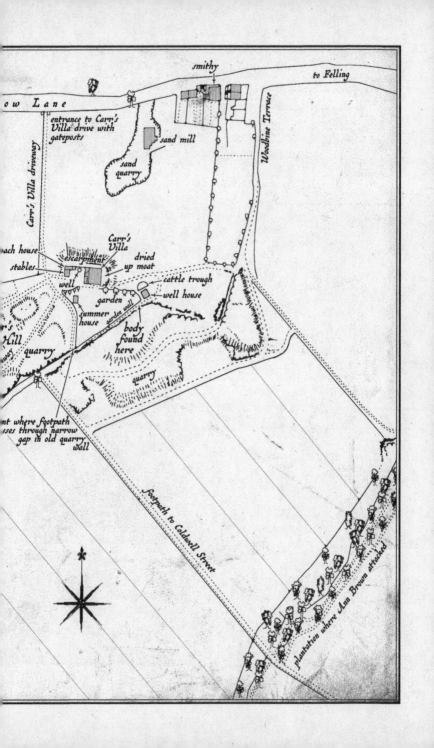

Foreword

It won't be giving anything away if I say that this book concerns a murder. That much is clear from the subtitle. It's a true story. Everything in it is based on contemporary records and reports that I have researched as thoroughly as possible. Until I became interested in the case, as far as I'm aware no one had given it any thought for well over a century. It was not a famous case, although interest in it from various quarters persisted for a considerable number of years after it happened. During the time that I was writing the book, I became very caught up in the first season of the *Serial* podcast, presented by Sarah Koenig.[1] The question of whether Adnan Syed murdered Hae Min Lee in January 1999 became an extraordinary obsession for millions of people around the world. Before Sarah Koenig agreed to look into the case and the possibility that there had been a miscarriage of justice, Adnan Syed had been in prison for fifteen years and the case had been all but forgotten by the world. Then, when the spotlight of diligent inquiry was focused on the details of the case, it sparked *huge* interest. Through the incredible capacity of social media to gather together a mass of information and opinion, people pooled their insights and debated infinitesimally small issues, with most coming to a view on what the 'truth' was. Most fascinating was how polarised these views were, for there was, tantalisingly, just too little that was certain about the case to allow a single, definitive interpretation. Many people felt that Syed had been correctly found guilty, but others felt equally strongly that he had been framed or that there were other suspects who were more likely to have committed the crime. I think most people agreed that no one involved was particularly well served by the great edifice of the law, as represented by the police and lawyers in the case.

Once the public, in their millions, were hooked on *Serial*, nothing about the murder of Hae Min Lee was overlooked. Every single detail became freighted with significance; every witness statement, every phone record was scrutinised; the very words that had been transcribed were questioned and in some cases rewritten (a surprising number of slips had been made both in the original note-taking by detectives and in the transcription of statements). The 'story' was impossibly baggy, a gigantic tangle of threads and contradictory accounts, full of holes and knots. It may never be neatly ironed out and concluded, even though, as this was going to press, Adnan Syed was granted a retrial: there may always be conflicting versions of what really happened.

My book is partly inspired by *Serial*. Not because it concerns a similar possibility of a miscarriage of justice (although there are hints of that), but because, in looking into this old, forgotten case, I became equally driven to find out every available detail. Nothing about it bored me, although I was sometimes frustrated that there was less 'scaffolding' holding it up than I would have liked. But there was nothing to be done about that. As with the elusive facts of *Serial*, I've made the very best of it I could. And when the story reached a denouement (literally, an 'unknotting'), I found that my interest didn't end there.

What happened afterwards was just as interesting to me – almost more so – as the murder itself. I was well and truly hooked.

When you follow a trail of real events, you don't have the same freedom as a novelist to shape your narrative, to introduce extraordinary twists and turns, to manipulate your characters. The reality of the Carr's Hill murder is extraordinary enough, and the fact that it took place a century and a half ago makes it all the more compelling as it affords us insights into the beginnings of various forensic procedures. However, recounting a true story as it unfurled means that you have to take it as it comes. If the fiction-reader in me might have wished it had sometimes happened differently, at the same time I find the strange, oblique truth just as fascinating. One of the most satisfying things about writing this book has been the discovery of scattered pieces of it in unexpected places. I won't refer to it as a 'jigsaw' as that implies there was once a straight-sided whole which simply had to be put back together. On the contrary, this story that begins with a murder has been pieced together from fragments that no one else has seen as belonging together. Now, from those disparate elements, a remarkable and disturbing story emerges.

First Finders

One fine but chilly evening in April 1866, after a long day's work, Joseph Bourne tried to cheer up his wife Ann, who was feeling under the weather, with a stroll and a drink at a local pub.[2]

Leaving their three young daughters at home (perhaps with a kindly neighbour keeping an eye on them) they left the house at about seven o'clock. First of all they had an errand to run. With most workers working a twelve-hour day from 6 a.m. to 6 p.m., shops stayed open late to catch wage-earners' business. The Bournes walked down into the Felling so that Joseph could order a new suit from Mr Greaves, but the tailor wasn't at home. They went on through the village, towards Gateshead. At the local landmark known as Robbers' Corner they took a footpath across the open fields towards Mount Pleasant, then crossed over Split Crow Lane and came up through the village of Carr's Hill to the Gardeners' Arms at the top of the hill.

Perhaps the fresh spring air had helped Ann Bourne's headache. Perhaps she was still feeling poorly. The Bournes only stayed at James Harvey's pub long enough to drink a glass of ale each before they set off for home. It was gone half past eight now, almost dark and a cold clear night coming. They took the most direct way home, along one of the many footpaths that criss-crossed the high, rocky outcrop that gave Carr's Hill its name ('carr' being an Old English word for a rocky shelf). Here quarry workings had been slowly altering the landscape for as long as memory served, the footpaths being constantly retrodden as the ground was dug away at different points. There was no gas lighting up on the hill and care was required. A young man, Joseph Reaves, had once met his girlfriend there after his shift at Carr's Hill glassworks had finished; he fell into one of the quarries and died after splitting his head open.[3]

Not long after they set off along the cart track towards home, just by a big rock that formed a natural landmark, the Bournes met a man and a woman coming in the opposite direction, from the Felling, the man walking a few yards ahead of the woman in silence. The Bournes didn't know them and passed by without greeting them. Their way took them past Rowell's Farm, until recently farmed by Matthew Laws, and then past Carr's Villa, home to the Carr family whose name had become associated with the whole district of Carr's Hill (though in fact it had been plain Carr Hill long before they arrived). At this point the track narrowed down to a footpath between the garden wall of the Villa and the high, rough wall of the quarry just behind it. Enclosed in this way, the path must have become even darker as twilight turned to night. Just at the point where the Carr's Villa garden wall turned sharply to the left and the path opened up, Mr Bourne stumbled over something in his way. It was soft but heavy. He nearly lost his footing then peered down to see what had tripped him up.

'Oh, Ann, here's a child asleep!'

It seemed very odd that a child should be sleeping out on the path, stranger still that he or she hadn't stirred when accidentally kicked by Joseph. They saw that it was a young girl and, to their horror, that she had her hands tightly tied together in front of her. She was lying on her back, right across the path. Joseph Bourne scooped her up into his arms and, almost without thinking, they started back to the Gardeners' Arms with her as fast as they could manage. She was fully dressed apart from bare feet and legs, completely limp, and so cold that she chilled Joseph's hands as he carried her. Without stopping to check whether the child's heart was beating, the Bournes hoped she was still alive, but once they got her to Mr Harvey's pub and he had quickly ushered them into a back room, it was obvious that she was dead. Joseph Bourne laid the little girl on a table and desperately felt her chest to see if there was any heartbeat. There was none.

Both Ann and Joseph Bourne kept their heads in spite of their ghastly discovery. They left the pub straight away to fetch a police constable. They went down into Carr's Hill village but didn't know where to find the local bobby. Almost immediately they met the same man they had passed earlier, the man who had been striding ahead of the woman the Bournes had assumed was his wife, up on the Carr's Hill footpath. Now he was with a girl who looked about fourteen.

Joseph Bourne stopped the pair.

'Will you be so kind as to tell us where the police officer lives?'

'What's the matter?' asked the other man, revealing himself by his accent to be Irish.

The Bournes said they had found a dead child, but even as they started to speak, the Irishman stuck out his hand to Joseph Bourne.

'I know you. Shake hands! If it's not you I know, it's your brother.'

Bourne felt a sudden stab of anger. What was wrong with this fellow? Awful Irish blarney.

'I don't shake hands with strangers. We need to find the police constable.'

It was as if the other man had not heard the awful news the first time. Was he drunk? Now he said, 'Why, what's the matter?'

Joseph said again, 'We've found a dead child. We've taken her to Mr Harvey's.'

Now the man began to cry out and the girl clutched at his arm.

'Oh, Father, it must be our little Sally. Where is she, sir? We were just looking for her.'

Told again that the child was at the Gardeners' Arms, the pair started off towards the pub, quickly becoming distraught, while the Bournes carried on down into the village, looking for someone who would tell them where to find the constable. They met a woman who had once kept company with Joseph's brother and she told them where the local bobby, PC Alexander Kemp, lived.

Before long they had found PC Kemp and he hurried back to Harvey's public house with them. Kemp was a police officer with a real knowledge of his community. He recognised the child at once: he knew her family; he knew the poor father and older sister who had come to the Gardeners' Arms and who, having seen the body for themselves, had now had their worst fears confirmed. She was Sarah Melvin, 5½ years old, the youngest child of Michael Melvin and his wife Mary.

By now it was around a quarter past nine. The room where the dead child was lying on a table was crammed with people keen to see the corpse and play some part in the terrible events as they unfolded: the spectacle of the child's father and sister confronted by her bound corpse was a horror no one would easily forget and in the coming days there would certainly be something to boast about. PC Kemp turned them all out apart from two men, one of whom was Joseph Bourne: as the 'first finder', he had earned his place at the heart of the affair. Ann Bourne was not allowed to remain in the room: the macabre business of examining the body was a job for men to carry out. She waited for

4

her husband in another part of the pub. Even the child's father was obliged to leave, weeping and in shock. There was no question of his being able to stay with his dead child.

Once the room had been cleared, Kemp focused on the little girl.[4] Not only were her hands tightly tied together but a length of the same cord was knotted around her neck. The garrotte was too deeply embedded in the child's neck for him to be able to insert a knife blade in order to cut it, so he carefully untied the knot. He cut the cord from around the wrists and put all the lengths safely away in case they should need to be produced later as evidence.

Next Kemp faced the harrowing task of examining Sarah Melvin's clothes and body, an intrusive act that forced him to break deeply ingrained social prohibitions. The Melvins were a poor family and could not afford shoes and stockings for Sarah, but even the children of the poor wore one or two layers of petticoats over a chemise and drawers. Kemp worked diligently, keeping notes as he would surely have to give an account of this examination at the inquest that would need to be held, as well as in any criminal proceedings. He found what he believed was 'night soil' (faeces) on the hem of her frock and also near the shoulder. There were bits of hay and straw in her hair and sticking to her clothes and he collected these as evidence as well. Carefully removing layer after layer of underclothes, Kemp saw a lot of blood on the child's upper legs. He covered her again to await further examination by a doctor.

Securing the room, he then asked Mr and Mrs Bourne to show him where they had found Sarah. They led him back along the footpath to the place where she had been lying and he examined the area as best he could by the light of his lamp. There were no signs of a struggle and no bloodstains, at least none visible in the limited light. He found no straw either.

Kemp's next task was to head down into Gateshead (just under two miles away) to alert his superior officers to the crime, but on the way he met them already coming up: Chief Constable John Elliott and Detective Brown. All three went to the Gardeners' Arms. Mr Elliott sent for Dr Benjamin Barkus, a Gateshead physician with an official role as police surgeon, to make a formal examination of the body. Dr Barkus arrived at around a quarter past eleven. The procedure for dealing with a dead body discovered in suspicious circumstances was well established and no doubt helped to contain the horror of what was swiftly being revealed as a vicious attack on a very young child.

Dr Barkus examined Sarah Melvin's body where it lay on a table in a downstairs room of the pub. He noted that the body was cold. She was a well-developed little girl, with stout limbs. Although her hair was very dishevelled, her facial features were placid in death, the skin pale, the lips bluish. There were deep marks around her neck and wrists where she had been bound. Barkus deduced from the coloration of the marks that the cord had been placed around her neck before death or at the time of death, before circulation had ceased, whereas he felt the cord around her wrists had probably been tied after death.[5]

Dr Barkus now had to examine the child's genitals, which were very bloody. He discovered a shallow wound just within the entrance of the vulva, about half an inch long and running upwards and outwards. Barkus felt it had been inflicted with a sharp instrument. There was another wound running from the upper part of the entrance of the vagina which had split open her urethra. This wound was about an inch long and running upwards, as if the instrument that had caused it had been drawn up. Additionally there was a large wound from the entrance of the floor of the vagina extending backwards almost to the anus, nearly an inch and a half long and about half an inch deep at its deepest part, gradually becoming more shallow as it extended

6

backwards. There were abrasions to the flesh and bruising too. It was
the doctor's opinion that all these wounds had been done after the
child's death or just as she died, when the blood was ceasing to circulate. To reach this conclusion, Dr Barkus studied the blood spots on
Sarah's chemise and petticoats and made a note that he believed some
of them were venous blood as opposed to arterial, due to their dark
colour. It was clear that Sarah had been subjected to a horrible sexually
motivated attack but for now Dr Barkus refrained from the even more
intimate examination that would be necessary in order to discover its
exact nature. He would perform a post-mortem the next day which,
in keeping with medical practice of the time, would be carried out in
the victim's home.

What then happened to Sarah Melvin's body? What little is known
is rather confused. Mary Melvin, Sarah's mother, sub-let rooms in
the house of Mrs Margaret Thorburn and her husband Thomas, a
shoemaker, in Carr's Hill village. Mrs Thorburn gave a statement a
few days later in which she said that Sarah's body was brought to
her house at about ten o'clock on the night she was found, Friday 13
April. Mrs Thorburn said that she herself removed Sarah's clothes and
that her body was warm (although her limbs were cold). But Sarah's
body must have been at the Gardeners' Arms until around midnight
as Dr Barkus only began his examination after eleven o'clock. And
PC Kemp said that he kept Sarah's clothes as evidence once they had
been removed. Perhaps Mrs Thorburn's memory was blurred by the
horror of what had happened to Sarah, or perhaps she tried to paint a
more acceptable picture of the violated body being brought home and
lovingly undressed and washed.

Very little can be discovered about Sarah Melvin. Her short life passed
more or less unnoticed by the authorities. Her birth does not seem to

have been recorded although she appears as a 6-month-old baby in Felling in the census of April 1861, so perhaps she was born around October 1860. No record of her burial has come to light either, nor is there any mention of her funeral in the extensive reports about her death. Beyond the detail that she was a 'well-developed, stout' child, no one described her as she had been when alive, not even the colour of her hair. The details of the horrible injuries to her private parts were published in newspapers the length of Britain but there was little to be said about her as an individual. She died before she was much formed as a person.

Even if she had grown to adulthood, the chances are that Sarah Melvin would have passed through life without drawing much attention. Her parents were Irish immigrants who both worked as hawkers, selling goods door to door (like many such hawkers, they may even have been Irish Travellers, that is to say Gypsies,* but this would be little more than a guess). Mrs Melvin had a line in earthenware which she obtained from the Carr's Hill pottery and took around the local area looking for buyers. It must have been a hard life. At the time of the murder, Mary and Michael Melvin had six children: James, 19, who worked at a local coalmine, Catherine (known as Kitty), 17, Mary Ann, 14, Margaret, 12, and Jane, 11. Sarah (also known to her family as Sally) was the youngest child.

The Melvins' marriage was under strain. Three months before the calamity that had now befallen them, not long after Christmas, they had separated. Michael Melvin was lodging in rooms in the Felling and had their son James with him. Mrs Melvin had taken all her daughters to lodge in Carr's Hill, ostensibly so that they would be nearer to the

---

* The terms 'Gypsy' and 'Traveller' are often used interchangeably (along with 'Roma') for Romani people. English Romanis often self-ascribe as Gypsies whilst Irish Romanis more often refer to themselves as Travellers.

pottery, where the older girls had jobs. They had been afraid to walk home to the Felling at night when they left work, she said (those fears now seeming horribly justified). Perhaps, for the sake of appearances, it was necessary to have a public explanation for what was really a simple falling-out. Michael Melvin was supposed to be moving to Carr's Hill to join them again, as soon as things worked out, but it wasn't all plain sailing.

On the morning of 13 April, when Mary Melvin set off on her selling rounds, her youngest daughter was left to her own devices, as she must have been most days. Perhaps Jane, the next youngest child, was supposed to keep an eye on her. Though not really old enough to earn a living, even Jane may have had some work to do – every member of a poor family had to earn their keep as soon as they could and even if a child hadn't yet started paid work there would be jobs to be done such as fetching milk or keeping the fire going. Very young children were expected to entertain themselves, probably out in the streets or in the alleys at the back of their houses and to turn up for dinner and tea by the clock in their hungry stomachs. No doubt older women in the village would know which family young children belonged to, and there was very likely an informal arrangement that Mrs Thorburn would watch Sarah. The policeman, Alexander Kemp, knew Sarah Melvin by sight. In spite of the huge influxes of workers over the previous two decades, drawn to the mass of manufactories and foundries that had grown up all along the river Tyne, these villages were communities, people who knew and would look out for each other.

At midday Mary Melvin returned home and made the dinner. Sarah ate with her mother. It was a very simple meal, mainly bread. Then, driven by the need to keep money coming in, Sarah's mother headed off to work again. She would not return until six o'clock that evening. In the meantime, Sarah was once again unsupervised.

We don't know whether Sarah was upset about something; perhaps she was just bored. Her parents' separation, however pragmatic, had no doubt unsettled her as it would any child. It seems she decided to walk over to the Felling to see her father. Going by one or other of the footpaths past Carr's Hill quarry, it was less than a mile's distance between Mr and Mrs Melvin's respective lodgings. The walk would not have been unusually long and she had already developed sturdy limbs, no doubt from walking everywhere. Setting off not too long after dinnertime, Sarah knew the way past the quarry and arrived in the Felling at around half past one. She also knew where her father was living but when she got there he too was out working. There wasn't much for Sarah to do and her instinct was almost certainly to set off home again. She may have waited around a little, in the hope that her dad might turn up.

Two boys, young men really, James Mullen and Patrick Cain, were just then coming up another path that ended at Split Crow Lane near the Felling. They had been looking for birds' nests in the plantation near William Falla's nurseries, just to the east of Carr's Hill. James Mullen was 14 and had a job at the local pit; Patrick Cain was 19 and worked at the Felling Chemical Works. James knew Sarah as they had played together at one time. The boys saw Sarah standing in the gutter at the edge of the road and asked her if she was lost, but she told them she wasn't. Then James went into a nearby pub to ask the time, because he didn't want to be late for his three o'clock shift at work, and was told it was ten to two.

Sarah Melvin set off back home to Carr's Hill, retracing her steps along the footpath by the side of the quarry.

Mr Melvin was having a busy day, following up leads in the hope of getting some work. His work as a hawker seems to have been less steady than that of his wife. At five o'clock he went to see a Mr Alexander at the Brewery Field in Gateshead. Mr Alexander wanted a cellar 'taking out' (meaning digging out). The two men walked back together to the top of Mount Pleasant, at the Gateshead end of Split Crow Lane. Perhaps they had a quick drink together to cement the deal. By six o'clock Michael Melvin was hurrying home to the Felling to let in his son James, who would be wanting his supper. James was waiting for his father with the upstairs neighbour, Alexander Mullen (a relative of the boy James Mullen who had spoken to Sarah earlier, probably his uncle; James Mullen's father was dead). Together they got the fire going and ate something. Then Michael went over the road to Mrs Atkinson's pub, the Shakespeare (now renamed the Portland Arms) to ask for the loan of a barrow. Back home, he was standing at his front door when an acquaintance of his named Harry came to call on him. Harry was going to help him with the cellar job. Looking like a man diligently in pursuit of paid employment, Michael next walked down to the police station at the bottom of Felling High Street, where he had to see Mr Thompson, the Inspector of Nuisances, about another bit of work, digging drains for 'netties' (lavatories). In fact Thompson wasn't there. Michael walked back towards home, passing the local butcher, Mr Makepeace, standing in his shop doorway. They stood and chatted for about ten minutes, then Michael set off towards home again. It was seven o'clock by the time he got back.

In the meantime, Mary Melvin had returned from her afternoon's work at around six o'clock and found that Sarah wasn't at home. She asked the neighbours if they'd seen her and then, at around half past six, decided to walk over to Michael's lodgings as the most likely place for Sarah to have gone. She arrived just as Michael was coming back from the police station and she went inside with him. Of course, he hadn't seen Sarah at all. Their son James had gone back upstairs for company but now he came down to see his mother. Alexander Mullen came down too. Mary asked Michael if he would go over to the Shakespeare and stand her a glass of whisky, so the two of them went across to the pub. One thing led to another. There was a man called Forster in there and he bought Mary a whisky as well. Michael stuck to mild. Mary cajoled Michael into buying her a third whisky. She was surely not the only woman around who needed a few stiff drinks to ease her sorrows but this was not a good call. All sense of urgency about Sarah's whereabouts seems to have drained away at this point.

At around half past eight, Mary was ready to return to Carr's Hill but she wanted Michael to walk her back. He said no.

'It's turning dark. Will you just come up a piece of the road with me?'

'Alright.'

They came part way along Split Crow Lane, past Woodbine Terrace where the first path to Carr's Hill began. Instead of taking that path, they went on further to the drive leading to Carr's Villa, which was also a public right of way. This path would take them around the other side of Carr's Villa from the first path. Just at the bottom of the drive they passed a young man coming the other way but by now Mary and Michael had started arguing quite vociferously and barely took any notice of him. They had the impression that he was quite tall but, later, that was all they could say about him. He stood still as they went past. After a while they fell into an angry silence, Michael walking ahead of Mary. At this point the two paths converged and it was here that they met another couple coming arm-in-arm from the direction of Carr's Hill – Joseph and Ann Bourne. Again, they didn't take much notice of them, being wrapped up in their own troubles.

When the Melvins reached Mary's place they found that Sarah still hadn't come home. Mrs Melvin was too upset to go out looking for her, so Michael took another of their daughters, Mary Ann, and they

12

set off to search again. Almost immediately they met Joseph and Ann Bourne coming down from the Gardeners' Arms to find the police constable. They heard the dreadful news that the Bournes had found a dead child up by Carr's Villa and knew almost at once that it could only be their Sally.

2

One of the Most Wicked Counties
in the Country

Before dawn the next morning, despite having worked long into the previous night, PC Kemp went back to the place up on Carr's Hill where Sarah Melvin's body had been found. By half past four on Saturday 14 April, Kemp was at the corner of the footpath where the wall of Mr Carr's garden turned away from the quarry – the spot where Sarah's body had been found – searching for any sign that violence had taken place there. He found nothing.

While he was there two men came along. Kemp knew them by sight: they were Robert Bell and Dennis McClure, who both worked as teazers* at the Carr's Hill glassworks. They were in their shirt-

---

* 'Teazer' was another name for the furnaceman at a glassworks. Teazers mixed up the powdered silica and other elements that were melted in the furnace to make glass and they were also responsible for calling the rest of the work team, boys and men, in to work when the furnace was reaching the right temperature to work the glass – as the heating process took around three hours, there was time to go round and knock them all up individually.

sleeves, either on their way to an early shift or returning from a late one, most likely going home still hot and sweaty. They sat on the wall to watch Kemp and perhaps to give their opinion on the child's death. Kemp said, later, that Bell and McClure 'came to me', suggesting perhaps that the men sought him out to tell him something in particular.

At about twenty minutes past six John Elliott, the Chief Constable, turned up, accompanied by Detectives Brown and Leech, and together the four men conducted a meticulous search of Carr's Hill quarry, which could be reached through a narrow gap in the high quarry wall next to the footpath. As the quarry was so enclosed, it seemed very possible that Sarah's killer had committed the murder there before moving her body out onto the more exposed path, perhaps intending her to be found more quickly (although such behaviour in an assailant would be unusual; a killer's instinct is more often to conceal their crime for as long as possible). But no evidence was found: no signs of a struggle, no footprints, no bloodstains. The men also scoured the ground for hay and straw, mindful that it had been found on Sarah's clothing and in her hair, but, again, none was found.

It was still less than twelve hours since Sarah's body had been discovered; the post-mortem examination of her body was not due to begin until noon. There would be an inquest but not until the beginning of the following week. The first reports of the crime would be published in the local newspapers almost immediately, but for now knowledge of what had happened to Sarah was still limited, both in extent and in terms of who knew about it (although word of mouth would be spreading like wildfire through Carr's Hill and the Felling). These policemen were already at the heart of the nascent investigation and must tamp down any emotional response to the horror of a child having been mutilated and, as seemed very likely, violated, before being killed and dumped on a footpath; they must carry out a professional investigation and find the perpetrator.

Both Elliott and Kemp had young daughters of a similar age to Sarah. Both were also under unprecedented pressure in the face of a huge increase in crime in the area over the past few months. Indeed, on Kemp's own small patch of Carr's Hill there had been what amounted to a crime wave. Yet the person or persons responsible for the growing notoriety of Carr's Hill remained at large.

Gateshead first recruited police constables in 1836. In the early years, when local administration was still run by the Select Vestry (a group of influential local citizens) it was the vestry who put forward the names of suitable men, from whom local magistrates then chose a skeleton force. Every man who stepped up to be a constable had to take an oath of allegiance:

> You swear that you will well and truly serve our Sovereign Lord in the Office of Constable for the Borough of Gateshead and good attendance give as well by night as by day. And that you will truly present all vagabonds, rogues and other suspected persons within your Constablewick. And all things that belong to the Office of a Constable you shall do according to the best of your skill and knowledge. So help you God.

The oath was written out (by hand) on the first page of the Attestation Book[6] and every constable who swore signed the book. Such was the continuity of practice that the word 'Lord' (referring to William IV) in the oath has been crossed out and replaced first by 'Lady' (for Queen Victoria), then by 'King' (for two Georges and two Edwards), then finally by 'Queen'. The list of policemen's signatures stretches unbroken from 1836 to 1968, with only the style of the handwriting changing over the years and fountain pens giving way to ballpoints.

John Elliott had signed the book in March 1839 and his was to be a very long and loyal career in Gateshead police force – he was known by the affectionate nickname of 'the Journeyman' for his long-serving solidity. Kemp's name first appears in February 1859. Later he was given Carr's Hill as his 'constablewick' and he certainly gave good attendance 'by night as by day'. It nearly killed him.

The sequence of events that was eventually to threaten Kemp's very survival began quite far away, at Byerside near Ebchester, about fifteen miles south-west of Carr's Hill. On a Monday night in September 1865 a fire broke out in one of the stackyards of Edward Davison, a farmer. Stackyards were effectively open-air warehouses where farmers kept their harvests of hay and grain, and a fire could be disastrous. The first fire at Byerside was followed by another on the same farm just three days later and the *Newcastle Courant* reported that 'the whole fell a prey to the devouring element . . . [Mr Davison's] crops for the present year are thus all destroyed, and it is stated that he is uninsured.'[7] As far as pointing the finger of blame went, the first fire was suspected to be the work of 'navvies who were smoking near the stacks' and the second to be the work of an 'incendiary'.[8]

On the very same night as the first Byerside fire, another blaze took hold in a stackyard roughly halfway between there and Carr's Hill, at Dockendale Farm near Winlaton. This time two boys were seen running away from the yard, 'one of them having a pipe in his mouth and shouting "Fire".'[9] At this point in the mid-nineteenth century, local fire brigades were rudimentary, where they existed at all, and there was no fire engine in nearby Blaydon. The police had no leads as to the firestarters either.

1865 was a year of heatwaves. The average temperature in April that year remained the highest on record until 2007, and on Midsummer's Day temperatures hit the high 80s Fahrenheit across most of England. By harvest time haystacks were tinder-dry and very easily set alight by accidental sparks. A fire in the stackyard of a farm near Kelso in Northumberland was thought to have started innocently when a spark fell from a farmhand's pipe.[10] But another fire the same night, near Hexham, was blamed on an arsonist because the stack was seen to be burning in two or three separate places at the same time. The stack belonged to Mr Stephenson, the superintendent of the local constabulary, so it seems likely that one or more miscreants with a grudge against their nemesis in the police force might well have set to with lighted rags. The newspapers reported that 'several fellows were seen lurking about the place'.[11] And it's well documented that very hot summers often lead to a rise in crime, tempers rising with the mercury.

There had been many incidents of incendiarism throughout the whole of England for decades, in particular during the Swing Riots of the early 1830s; other peaks were in 1844 and 1863. In fact the high levels of arson drove forward the setting up of professional police forces throughout the country. The new officers did make some inroads into rural criminality, even if resentment of their presence might have incited even more crime. Disaffected locals quite often wrote threatening letters to the police, as in this letter written by Samuel Stow of Polstead, Suffolk in 1845:

> . . . you can Doo As you please about keeping on These piece on if you doo you both Shall have a blaze very soon you May Watch day and night you Shall be sure to have it. And both These plecemen Shall have their Brains blown out.[12]

Policemen's homes were also attacked, their families taunted or assaulted.

Including the second fire at Byerside, six stackyard fires broke out within the space of four days in scattered locations around Tyneside. The earliest newspaper reports of the first appeared on the day of the last so it seems relatively unlikely that these first fires were started by copycats. Perhaps they can be put down to coincidence and the unusually dry conditions. But once the newspapers started to run stories about incendiaries, the number of fires increased alarmingly.

One week later, at Windy Nook, the next small village along from Carr's Hill, fire broke out in the stackyard of White House Farm. A farmhand was thatching the top of a stack when he was enveloped in smoke, suggesting a very daring incursion if this was the work of a firestarter. Luckily for the farmer, a Mr Richard Carnaby Forster, Felling Chemical Works, nearby, had its own fire engine and it was soon on the scene. Then the Gateshead borough fire engine arrived shortly afterwards, brought by Chief Constable Elliott and fifteen of his policemen. The fire service and the police service were one and the same (all thirty-three police officers doubled up as firemen and the service had acquired its first fire engine, secondhand, in 1862).[13] Again, this was particularly fortunate for Mr Forster as an opportunistic thief had opened one of the farmhouse windows and was just about to break in while all hands were tackling the blaze; he was spotted and arrested by a sharp-eyed officer.[14] Around a thousand pounds' worth of damage was caused – hundreds of thousands of pounds' worth at today's prices – but thankfully Mr Forster was insured. The *Newcastle Courant* reported that 'large crowds of spectators visited the scene in the evening,'[15] and perhaps, if the fire really had been started deliberately, the perpetrator stood among them enjoying the secret knowledge that he or she was responsible for the excitement.

That same night, Thursday 28 September 1865, while the fire still blazed at White House Farm, more fires were set, at Plawsworth, near Durham, and at Mr Thomas Robson's farm at Barlow, near Winlaton. Once again, there was speculation that a spark from a workman's pipe had started this fire, but as three or four more fires broke out at the farm in the course of the next few days there seemed to be more determined mischief afoot. Perhaps there was excited talk of a polter-geist amongst the agitated farm workers, but as an old shirt was found smouldering in a shed suspicion fell increasingly on a human arsonist.

Still more fires broke out – at Busty Bank Farm near Rowlands Gill and at Mountsett Farm near Lintz Ford (where a burning bundle of rags was again found near the fire). It was as if a ring of fire were beginning to enclose Newcastle and Gateshead.

Although this was the height of the Industrial Revolution and 35 per cent of the working population toiled in manufacturing, around 20 per cent still worked in agriculture; farming continued to be a huge source of wealth. Each haystack fire caused the loss of valuable produce whose worth was readily given in newspaper reports. The farms were entirely at the mercy of firestarters and little could be done to stop someone determined to start a blaze.

The *Newcastle Chronicle* published an editorial about the incidents:

For the last fortnight we have had to record almost daily some conflagration, more or less serious, in the homesteads of this neighbourhood . . . A recurrence of fires in the same stackyard, as at Barlow, and the almost simultaneous bursting out of fires in stackyards in the same vicinity can lead to but one conclusion, that these catastrophes are wilfully produced, this conviction being strengthened by the finding of the bundles of burning rags.[16]

The day after the blaze at Lintz Ford, fire broke out at Matthew Laws' farm at Carr's Hill. The farm buildings lay just behind the Gardeners' Arms public house where Sarah Melvin's body would be taken in April the following year. Mr Laws' workers were sitting eating their bread and cheese at midday when they saw smoke from a stackfire. Men from Carr's Hill quarry close by came running to help and the burning straw was pulled down from the stack, saving the rest from catching fire. As at Windy Nook, both the fire engine from the chemical works and that of the Chief Constable rushed to lend assistance. Also on hand was a Mr R.R. Vanderkiste of the head office of Mr Laws' insurance company, who happened to be visiting Newcastle from Liverpool, and he was able to settle the loss 'very satisfactorily' on the spot.[17] He also paid all the men who had helped to put out the flames 'in a liberal manner'.[18]

It was at this point that PC Kemp began to keep watch over Matthew Laws' surviving haystacks (only one of fifteen had been destroyed thanks to the prompt action of all who had come to help). In November 1863 Kemp had been one of eight police officers in the Gateshead force to be awarded a good-conduct badge.[19] He seems to have been an exemplary officer who would push himself to the limit to protect his territory. Policemen who, like Kemp, went on night patrol to try to protect farmers' property risked their lives: PC James McFadden was killed in 1844 at Gisleham near Lowestoft while trying to protect a farm from arsonists and thieves.[20] And in fact it was virtually impossible to protect a farm at night. Under cover of darkness it was easy to evade any nightwatchmen and light a fire with a lucifer match.[21] In spite of Kemp's keeping vigil through the chilly autumn nights, a second fire broke out at Matthew Laws' farm just three nights later. Another large haystack was destroyed.

Chief Constable Elliott was being kept busy by the fires as well, in his capacity as head fireman. A week after the second fire at Matthew

Laws' farm, the Gateshead engine was called out to yet another stack-yard fire, this time at Mr Snaith's farm at Claxton, about a mile from Carr's Hill. Mr Elliott and his crew had to use their wits. Although there was a pond close to the farm, it was muddy and full of 'ingredients that threatened to fill up the suction pipes' of the fire engine, so they commandeered a wicker basket which was used as a filter. The fire was out within two hours.[22]

At nine o'clock on the evening of Wednesday 18 October, three days after the Claxton fire, a third fire was discovered at Matthew Laws' farm on Carr's Hill. This marked the limit of Alexander Kemp's endurance. He was 'compelled to go off duty in consequence of a severe illness, brought on through cold, caught through his nightly watchings'.[23] Another newspaper added, 'fears are entertained as to his recovery'.[24] He had caught pneumonia but no arsonists.

Who knows how closely those responsible for the fires were watching the reports of their crimes? One can only speculate about their motives and the feelings that seeing their fires taking hold provoked. If a single perpetrator was behind the cluster of fires centred on Carr's Hill and the Felling and they were keeping a close eye on the newspapers, perhaps they decided to give Alexander Kemp a break in which to recover, because the next fire in the area was not until eleven days later, at a farm in Low Fell, two miles from Carr's Hill. Perhaps it was not so much fun to start a fire when you knew your chief adversary was *hors de combat*. On the other hand, two tramps had been turned out of the farmyard at Low Fell that same morning and there was specu-lation they had returned and either set fire to the stack deliberately in revenge or accidentally while smoking their pipes. The ubiquitous clay pipes were a menace. The tramps and lads and navvies who were so often reported as having been sighted just before fires broke out take on almost mythic status as they were never caught. A fire was less frightening if a prosaic reason could be found for its breaking out. How did the farmhands and other local people feel when they saw the farmer's profits going up in smoke? Perhaps there were resentments at low wages or harsh treatment, perhaps some of them even knew who the culprit was but said nothing. Were the rumours about malign outsiders spread precisely to divert suspicion from a hot-headed local with a known grudge?

The spate of fires burned itself out, as such episodes will, and by early 1866 reports of arson had dwindled. There seems to have been a strong copycat element, with different perpetrators 'catching' the firestarting bug through newspaper reports and word of mouth. In some instances the motivation behind the fires was laid bare, in most cases it was not.

While PC Kemp survived his illness, the fires did claim a victim. On 7 December 1865 farmer Matthew Laws died at his farm on Carr's Hill. The stress of being the victim of arson three times in quick succession surely contributed to his death. He was 74 years old.

During these same months, other, more disturbing crimes were being committed in and around Gateshead. The case which particularly darkened the reputation of the district took place in mid-January 1866. Mary Ann Thirlwell, who was about 42 years old, was coming back from the pub with her husband. Mary Ann and George Thirlwell lived at the Felling; George worked down the pit. According to Mary Ann's account of events, the couple hadn't lived at the Felling for very long, so when George went ahead to stoke up the fire and warm the house, it was easy for Mary Ann to miss her turning and lose her way. By this time it was about nine o'clock in the evening. A man called Thomas Bell, 22, came up to Mary Ann with some other men. Mary Ann said she had known Bell by sight for years, so when he threw his arm around her neck she thought it was a joke and shrugged him off.

But Bell grabbed hold of her neck again and threw her down by the side of the road. One by one, Bell and the four men with him raped Mary Ann. Finally she was let go and tried to scramble over a wall to get away from them, but she was unable to get over and fell to the ground. Then the men came back and hit her on the head; Bell raped her a second time. By the time they left her she was unconscious. She finally managed to get home and, the next day, having told the local police sergeant what had happened, she identified Thomas Bell when he was brought to her house. Bell tried to blame two of his friends for the attack and Mary Ann identified two more of the men subsequently.

Thomas Bell, Joseph O'Neil, David Gaffin, Patrick Curo and Thomas Scanlon, all aged between 19 and 22 and all coalminers, were tried at Durham Crown Court at the Spring Assizes of March 1866. It was an interesting case because while it illustrated the tendency of rape victims to be vilified for being drunk and accused of lying about consensual intercourse later regretted, the jury found the five men guilty. Looked at dispassionately, from the detailed accounts of the trial given in local newspapers it does seem possible that Mary Ann lied about her ordeal. While she did have bruises on her neck and arms that could have been made by fingers, there was no physical evidence of rape, such as cuts or bruises on her genitals, according to the doctor who examined her. Also tending to undermine her account was the evidence given by PC Mallaby, who had been standing in the doorway of Felling Police Station when he heard a woman cry out. He went to see what had happened and found Mary Ann lying on the ground (she had just fallen off the wall), with all the accused near by. Mallaby helped Mary Ann to her feet and the young men then offered to see her home as they knew her. Since she didn't protest, he left her with them. Mary Ann swore she had no recollection of the policeman coming (and perhaps what Mallaby took for a lack of distress on Mary Ann's part was actually shock or even concussion). Although the men's barrister seemed to make a powerful case for their innocence, dismantling Mary Ann's account inconsistency by inconsistency, the jury nonetheless found against them. Thomas Bell was sentenced to fifteen years of penal servitude and the rest to twelve years.[25] Bell's punishment was more severe because he had known Mary Ann, because he had raped her twice and also because he had stolen money from her during the attack.

The verdict in the Thirlwell case was reached just a month before Sarah Melvin was murdered. On the same day that the case was heard, another terrible sexual crime was committed near the Felling. Several newspapers[26] carried the story that a little girl named Hannah Bell, aged 6, had been attacked by two men in a plantation halfway between the Felling and Carr's Hill. According to the newspapers, Hannah was the daughter of John Bell, a labourer at Felling Chemical Works, and the family lived between the Felling and Windy Nook. Hannah's mother had sent her to fetch milk at Carr's Hill Farm. On the way to the farm, Hannah had noticed two men standing in the lane and, as she returned, one of these same men grabbed her and carried her into the plantation. Both men then raped her and left her insensible. When she came to, Hannah managed to walk home and told her mother what had happened. A Dr Robinson was called and he confirmed that Hannah's account was consistent with injuries she had sustained. A further sad detail was that, after the police had been informed of Hannah's ordeal, they went to the place where she said it had happened and found the spilt can of milk as well as her little jacket. At the time the crime was reported in the newspapers, the two men had not been identified.

Yet another disturbing case was tried at Gateshead Magistrates' Court just two weeks before the murder of Sarah Melvin. Sarah Davison, who was described in the local paper[27] as an 'old married woman' (Mary Ann Thirlwell had been similarly described and she was only 42), had been travelling back to Windy Nook from South Shields by pony and cart with her 10-year-old son. They had been selling tripe all day, which was how Mrs Davison made her living. The newspaper said that the horse 'took bad' on the journey home, an echo of Mrs Davison as she had spoken in court. It was eleven o'clock at night by now and they stopped at a pub near Heworth (close to the Felling) to see if anyone could help them, but no one offered any assistance. As they were only a few miles from home they set off again. A man started walking along with them. This was John Wilson, a local joiner. Before long the horse had to be abandoned as it was 'very bad'. Then Wilson began to 'take liberties' with Mrs Davison: he threw her down on the ground and tried to rape her, but both Sarah and her son shouted as loudly as they could and Wilson ran away. In his defence Wilson said that he had been drunk but, although drunkenness was often accepted as a defence for many different crimes at this period, the magistrates sentenced him to four months' hard labour. In summing up, one of the magistrates, Mr Ramsay, said that the county of Durham was 'one of the most wicked in the country'.[28]

So, this place where Sarah Melvin had been robbed of her life was already notorious. It even came to the notice of the London *Times*, which published an article about Sarah's murder on 26 April:

The most extraordinary circumstances in connexion with this crime are that within a quarter of a mile of where the body of the poor child was found several incendiary fires have occurred within the past six months; that a most diabolical rape was committed six weeks ago upon a little girl, who was going for milk to a farm, and of the same age, by two villains who left her nearly murdered and insensible and that the police have been unable to discover the perpetrators of any of these outrages.[29]

*   *   *

26

The fingertip search of the crime scene by PC Kemp, Chief Constable Elliott and the two other detectives had turned up no clue. The next day, Sunday, crowds of Tynesiders made a trip out to Carr's Hill to visit the scene of the crime. As described by the *Dundee Courier & Argus* (in a singularly detailed report of all aspects of the crime so far):

> The house of Mrs Melvin was an object of eager curiosity. A crowd of persons stood about the doors the whole of the day, watching with keen interest the visitors to the humble dwelling. The place where the body was found was visited by some hundreds of persons during the day. Groups collected about the spot, the details of the crime furnishing ample topics for comment and speculation. Attention was directed to the spot by someone having written upon the face of the rock [presumably in chalk] an intimation that that was the place where the body had been found. The police have been indefatigable in their investigation, but we regret to say that up to Sunday evening they had not succeeded in apprehending the guilty party.[30]

If John Elliott had not yet completed his crime-scene investigations, it would be too late now: no potential clue was likely to have survived the desecration by throngs of sightseers of the place where Sarah's body had lain. The growing notoriety of Gateshead and its surrounding villages surely added to the sense of excitement and swelled the crowds keen to experience a frisson of outrage and horror. And if the shameful crimes of the past few months had put Gateshead in the headlines all over the country, the town's history of lawlessness went back much further than that.

3

'Carefully Planned by an Enemy
of the Human Race'[31]

In July 1811 the engraver Thomas Bewick was obliged to leave the modest house in Newcastle that had been his home for thirty years. Perhaps surprisingly, he chose to move across the river Tyne to Gateshead.[32] He was 58, so a fairly old man for the period (he would live for a further seventeen years). The relocation seems to represent that definitive move out of the mainstream that hardworking people so often decide to make towards the end of their career, but it was odd that Bewick should have chosen to live in Newcastle's less glamorous neighbour. He moved to a townhouse on West Street, which at the time was on the edge of Gateshead, looking out across fields to the Windmill Hills. In these first decades of the nineteenth century the main residential areas of the town were still clustered around the Tyne Bridge, in Pipewellgate, Hillgate and the High Street – though these were also the main manufacturing areas as well, for everything was mixed in together. From the first steep climb up Bottle Bank from the river, the town was all aslope on the flanks of Gateshead Fell. After that initial steep incline the High Street levelled out for a while, only for the climb to begin again, long and sustained towards Deckham and Carr Hill and the Fell proper.

In Bewick's day the Fell was still common land, 'a wide, spongy, dark moor' according to Robert Surtees in 1820.[33] This high, rocky landscape of gorse and briars had been a no man's land for centuries. Gypsies and other people thrown to the margins, such as miners evicted from tied cottages when coal seams ran out, built illegal lean-tos on the Fell made from mud and turf (commemorated in the name of Sodhouse Bank, now renamed more grandly as Sheriffs Highway). It was said that you could farm an illegitimate baby out to a foster-nurse up on the Fell with no questions asked. Gypsies and tinkers (or 'faws' as they were often called, a corruption of the common Gypsy surname Faa) pursued various ways of making a living there, including clog-making, pot-throwing, besom-making and rag-collecting.

The main turnpike road from Durham to Newcastle came up from the south and was confronted by Gateshead Fell, a great natural obstacle between the relatively gentle landscape of County Durham and the north country of Tyneside and the Borders. At nearly 600 feet above sea level, the Fell afforded wonderful panoramas in every direction, but no one would linger up there to enjoy the view when there was a constant threat of being robbed by muggers and cutpurses. The most notorious of these was Robert Hazlitt, who robbed a coach and a postman in 1770. After he had been tried and hanged, his tarred corpse was returned to the Fell and hung from chains, presumably to act as a deterrent. But reports of a 'Gateshead Fell Gang' in the local papers in the 1780s suggest this had not been entirely effective.[34]

Less than a year after he moved to Gateshead, Thomas Bewick fell ill and after several months of sickness he travelled the few miles to the village of Carr Hill to convalesce. He stayed with his friend Matthew Atkinson, the wealthy owner of Carr Hill House. Although it was only two miles from his home, this was essentially a retreat to the countryside. Carr Hill House was a large property with several acres of garden and a working windmill, just south of Carr Hill village. It had previously been used as a private lunatic asylum. The Fell villages, of which Carr Hill was one, were still very small and isolated, separated by tracts of wild moorland. Bewick's stay at Carr Hill seems to have restored him to good health.

From Carr Hill, one of the highest points on the Fell, the views extended to the sea to the north and east and also took in 'the whole navigable course of the river Tyne, the Cheviot hills . . . the Cathedral of Durham, and numerous seats'.[35] But the immediate scenery cannot have been so picturesque, for the Fell itself represented a rich natural resource which had been exploited, albeit in a piecemeal way, for centuries. Spoil heaps from coalpit workings and quarries lay everywhere as men discovered the extent of the 'great sweep' of sandstone layered above and between seams of coal. The stone 'was consistently superb for building and for making grindstones and millstones'.[36] Quarrying was a free-for-all: quarries changed hands frequently and were poorly regulated – leases might only be for a year or two and owners dumped their spoil heedlessly. Finished quarries were simply abandoned and usually filled in with refuse, sometimes storing up problems for future generations.

There was a powerful entrepreneurial spirit in Tyneside. Every natural resource needed to get rich was readily available. And if it wasn't naturally embedded in the earth, then it seemed that ships would bring it right to the doorstep. Waste was used as ballast in ships sailing to Newcastle to pick up cargoes of coal and other goods. When they arrived at the Tyne quayside the ships simply dumped the ballast (for a charge) but this waste contained elements such as sand and flints that took on new value as the raw material for emerging industries, particularly glassmaking.

Coal and iron were the foundations of the Industrial Revolution on Tyneside as elsewhere in England. The manufacture of sheet iron at rolling mills rapidly became a key industry in the mid-nineteenth century. Joseph Bourne, who found Sarah Melvin's body, worked as a roller at Fraser's ironworks down on the south shore of the Tyne near the Felling.

As well as quarries, Gateshead Fell was also dotted with windmills. Not for nothing was one of the villages on the Fell named Windy Nook. Almost certainly using grindstones made from the local stone, these had milled grain since the Middle Ages and, by the end of the eight-eenth century, they also ground sandstone to make sand for the glass industry. There were two windmills at Carr's Hill: as well as the one on Matthew Atkinson's land there was one next to Carr's Villa. We think of windmills now as quiet, graceful structures, but, as an early means of powering machinery, mills drove the development of manufacturing.

Pottery was the first industry to be established at Carr Hill (in the mid-eighteenth century), then glass started to be made there in about 1830.[37] There seems to have been quite a manufacturing complex in the small village, providing employment for many of the locals. Both pottery and glass used three ingredients that were available locally: clay, which could be dug up by the river; coal to fire the kilns; and sand, pebbles, lime and flints gleaned from ballast.[38]

In the headlong rush for profit from the new industrialisation, no trade was too noxious for Gateshead to try. By the 1750s there was a whale-blubber boilery at the Felling and also several glue factories.[39] In Thomas Oliver's *New Picture of Newcastle upon Tyne*, published in 1831, his 'Perambulatory Survey' of Gateshead mentions a paper mill, a flint-glass house, a cable-chain works, gas works, a cudbear manu-factory,* lime kilns, pigment factories, pipe makers, an oil mill and a vinegar works.[40] By mid-century the area was dominant in chemical manufacture – and all of it both fouled the environment and damaged its workers.

The alkali industry produced soda crystals, caustic soda, bleach, soap, disinfectant and fertiliser; this was a filthy and dangerous business. Workers at Allhusen's alkali works in Felling (who were mainly Irish immigrants) would wrap their heads in layer upon layer of flannel in a bid to filter out the corrosive and dehydrating chemicals from the air they breathed in. Some of the men drank tea with butter in it as a homemade remedy to try to counteract the effect of a day's work.[41]

In parallel with the industrial development of Gateshead came changes to the town as a place to live. Many of the large estates on Gateshead Fell were sold off for housing (partly because it was no longer such a desirable place for wealthy landowners to make their homes) and residential suburbs began to be built. Endless terraces of mean houses were quickly thrown up for the factory workers pouring into Gateshead and Felling, but there was still overcrowding.[42] The population of Gateshead grew more than tenfold over the course of the nineteenth century and the character it took on was tough and unlovely, a dark place of endless work for survival. It would be almost impossible for the town to throw off this mantle until most of the industry was long gone and it began to reinvent itself at the end of the twentieth century with the Angel of the North, the Baltic art gallery and the Sage concert venue.

The title of this chapter is J.B. Priestley's comprehensive put-down of Gateshead, which he visited in 1933 on his 'English Journey'. Suffering

---

* Cudbear is a purplish-red dye extracted from lichen

from a bad cold for the north-east leg of his trip, Priestley's condemnation of Gateshead's 'lack of civic dignity' and his broader swipes at Tyneside's 'slatternly women' and 'stocky, toothless' men smack of curmudgeonliness rather than considered criticism. His aim in writing the book was to paint a realistic portrait of industrial England, because 'Londoners have no conception of life as it is being lived in other parts of England; if they had, they would not feel so comfortable'.[43] That was a decent intention for the project, but as Priestley trudged ever northwards he lapsed into taking easy potshots at people enduring real poverty. However, when he said, 'If anybody ever made money in Gateshead, they must have taken great care not to spend any of it in the town,' he was perceptive, for the local businessmen who served on the town council had been concerned, for centuries, to keep their rates down, and spending their hard-earned money on relief of the poor was something that had to be kept firmly in check.

From the 1840s onwards, an increasing proportion of those Gateshead poor were Irish as huge numbers were driven out of Ireland by famine. The north-east was a magnet for many of them, not only because of the promise of work in the factories but because of its long-established reputation for tolerance towards Catholics.[44] There had been a Roman Catholic church in the Felling since 1842, and by 1850 there were so many Irish immigrants living in the village that the church had to be extended and have a gallery added, doubling the number who could worship there.

But tolerance was relative and anti-Irish feeling began to intensify across England in the mid-nineteenth century, partly because of the sheer numbers arriving in the country and partly as a result of political developments. Just three days after Sarah Melvin's murder, the first of five 'Fenian outrages' in Canada was sensationally reported in the British newspapers. During the first six months of 1866, there was barely an edition of the *Gateshead Observer* that didn't contain a headline referring to the 'Fenian Conspiracy', and on 3 March 1866, the Dublin police were 'exhibiting the utmost vigilance in unearthing the leading or most dangerous members of the Fenian conspiracy, nor is their activity less prominent in searching for arms'.[45]

Ten years earlier, in July 1856, sectarian violence had broken out in the Felling for the first time, when a parade of fifty or sixty Protestant Orangemen who were marking 'the Twelfth' with a march from Newcastle to an Orange pub in the Felling were ambushed by a much bigger group of Catholic 'Ribbonmen' armed with 'guns, pistols, swords, bludgeons, Morgan-rattlers* and a scythe'. A 13-year-old boy, Edward Badger, was shot in the thigh with a jagged homemade bullet. Several people received serious head wounds and it was lucky no one was killed. The Catholic Irish of Gateshead perceived the march as an intolerable provocation, although the local papers, perhaps disingenuously, reported it sympathetically as a harmless and merry parade.

By 1866, then, local tensions were running high. There was sectarian hostility between Catholic and Protestant Irish immigrants and general anti-Irish feeling from the indigenous locals, exacerbated by fears of an Irish uprising and acts of terrorism. All this fuelled the response to Sarah Melvin's murder and the suspicions that fell, almost immediately, on her parents, particularly her poor mother, Mary.

---

* A Morgan-rattler was a weighted club or stick.

4

'Then and there lying dead'[46]

It's hard to imagine how Mrs Melvin bore not only the pain of losing her child but the attendant horrors that she was powerless to prevent – firstly, the crowds that gathered outside her house to gawp from the very first day after the murder. By the beginning of the next week at least one newspaper report had included the detail that Mary's house was 'about half-way up the street, on the right-hand side' in Carr's Hill, making it easy for anyone to locate it.[47] Since the advent of the railways, crime tourism had become a popular pastime.

The crowds were not there to offer their condolences but were probably hoping that the police would turn up and drag Mrs Melvin away to a cell. Mr and Mrs Melvin had been seen by the Bournes close to the place where they stumbled over Sarah's body and just a few minutes before they did so. Local people, and soon the newspapers too, jumped to immediate and unsympathetic conclusions. The murder of one's own children as a desperate response to poverty was far from uncommon, though it more often took the form of stifling unwanted newborns at birth. A poor Irishwoman, a hawker no less, and – this was the clincher – separated from her husband: how could the suspicion that she had murdered her own child not fall on her?

As we have seen, there was anti-Irish feeling in Tyneside, partly because of the sheer numbers of Irish flowing into the area. As the incomers put pressure on chronically inadequate housing and crowded into tenements that were already overfull, tensions were almost inevitable. The ratcheting up of sectarian politics at a national level only made things worse.

Mr and Mrs Melvin were almost certainly pushed into leaving Ireland by hardship, as were hundreds of thousands of people during and after the Great Famine of 1845–52. Mary and Michael had arrived in the north-east of England some time in the late 1840s. Although they were in the Carr's Hill area in 1847 or so, when James Melvin was born, they also spent time in Berwick-upon-Tweed, living in a tenement in Black Bull Yard, a cramped alley off the main street, Marygate. A new child was born roughly every two years, until Sarah, their sixth and youngest, in 1860, by which time they had moved back to Felling. This was by no means an unusually large family for the period, but they all had to be fed and clothed, money had to be earned. Mary went out hawking, calling at houses to sell whatever she could offer, while Michael, also a hawker, seems to have looked to supplement that poorly paid work with whatever casual work he could get.[48]

The pottery firms actually depended on hawkers to fulfil local distribution. Sheriff Hill potter Paul Jackson had advertised that 'Hawkers from Northumberland and Cumberland may be supplied at the shop'.[49] Hawkers sold glassware too and, if they were homeless, might arrive at the works in the evening and sleep in the warm near the furnaces before setting out with new stock the next morning.[50]

Mary's work as a hawker was probably very similar to that of 'Pot Nelly', as a hawker called Eleanor Brownlee was known. She travelled around Gateshead Fell in the first half of the nineteenth century with a basket containing nuts, oranges and a few pieces of the local pottery. It sounds as though Nelly was a favoured employee at one point in her career as she had reputedly attended trade fairs at Leipzig on behalf of Warburton's pottery in Carr Hill. She died from exposure in the winter of 1838 when she was overtaken by nightfall, refused shelter at a farmhouse, and lost her way in woods on a night of heavy rain.[51] Hawking heavy pottery was drudgery and very unlikely to have made Mary Melvin much more than a pittance.

After Sarah's death, poor Mary took to her bed. On the Monday, three days after the murder, it was reported that, 'the mother of the deceased was in bed, and appeared to be in fearful agony, tossing backwards and forwards, moaning and crying, while a weeping daughter sat at the bedside evidently trying to soothe her mother. There were several people in the house besides, and many of them were bathed in tears.'[52]

At noon on Saturday 14 April, the day after the murder, when crowds had already started to mass, Doctors Benjamin Barkus and Robert Banning arrived at Mary's house to perform a post-mortem on Sarah's body. Mortuaries and pathology labs were rare in England before the end of the nineteenth century and only really began to be built after the passing of the 1875 Public Health Act. In Portsmouth in 1873, the medical officer for the town, George Turner, complained that he had to carry out post-mortems within the sight of prisoners at the police station or before crowds of bystanders.[53] It is to be hoped that the curious crowds were kept out of Mary's house when the doctors entered to do their grim work.

Victorian post-mortems were gruesome dissections that, perforce, took place in the victim's own home more often than not. In his *Practical Pathology: A Manual for Students and Practitioners* of 1885

Sir German Sims Woodhead wrote that 'where the examination has to be conducted in a private house . . . a good firm kitchen table is to be placed in the room where the cadaver is lying. (If this cannot be obtained, the coffin lid makes a very fair substitute.) . . . A piece of stout Mackintosh should be spread over the table.'[54]

Reading Woodhead's list of knives, saws, mallets and chisels, the requisites of the pathologist, together with his direct and unflinching instructions for cutting open a human body in order to lay bare its secrets, it is hard to imagine it being done to your own child in the very place where the child ate and slept and played. How would one cope with such an experience? Mary Melvin must have been beside herself.

Dr Barkus carried out his autopsy on Sarah's body according to established procedure. Although men had dissected corpses for centuries, forensic pathology was a relatively new science. The pre-eminent doctors driving the development of strict methodologies for establishing the cause of death were two Germans, Carl von Rokitansky (1804–78) and Rudolf Virchow (1821–1902), the latter known as the 'father of modern pathology'. But Virchow would not publish his seminal book on autopsy procedure until 1876. In England the leading authority on forensic pathology – or 'medical jurisprudence' as it was more commonly referred to, was Alfred Swaine Taylor (1806–80). His *Principles and Practice of Medical Jurisprudence*, one of many works, was first published in 1865. Taylor was a lecturer at Guy's Hospital and had an insatiable appetite for the details of forensic pathology to be gleaned from trials. In his *Elements of Medical Jurisprudence interspersed with a copious selection of instructive cases and analyses of opinions delivered at coroners' inquests* of 1843 he wrote, 'Trials for murder and manslaughter by wounding are very frequent in our Courts of Law; and I flatter myself that the copious selection of modern cases which are dispersed through the concluding chapters of the volume, will point out to the practitioner those questions which he is most commonly required to answer.'[55]

Armed with one or other of Taylor's exhaustive volumes, Dr Barkus would have been guided in his probing of Sarah's corpse, even if he had to do so in the, to us, highly inappropriate setting of her home. He made a record of his findings which he would be required to convey to the coroner when the inquest opened in two days' time.

When the Bournes found Sarah Melvin on the footpath at Carr's Hill Joseph had no hesitation in picking her up and carrying her straight to James Harvey's pub. This instinct was built on centuries of custom, now lost, in which public houses were used as democratic spaces. Pubs were among the few buildings to which all citizens had free access, access that took on a political dimension over time. As well as being makeshift mortuaries and the venue for inquests (well into the twentieth century in some rural locations), pubs were also used to try grievances, to register births and deaths, and for tax collection. They were bastions of citizen-based civic responsibility.[56] And they were also, of course, places where civil disobedience might be planned – almost all radical groups held their meetings in pubs. Pubs were the people's spaces.

Joseph Bourne was following custom in carrying Sarah's body to the Gardeners' Arms, but publicans did not necessarily welcome this particular use of their premises. As late as 1906 the publicans' trade journal, *The Licensed Victualler*, declared: 'In some quarters there is a belief that an innkeeper is compelled by law to receive into his house a dead body, found in the street or washed ashore, for the purpose of an inquest, but such is perfectly erroneous. Inns are established to supply the wants of the living, and have nothing to do with the dead.'[57]

Although inquests were routinely held in public houses, pressure grew towards the close of the nineteenth century to end the practice.

A petition to central government drawn up by local officials in Sheffield in 1889 stated that, 'Nothing can be more repugnant to bereaved relatives than to have their natural sufferings accentuated by being the objects of what often proves to be unjust suspicions, exhibited to the gaze of persons surrounding a Public House bar.'[58]

This situation certainly pertained during Sarah Melvin's inquest, which opened at three o'clock on Monday 16 April 1866 at the Gardeners' Arms. Michael Melvin attended the hearing under a dark cloud of suspicion. The *Newcastle Courant* observed archly, 'The father of the deceased was present in the Gardeners' Arms during the inquest, but not in the room where the inquiry was held. He did not display any particular concern.'[59] It's interesting that the reporter should have made a note of Michael's demeanour: it's possible he was making an effort to appear at ease. Back in 1849, when the Melvins were up in Berwick-upon-Tweed, Michael had been tried for larceny, along with another man. They were accused of stealing three steel bars from the yard of a railway contractor. Mr Morris, the contractor, was unable to identify the bars found in Michael's possession as the actual ones stolen from him and so Michael and his accomplice were found not guilty.[60] It sounds as though they had a lucky escape. Then, in May 1857, Michael and another man were given a month-long sentence for robbing a man at knifepoint in Forth Banks, just across the Tyne from Gateshead. And later the same year he and a different sidekick were given two months for robbing a woman in a pub in the same street.[61] The sentence clearly didn't have much deterrent effect as by January the following year Michael was being tried at Durham Assizes for stealing some lead weights from a chemical works in December 1857 (again with an accomplice). This time the stolen goods were positively identified from traces of chemicals on them and Michael got eight months.[62] So it's likely that Michael would have felt very uncomfortable indeed in such close proximity to the workings of the law. Extraordinarily, Michael's criminal record was never mentioned once in either the newspapers or the official record, throughout the entire inquiry into his daughter's death.

As is the case today, inquests were not held into every death but only into those that were deemed 'worthy of inquiry' by virtue of the circumstances. An accidental, violent or otherwise unnatural death would be drawn to the attention of the local coroner who would attempt to come to a reasonable account of its cause. Around 6 per cent of deaths each year were subject to an inquest.[63]

Coroners were usually picked from the legal profession, most often solicitors, and John Milnes Favell, the Coroner for the Chester Ward of Durham, was no exception to this. At the time of the inquest into Sarah Melvin's death Favell was 59 and would have been elected to the role by local freeholders. Although for many years coroners had been paid on an ad hoc basis – that is, given a fee for each inquest they held – since the 1860 Coroners Act they were paid a salary (perhaps to discourage them from ordering more inquests than were necessary). The coroner would appoint a jury of as many as 23 local men (never women) and their job was to carry out a wide-ranging investigation into all the circumstances surrounding the death under scrutiny: it was more akin to a police investigation than is the case today. The formal purpose of the inquest was to discover the *corpus delicti* – the 'body of evidence' proving that a crime had been committed (although the term was often applied in common parlance to the body of the victim). The coroner also had the power to make a formal accusation against a suspected perpetrator, directing legal action to be taken.[64]

The first formality was for the coroner and his jury to walk the few hundred yards up to Carr's Villa to inspect the place where the body had been found. From there they trooped back down into the village to view Sarah's body at Mary's house. Further racking misery was no doubt caused for Mary Melvin by this invasion of her home by unfamiliar men who had quite possibly already formed opinions as to her likely role in her child's death. As Sarah's body had been autopsied two days earlier, it was presumably no longer able to be viewed as a 'touching' little corpse (of the kind regularly photographed by grieving Victorian parents as a *memento mori*). Sarah's remains must have been placed in a coffin, the worst of her wounds and the most unsightly of the pathologist's incisions no doubt covered by a nightdress.

We might wonder why the jurymen needed to look at the victim's body, but the viewing was an important part of the process and had a symbolic function: 'It is the view of the body that gives jurisdiction.'[65] The symbolism was a throwback to much earlier times when the entire inquest had to be held in the presence of the body under scrutiny. By the mid-nineteenth century the physical body was gradually being distanced from the inquest procedure but if the viewing did not take place, the inquest itself would be considered void.[66] Again, some local officials campaigned for an end to these viewings – 'an intrusion into a home rendered sacred by extraordinary grief and trouble'[67] – and indeed these words seem singularly apt as a description of Mrs Melvin's house at this time. But it would be 1926 before the practice of viewing was formally ended by a change in the law.

The formalities of an inquest (and the documents that recorded them) enshrined the importance of the viewing of the body. Setting eyes on the corpse was the only sure way for the jury to confirm the existence of the corpse (and thereby the necessity of the inquest itself). The formal record of the inquest into Sarah's death, now held in the National Archives, is handwritten on a pro forma pre-printed with John Milnes Favell's name and with spaces for the relevant details to be filled in. It reads, 'Informations of Witnesses severally taken ...

touching the death of Sarah Melvin on the sixteenth of April [1866] on an Inquisition, then and there taken, on view of the body of Sarah Melvin then and there lying dead . . .'[68] The coroner and jury then returned to the Gardeners' Arms for the inquest proper to begin.

The first witness to be called was Margaret Thorburn, in whose house Mary Melvin lived with her daughters. Mrs Thorburn was questioned as to the temperature of Sarah's body when it was brought to her house on the night of the murder. It was one of the coroner's key objectives to pin down the time of death as accurately as possible and the warmth or otherwise of Sarah's body and limbs was clearly thought to be significant in this respect. However, as detailed in Chapter 1, Mrs Thorburn's statement seems to contradict those of PC Alexander Kemp and Dr Barkus, both in terms of the time when Sarah's body could have been taken from the pub to her mother's house and in terms of what she was wearing. Some vagueness may well have crept into Mrs Thorburn's recollection as a result of the intensity of emotions felt by all in the house; it is also possible that there wasn't a clock in the house so that times were simply estimated. She said: 'About ten o'clock on Friday night, the deceased, Sarah Melvin, was brought to her house. I took her clothes off. She is five years of age. She was warm about her body when brought home. Her limbs were cold.'[69]

Not every witness who was questioned at the inquest had their statement transcribed for the official record; nor were the statements transcribed in the exact order in which they were given. The official transcription boils down what was actually said (which can be picked up from the newspaper reports) to a succinct statement that was signed by the witness, while the very full newspaper reports of the inquest convey a more vivid sense of the questions and answers that were exchanged. Mrs Thorburn's statement was not entered into the record.

Next to be questioned was PC Kemp. He went over his part in the events of Friday evening in detail, from the moment when Joseph and Ann Bourne found him at his home in Deckham Place (the village closest to Carr's Hill, just to the west) at about 9.15 p.m. As he recounted his examination of Sarah's body and how he had removed the cords from around her neck and wrists, he produced the cords themselves as evidence. The *Courant*'s reporter described them as 'very strong and of small size'.[70] The two cords were of equal length. PC Kemp also produced Sarah's clothes, which he had taken off her body whilst it lay in the Gardeners' Arms (even though Mrs Thorburn had just said that she removed Sarah's clothes after her body had been taken to her house; no one seems to have been concerned about the conflict in their accounts). Kemp described the 'night soil' on Sarah's dress (the topmost layer of her clothing beneath which were two petticoats and a chemise). He added that there were fine spots of blood on her chemise and on one of her petticoats, whilst the other had no marks on it.

Mr Favell then asked Dr Barkus, who was present (and waiting to give his own statement), to take Sarah's clothes from Kemp 'with a view to his making a careful microscopial examination of these suspicious spots, and of the garments generally'.[71] It's clear that the coroner was aware that bloodstains might offer up significant information and, indeed, in his *Principles and Practice of Medical Jurisprudence* Alfred Swaine Taylor wrote that 'stains of blood on the dress of a wounded person or dead body may often furnish important circumstantial evidence'.[72] Furthermore, 'when spots of blood are found upon articles of dress or furniture, their *form* and *direction* may occasionally serve to furnish an indication of the position of the person with respect to them when the wound was inflicted. Thus if the form of a spot is oval and elongated, the . . . force with which the blood has been thrown out will be in some measure indicated by the degree of obliquity and length of the spot'.[73] It would remain to be seen whether any meaningful information could be gleaned from Sarah's clothes.

After the police constable, Joseph Bourne stepped up to be questioned by the coroner and jurymen. He gave a clear and coherent account of his and his wife's movements that evening. He described how, just before coming across Sarah's body on the narrow footpath, he and Ann had passed Michael and Mary Melvin coming in the opposite direction. Although this might seem to imply that the Melvins must have either passed their own child lying on the ground or, worse, that they had had some part in her death, in fact at least two other paths joined the 'cart road' where the two couples met at a point beyond Carr's Villa, thus making it very possible for the Melvins to have come by one of these other routes and to have missed the place where Sarah lay entirely.

About the Melvins, Joseph said, 'We met Michael Melvin and his wife about half-way down the lane. We did not know then that they were the father and mother of the deceased, but they afterwards acknowledged it. He was walking first, and she was walking behind him. They were coming in the direction of [i.e. towards] Carr's Hill. She would be about a couple of yards behind him. They were not talking. We did not speak to them.'

Pursuing his line of questioning about the temperature of Sarah's body when she was found, the coroner questioned Bourne about the state the child was in when he found her.

He answered: 'Her clothes were down to about her knees, and they were straight. I picked her up. She appeared dead, but I thought she might not be, as she was not stiff. She starved my hands carrying her. When I caught hold of her hands they were cold . . . When we got to Mr Harvey's, we put our hands up her clothes, and felt that her breast was cold. It is my opinion that she must have been dead some little time.'[74]

The words 'She starved my hands' startle with their metaphorical force but this is simply a now-archaic usage of 'starve', which originally meant to 'freeze' with cold. Sarah's cold body chilled Bourne's hands as he carried her. How long would it have taken for the dead child's body to lose this much of its stored heat? This statement also contradicted Mrs Thorburn's testimony that Sarah's body had been warm when it was brought to her house.

Now one of the jurors questioned Bourne about his second meeting with Michael Melvin.

'We met Melvin and his little daughter, a girl about fourteen.' This would have been Mary Ann Melvin, the Melvins' third child, who was 14 at the time. Mrs Melvin had gone home by this point and Mr Melvin had gone out to look for Sarah again, accompanied by his daughter. This was the moment of the strangely awkward exchange between Michael Melvin and Joseph Bourne. By Joseph's account, he had already told Michael that he and Ann had 'found a child strangled'. And then Melvin said, 'I know you. Shake hands!'

This demand to shake hands seems to have struck the coroner and several jurors as strange, false. Bourne was questioned closely about it:

'Did Melvin seem to be the worse of drink?'

'Did Melvin and his wife appear drunk when you met them?'

Joseph said neither of them seemed drunk.

'There was no reason for his wishing to shake hands with you?'

'No, but he afterwards said that he knew a brother of mine.'

The coroner's opinion on the matter was, 'If he had been drunk I could have understood it, for drunken people often wish to shake hands with everybody they meet.'

Joseph said, 'I suppose it is the custom of the Irish to shake hands with people.'

The truth was that Joseph's own parents, Thomas and Willett, were both Irish. They had emigrated to the textile town of Bury, Lancashire in the 1820s and married when Willett was only 14 years old (and probably pregnant with their first child, Michael). The rest of Joseph's family spelled their surname Burnes whereas Joseph seems to have adopted a more anglicised version of the name. So he may have been keen to pass as English born and bred (he was born in Bilston near Wolverhampton in 1830). Several newspaper reports spelled Joseph's surname Burns or Byrne, perhaps more familiar – and more Irish – forms of the name to them. Joseph turned his nose up at Michael's Irish gladhanding. Everyone who spoke seemed to agree that Michael Melvin's overfriendliness was in poor taste – perhaps even a little suspicious . . .

Ann Bourne gave a statement that echoed her husband's in every detail. She referred to Joseph as 'the master'.

Next to be called to give a statement was a young woman named Catherine Forster. She was 32 years old, married, and lived at the Felling. She said she worked at Carr's Hill pottery, so would have been back and forth along the paths by the quarry at least twice a day:

The last time I saw this little girl, Sarah Melvin, was on Friday, about twenty minutes to seven. When I got down to the footpath where the body was found, she was crying at the bottom of the narrow lane. I asked her what she was crying for, and she said she wanted her mammy. She said she was looking for her. I saw a man near there. I took her by the hand and brought her up to the end of Harvey's house [i.e. the Gardeners' Arms]. I told her to go home, and not to come down there any more for fear the bad man got hold of her. I merely said that to frighten her from coming back again. She was crying sore. She did not give any other reason for crying but that she had lost her mammy.[75]

The *Dundee Courier & Argus* added a note of pathos in their account of Catherine's part in the tragedy: 'The young woman very kindly turned back and set the little wanderer into the cart road near the end of the village, and saying, "You'll soon be at home, hinny," left her. The poor little girl was never seen alive again after this, except by her cruel murderers.'[76] That Geordie 'hinny' is very touching.

Naturally the fact that Catherine had seen a lone man up by Carr's Hill quarry was of great interest to the inquiry. The coroner asked Catherine, 'With reference to the man you saw, where was he?'

'He was sitting between the green field and the quarry. There was a great noise in the wood, and as I took hold of the child's hand the man got up and went away towards the nurseries.'

The coroner pressed her. 'I wish I could get out of you exactly where he was sitting?'

'I could show you the place.'

'Was he between the footpath and the quarry?'

'He was between the footpath that leads down to Split Crow Lane and the quarry . . . He was sitting between the path to the Felling and the quarry.'

'Did you see how he was dressed?'

'No, I did not take any notice.'

'When you saw him, what position was he in?'

'He had his head down towards the ground.'

Then, pressed still further about the man, Catherine said that the man appeared to be there 'for a natural purpose'. This was a widely understood euphemism for defecating.

A juror chipped in to ask, 'Would you know the man again if you saw him?'

'No, I did not see his face. I saw him go away towards the nurseries when I met the child, and I did not see him when I came back again.'

Another juror said it was 'a singular thing that the child should have gone down again' towards the Felling after Catherine Forster had brought her up to the top of Carr's Hill village. The child surely knew the road home well enough?

But then another juror countered that Sarah knew her father and mother were at the Felling, so it was understandable that she would have been drawn back towards the Felling. However, Sarah did not know that her mother had gone to the Felling to look for her: as far as anyone knew, there had been no contact between them since midday.

There were no suggestions as to who Catherine's defecating man might have been and Catherine was finally allowed to step down. She was the only witness who was pushed to stand by her account by the coroner and jury. She was also the only witness who signed their statement with a mark because she couldn't write her own name.

Last to be called on this first day of the inquest was Dr Benjamin Barkus. First Dr Barkus went over his initial examination of Sarah's body at the Gardeners' Arms on the night of the murder. The cords kept as evidence by PC Kemp were brought out again and the doctor confirmed that they matched the marks he had seen around the child's neck and wrists. After giving a careful and detailed account of the damage that he had discovered to Sarah's genitals during that preliminary examination, Dr Barkus went on record as saying that he believed these wounds had been 'made immediately after death'.[77] He added, 'I don't swear it positively, but that is my opinion. Very probably it might be immediately after death, just as the blood was ceasing to circulate.'[78]

Asked about the temperature of Sarah's body when he first examined it, Dr Barkus said that her legs had been cold and that there was little warmth in her torso either. Mr Favell, the coroner, asked him how long a child clothed as this one was could be dead before it became cold.

The doctor's opinion was that the limbs could become cold in about an hour but not in less time than that, which seemed to corroborate Catherine Forster's having seen Sarah alive at twenty to seven, roughly two hours before she had been found dead.

The coroner: 'What sort of a night was Friday night? Was it a very cold night? It depends, of course, very much upon the nature of the night.'

A juror piped up: 'The stars were out, and it was very frosty.'

Dr Barkus said, 'That would also assist towards the limbs getting cold.'[79]

Now it was time for the doctor to give his autopsy report. Although the inquest was proceeding very properly and giving every appearance of falling within the realms of 'business as usual' for the participants, surely this moment must have drawn them together in a collective sense of dread. The man who had been required to go to Sarah Melvin's home and dissect her small corpse in order to look for answers about her violent death was about to reveal his findings.

'I made a post mortem examination on Saturday the 14th inst.* at noon, in company with Dr Banning.'[80] As was standard practice, Dr Barkus began by examining Sarah's head, then worked his way down her body:[81]

I noticed a slight external contusion [i.e. a bruise] on the left side of the forehead. On removing the covering of the skull, I found extravasated blood† between the scalp and the bone on the upper and back part of the head towards the left side. There was no external mark to lead me to that at the time.

---

* 'Inst.' comes from the Latin *instante mense* and means 'this month'.
† 'Extravasated' blood is blood that has been forced out of blood vessels into the surrounding area of the body by the rupturing of the vessels. It implies the use of force to cause injury.

Dr Barkus went on:

> On removing the skull cap I found the membranes of the brain congested with dark blood, and also the surface of the brain itself and its interior. I reflected [i.e. peeled back] the skin in front of the neck, and found extensive extravasation of dark venous blood in the course of the mark made by the cord round the neck in front and particularly on the left side.
>
> On opening the windpipe I found the lining membrane congested and dark at the upper part of the windpipe. On opening the chest I found the lungs very much congested with dark blood; the right side of the heart was nearly filled with dark blood, coagulated; the left side was empty. On opening the abdomen I found the organs generally somewhat congested. The bladder was empty. I might mention that the stomach contained some half digested farinaceous food.

'Congestion' is the abnormal flooding of organs with fluid, in this case blood. So much blood was evidence of the extreme violence done to Sarah. Dr Barkus also saw the remains of Sarah's last, very ordinary meal consisting mainly of bread.

At this point, the coroner perhaps grew a little impatient. He sought to move Dr Barkus to his key evidence: 'You did not discover that she had been violated?'

Barkus said, 'There was no trace of it.'

'You could not make out that she had?'

'No.'

Mr Favell pressed the point: 'Could there have been any attempt without your discovering it?'

'It is possible, but I think I should have found traces [of semen] if there had.'

Favell: 'And a more bruised appearance [to Sarah's genitals]?'

'Not a more bruised appearance. The wound had been caused by a knife.'

There is a slight ambiguity here. Favell is asking a hypothetical question: if Sarah had been raped, would her genitals have been more severely bruised? But Barkus doesn't answer that question: because he has made up his mind that Sarah's injuries were caused by a knife, he doesn't consider the possibility of bruising at all.

Switching to the idea of wounding by knife, Favell now asked whether the harm was done 'Either at or after death?'

Barkus answered, 'Shortly after death. I am pretty strongly of opinion that it was after death.' As we have seen, the doctor had already formed this view when he first examined Sarah in the Gardeners' Arms.

Favell: 'Then it would be more difficult to bruise the parts at that time [i.e. after death]?'

Barkus: 'Yes, more difficult to bruise them without showing appearances. If this wound had been inflicted during life, there must have been [i.e. would have been] considerable haemorrhage.'

This creates a further ambiguity. Barkus alters the coroner's intended meaning so that, rather than answering a simple question about bruises not forming so readily once the blood has stopped flowing, he instead talks about bruises that *do* form readily *because* blood is still flowing. It's almost certainly just a misunderstanding and no notice seems to have been taken at the time.

The coroner pressed Dr Barkus further about the key issue: 'There could not have been an attempt made upon the person [i.e. sexual penetration] of a child like that without bruising the parts?'

'Not during life.'

Taking all the salient points of Dr Barkus's testimony together, the conclusion was drawn that Sarah was not actually raped, and also that the injuries to her private parts were inflicted after her death.

Mr Favell again moved the inquiry on: 'Now, Dr Barkus, after this, what is your opinion as to the cause of death?'

'I think she died from strangulation, and had previously been rendered insensible by a blow on the back of the head. That would account to me for the appearance of non-resistance about the body.'

'Then the cause of death was strangulation?'

'Yes, strangulation with a cord.'

'But you are of opinion that she had been previously stunned by that blow on the head?'

'Yes.'

'What leads you to think that?'

'The want of any appearance of resistance, the placid appearance of the features, and the absence altogether of any appearance of struggling about the body, make me think that she had been rendered non-resistant by that blow.'

At this point the coroner abruptly adjourned the inquest in order to give the police more time to carry out their investigations.

There must have been a sense of growing horror among those present as the significance of Dr Barkus's statement sank in, for it was understood as implicating Sarah's mother in the murder of her own child. The details of the child's injuries suggested an abominable degree of calculation, if that were the case: as a woman, Mary Melvin was physically incapable of rape, but it seemed that, *after* killing her, the perpetrator had tried to make it seem as though Sarah had been violated. No actual rape had taken place, according to Barkus. Was this a way for a murderous mother to divert suspicion away from herself? Such a possibility seems too horrible to contemplate but it is hinted at in several newspaper articles. It may even have been the case that the inquest was adjourned at this particular point because of the newly strengthened suspicions against Mrs Melvin. Was there a feeling that the police must now act?

At the end of a very long article about the murder, the *Dundee Courier & Argus* spoke its mind:

> The diabolical cruelty by which the supposed violation seemed to have been accompanied induced a suspicion that no rape had taken place; but that the appearance of an outrage of this nature having been committed had been given to the body of the unfortunate child, with a view to divert suspicion from the real criminal. From what we can learn of the result of the *post mortem* examination, the fact that no rape at all has been committed is conclusively proved, and more astounding still that the wound on the lower part of the body had been inflicted after death.
>
> This disclosure undoubtedly deprives the crime of its more revolting features; but naturally suggests the question: What motive could lead to the perpetration of this cold-blooded murder? All at present is shrouded in mystery.[82]

Now under a dense cloud of suspicion, based entirely on prejudice and circumstance, Mr and Mrs Melvin were taken in for questioning by the police. These interviews were discreetly managed and hardly anyone was aware they had taken place. Later, the *London Evening Standard* would be one of very few newspapers, if not the only one, to report explicitly that 'at that time, the father and mother were suspected of having murdered their child, and were taken into custody, but after an examination before the magistrates, were released.'[83]

It seems that the Melvins' detailed alibis had withstood all efforts to demolish them. 'They both gave a straightforward account of their movements on the night of the murder . . . Chief Constable Elliott had had questioned every person mentioned as having been seen by [the Melvins] during that night, with one exception, and the statements of the whole of these persons corroborated in the minutest detail the account given by the parents'.[84] Having failed to undermine the veracity of their alibis, the police had little choice but to let the couple go. However, when the inquest was reconvened just over a week later, the Melvins were questioned publicly as well. This seems to have been done almost as a piece of theatre. Although the police were convinced, now, of the Melvins' innocence, it was necessary to re-enact the interrogation at the inquest, so that the public's suspicions could also be allayed.

The *Courant* gave an account of the questioning of Sarah's parents at the inquest:

'Considerable interest attached to the proceedings as it was generally expected that Michael and Mary Melvin, the parents of the murdered child, would be examined.'[85] The awkwardness of the situation comes across in the tortured grammar of the coroner's words:

The Coroner said it appeared that Mr Elliott had really no further evidence to lay before them; but he [Elliott] had the examination of several parties and he had asked him (the Coroner) to take these and examine the father [Michael Melvin] upon them. He made that request because he had been told that there were many people who would like to have it done. If the father were examined properly and with due caution, he (the Coroner) did not see why he should not be examined. He had every statement made by the father and taken by Mr Elliott before any deposition was taken. Mr Elliott had traced the people whom the father had said he had seen and had been with, and he had done this without those persons having an opportunity of communicating with Melvin, and he (the Coroner) had their statements here. If the jury wished, he would have the father brought in and sworn.

Needless to say, 'the jury expressed a desire that this [the questioning of Mr Melvin] should be done; and Michael Melvin, the father of the murdered child, was brought into the room.'

The coroner: 'Your name is Michael Melvin?'

Mr Melvin: 'Yes.'

'You have no objection to be sworn in this case?'

'No, sir.'

The witness was sworn in.

'You will be bound to answer any question I put to you. What is the name of your wife?'

'Mary Melvin.'

'You do not live together?'

'No, not now.'

'How long have you been parted?'

'About three months.'

'Where do you live?'

'At the Felling.'

'What makes you live at the Felling when your wife lives up here?'

'The children work in the potteries here, and they were afraid to go home to the Felling through the Nurseries at night.'

'She left you to take this room at the potteries?'

'Yes, and I was to come up too, as soon as convenient.'

Although the fact that the Melvins were living apart at the time of the murder was taken as one more cause for suspicion, there is no reason to doubt Michael's explanation of the situation as given here. Indeed, it's possible to track Michael and Mary through subsequent censuses (in 1871 and 1881) in which they are shown to be living together again on Split Crow Lane. But that was the future and for now the police (and everyone else) would make their own judgements about the Melvins' situation. It seems unlikely that these would have been favourable.

Mr Favell now moved on to ask Michael to run through his movements on the evening of the murder. He specified that Michael should start his account from about five in the afternoon. So Michael recounted his visit to Mr Alexander, his supper with his son James, his going over to ask to borrow the landlady of the Shakespeare's barrow, his going to see Mr Thompson, the Inspector of Nuisances, and finally his chat with Mr Makepeace the butcher. Then Mary had arrived, looking for Sarah, and they had ended up going over to the Shakespeare again, so that Mary could settle her nerves with a whisky. At first, Michael said, she just had a half-glass, but then their acquaintance named William Forster* bought Mary another glass. Michael and Forster had glasses of mild ale.

'When she had drank the glass of whisky she said she did not thank me for the glass of whisky; would I not give her [another] half a glass? I gave her the half glass . . .'

Of course, for it to emerge that the Melvins had sat drinking in a pub when they knew their little girl was missing would do nothing to improve the poor impression the general public already had of them. It's notable that Michael took care to differentiate between his own modest consumption of beer and his wife's taste for whisky. Whatever the reason for his living apart from Mary, the fact was that their marriage seemed rocky: they had been seen arguing in public. At this stage, he may have thought to save his own skin if Mary were suspected of being guilty of murder. Perhaps he even suspected her himself for she had after all only turned up at his house at seven o'clock. It might have been hard for him not to have doubts, given the way the post-mortem evidence had been spun.

---

* William Forster was not Catherine Forster's husband (who was named George) but it's possible he may have been a relative of theirs. No such link was ever made; Forster was a common name, locally.

Michael carried on his account: 'We came away together. This would be about half past eight o'clock.' He went over how Mary had wheedled him into walking her back to Carr's Hill now that it was 'turning dark'. He went into the detail of which path they had taken back past Carr's Villa and Carr's Quarry. He mentioned the man they had passed near the entrance to the Carr's Villa drive and then of course the Bournes. When he got to the moment when he went up to the Gardeners' Arms and saw his child lying dead on a table, his ordeal was over.

Mary Melvin took the oath now, no doubt dreading the questions to which she was about to be subjected. Innocent or not, it must have been terrifying for such an uneducated woman to step into this arena of public scrutiny. Even if Mary knew that her alibi had been substantiated, she may not have been confident that she was no longer a suspect. If she had been suspected of killing her little girl and mutilating her body so vilely just a few days earlier, why would opinion be swayed now? And what if her alibi were not enough to protect her?

She said, 'I am the wife of Michael Melvin . . . My husband and I have been parted about three months. We parted because the little girls worked at the pottery. We have never been parted before. He was always a good man to me and his bit family.' She gave her own account of going across to the Felling to see if Sarah was there and asking 'Mickey' to buy her a drink. She said her head had been bad. She mentioned passing the Bournes but not the other man.

Mary's statement was quite a lot shorter than Michael's and when she had finished, the statements that corroborated their two accounts (which had been taken by John Elliott previously) were read by Mr Favell but not 'placed upon the depositions' (that is, not formally added to the inquest record). These were from Mrs Alice Atkinson, landlady of the Shakespeare pub in Felling; William Forster, the man who bought Mary a whisky in the pub; Alexander Mullen, Michael's upstairs neighbour; and James Melvin, the oldest of the Melvin children. The witness whom the police had failed to find was the man whom Michael said they had seen just before they walked up the drive behind Carr's Villa.[86]

Some interesting, if peripheral, details emerge from these four statements. The pub landlady had a precise memory of Michael and Mary both having 'three halfpennyworth'[87] – no doubt this price would have instantly identified the drink for readers. From the context it seems to have been ale as Mrs Atkinson then specified that Mary moved on to whisky. Mary's first glass was spilt, she said, and the couple were in the Shakespeare for no more than ten minutes. Then, when William Forster's statement was read, he confirmed that it was whisky that was spilt and said, tellingly, 'Mrs Atkinson wanted them to go home.' Was Mary possibly drunk and lairy?

Alexander Mullen, who lived upstairs from Michael Melvin, said that James asked him to go downstairs when Mary arrived so that they might 'have some fun' out of her. Mullen went down and 'took hold of her', he said. 'I then asked Michael Melvin for the loan of sixpence. He said I will not lend it you, and we did not get any whisky.'

Finally, in his statement 19-year-old James Melvin let slip something not mentioned in any other context. He referred to Mary twice as his stepmother. She had just referred to James as her son, in her own deposition. It's possible that Michael, who was around twelve years older than Mary, had been married before (or at least in a relationship with someone else) who had either died or left him. James' apparent lack of respect for Mary may be explained by this.

For those listening, all the statements would have added to the sense that these people were seedy and dissolute. The Melvins' behaviour was a long way from the uptight standards regarding personal conduct that characterised 'proper' Victorian society and no doubt many were quick to judge them unfavourably. But their alibis were accepted as rock solid. At no point does anyone suggest the possibility that when Mrs Melvin was out looking for Sarah between six and seven in the evening, she perhaps came across her up on Carr's Hill and, losing her temper, killed her in a fit of rage. Even if she had, could she really have been so evil as to have quickly thought up and carried out the faked violation of her own child? No one seemed to think so any more.

This completed the public demonstration of the Melvins' innocence. In one way, it was commendable that the authorities went through this process of exoneration. Whilst there was an element of prurience in wheeling out the Melvins, it also did the couple a huge service and effectively ended their role as suspects. As the *Courant* wrote, 'Speculation is, therefore, now completely at fault as to the perpetrator.'[88] Even *The Times* weighed in with an article that declared, 'The father and mother were examined at the inquest, and have been closely examined by the police, and the general impression is that they are absolutely innocent of any concern in the murder.'[89]

The desire to find Sarah's parents guilty of her murder had to be quietly shelved. There was a sense that time had been wasted while the police tried to challenge the Melvins' alibis but, however much the public might disapprove of their living arrangements, their Irishness, their being hawkers, or Mary's taste for whisky, there was no evidence to suggest that either of them had killed their youngest child. The fact that none of the statements (neither those of the Melvins nor their witnesses) was entered into the public record suggests that the coroner felt the less said about it the better. There was a hint of shame in the air.

The police now had no choice but to fall back on their sleuthing skills to try to find the murderer. They seemed to have few leads to follow. The inquest was adjourned again, this time for a fortnight, so that the police might do their best to crack the case. But when the coroner and jurors met again at the Gardeners' Arms on Monday 7 May, only one new item was entered into the record: Alexander Kemp had re-examined Sarah's dress and found, in addition to hay and straw, some hayseeds.[90]

After convening on three separate occasions, the inquest was now drawn to a formal conclusion. The coroner's jury reached a verdict of 'wilful murder' by some person unknown.[91] In his closing remarks, Favell said that 'the deed had been done in the dark, and it was difficult to find it out. He had great hope, however, of the ultimate discovery of the guilty party.'[92]

5

'The Particulars of the Present Revolting Case'[93]

As will have been very clear from the reconstruction of the inquest into Sarah's death in the last chapter, this book draws extensively on contemporary newspaper reports as well as on the original documents pertaining to the case. Although the formal record of the inquest and subsequent proceedings is crucial, it is surprisingly succinct, leaving out a good deal of material. For instance, several key witness statements are referred to in the documentation but not actually transcribed. Time may have been a factor when the formal record was still written out by hand. If accurate notes were not taken at the time, perhaps a decision would be made to leave things out. No doubt a degree of pragmatism was involved. But when journalists were also present a parallel record was created and, by stitching together details from both, a fuller account emerges.

Some newspapers' coverage stands out for its thoroughness and speedy response time. Only four days after Sarah's body was found and one day after the first session of the inquest, the *Dundee Courier & Argus* published an article about the case that sets it in context to a degree unmatched by any other paper. Often it is evident that newspapers bought in copy from other papers more local to the scene of a crime, so that very similar articles echo round from Newcastle to Leeds to Manchester and further afield. By contrast, the *Dundee Courier* had details other papers hadn't managed to get and it seems likely that they had their own reporter on the ground. Their piece opens with a description of the locus of the crime:

The village of Carr's Hill is composed of some straggling houses on either side of the road. The village is approached on the west by the road which leaves the old Durham road and runs past Deckham Hall. The village is principally inhabited by the labouring classes who are chiefly employed in the immediate neighbourhood.

About half-way up the street, on the right-hand side, is the house where Mary Melvin, the mother of the murdered girl, resides. Passing up to the east end of the village, a sharp turn to the left leads into a cart road past Laws' farmhouse. Continuing along this road for about 150 yards, a narrow passage through a wall gives access to a confined footpath, skirted on one side by the garden wall of Carr's House [i.e. Villa]; on the other by a rugged, rocky cliff of freestone, about eighteen or twenty feet in height. The garden wall is not quite five feet in height; and of either man or woman of ordinary height passing up this footpath a view is commanded from the windows of Carr's [Villa]. The garden in front of it is not of large extent, and after running parallel to the face of the rock a short distance, the wall turns off at right angles, the footpath following its course and leading into

Split Crow Lane past three or four houses known as Woodbine Terrace.

It was on the footpath at this angle of the wall that the body was found. From the spot, however, a short cut to the Felling could be made by skirting the quarry and crossing over into Nursery Lane near the plantation where the outrage was committed upon the little girl Hannah Bell. The quarry . . . has been somewhat singularly wrought. The rock on the side next Carr's [Villa] has been removed, leaving the cliff to which reference has been made. This cliff is continued some distance beyond the point where the angle of the garden wall is situated, and the stone having been removed on the south side, the cliff constitutes one face of a rocky wall of various thicknesses which screens the interior of the quarry completely from observation on all sides. Just at the spot where the body was found, a descent of a few feet leads to a high narrow slit in the rocky wall, through which easy access is gained to the interior of the quarry.[94]

Apart from referring to Carr's Villa as Carr's House (and risking it being confused with Carr Hill House just to the south-east of the village, the erstwhile home of Matthew Atkinson), this is a tremendously detailed and accurate description. The writer must surely have walked up to the quarry himself (he was almost certain to have been a man) and got a feel for the place and its criss-crossing network of footpaths. The Villa faced east (towards the Felling), but rather than having a garden in front of the house the Villa's main garden had been created in a triangular-shaped plot immediately to the south. It was separated from the house by one of the several footpaths running between Felling and Carr's Hill villages.

The *Courier*'s correspondent goes on to give a close account of

Sarah's movements on the day of the murder, followed by those of her parents. The piece was over two thousand words long and had ample space for details of Sarah's injuries as well as speculation on the murderer or murderers:

> The spot where the body was found precludes the idea that the crime was committed there. To believe that this was the scene of this shocking outrage is only reconcileable with a degree of recklessness on the part of the perpetrators which can scarcely be realised. The place is so open to observation that none but a madman would have attempted such a crime there ... Had the murder been perpetrated in the quarry, one cannot imagine conveying the body out of the quarry, and placing it upon the footpath. He could only be exposing himself to detection by any passer-by, and by placing the body where it was certain to be found ere long the officers of justice be brought all the sooner upon his track. Had the murder and supposed outrage taken place in the quarry, and the body being left there, it would probably have remained undiscovered until Saturday morning, when the labours of the quarrymen re-commenced.

The article gives another reason why the murder was unlikely to have been committed in the quarry: 'Carr's [Villa] stands close against the quarry, and in a garden within a very short distance a man was working until dark, which would not be until about eight o'clock. By no one was a single sound heard in the locality which would indicate that such a crime was being accomplished.' The only garden up on the hill was that belonging to the Villa. Did Mr Carr employ a gardener or had he perhaps been out working in his garden himself?

The *Courier* pulled together its observations: 'The conclusion inevitably forced upon the thoughtful mind is that the murder was not committed there, nor yet at the spot where the body was found . . . Where or by whom the murder was committed, the body was afterwards conveyed to the spot at which it was found by Burns [i.e. Joseph Bourne] and his wife.'

Perhaps the most striking aspect of this piece and others like it is the incredibly close focus – the report is published for readers in and around Dundee but is written in terms of such familiarity about the area around Gateshead and the Felling that most of those readers couldn't hope to share. In doing so, the writer renders the crime much more affecting. He takes the reader right to the heart of the murder scene, so that their emotions are aroused and their interest piqued. It is quite different from the emotional distance we feel when a terrible crime happens outside the area we think of as our own (the size of which has changed over time as a result of technological developments) – consider, for example, our emotional response to a terrorist act in our own country compared to one in a far-off place. It is very skilful and presumably reflects a deliberate editorial policy on the part of the newspaper. That they would publish such detailed and intimate coverage of a relatively far-away crime gives an indication of how important crime stories were to newspaper readers at the time.

After the repeal of the last penny of stamp duty on newspapers in 1855, newspapers finally became affordable by most people and the British press grew exponentially. Although the working classes had been able to access newspapers before their price fell (sometimes chipping in to purchase a paper between several people or listening to someone else reading out the stories if they could not read the paper themselves), the new affordability of newsprint nonetheless altered the make-up of readerships.

The *News of the World* had launched as early as 1843 and deliberately went after lurid stories in order to tap into what we now call the 'tabloid' market. Other newspapers followed suit. By the 1860s sensationalism was in full swing, with the middle classes as well as the lower orders feeding their insatiable appetite for crime on endless newspaper reports of battered wives, loose women and murders. It was at this time, too, that novels inspired by newspaper crime reportage began to appear, by writers such as Wilkie Collins, Mary Elizabeth Braddon and even Charles Dickens. Like any addiction, its hold over those who succumbed to it was strengthened as they consumed more and more of the gratifying substance – in this case heart-rending human-interest stories. Stories such as the rape and murder of a little girl had (and of course still have) a complex effect on readers: there were elements of fear (it could happen to you, or to your own child), moral condemnation and, hidden underneath it all, titillation, which could never be admitted to. The newspapers 'educated' their readers in the proper response to such events and also acted as a kind of open college where members of the public learned what would happen if they were called for jury service or to act as witnesses in criminal cases. People not only found out how trials were conducted and how the legal system worked but also absorbed all its unspoken values and inherent biases as well.

From a practical point of view, the use of telegrams (which developed massively after the founding of the Electric Telegraph Company in 1845) increased the speed and sheer quantity of newspaper reporting enormously. Another contributing factor was the growth of the railway network, which meant that copy could be conveyed speedily from all parts of the country to editorial offices where compositors toiled night and day to create two and very occasionally even three daily editions of the bigger newspapers, including those in provincial cities such as Newcastle (two editions to catch the morning and evening readerships;

three if there were a particularly newsworthy and fast-moving story with the potential to win extra sales). Economies could be made by carrying stories over from the second edition of the day before to the next day's first edition, and large areas of newsprint were filled with advertisements, turgid local news about council meetings and livestock prices and the like, as well as sports reports and cultural reviews. But the pages reserved for crime reporting had to be fed constantly with cases from the borough magistrates' courts, the quarterly or half-yearly assizes, and, of course, with the reporting of crime as it happened, before anyone had been brought to justice.

Readers may be surprised by the level of explicit detail given in the reports about Sarah Melvin's murder. In particular, the details reported of the wounds she suffered to her private parts are more graphic than would probably be found in today's newspapers. However, although the details are explicit, a sombre tone is maintained. The reporting is factual – and those facts are admittedly horrible – but there is little one can point to as gratuitous.

The historian Kim Stevenson, interestingly, has suggested that the local newspapers of northern towns were in the vanguard in terms of sexual explicitness in their reporting, and this is perhaps in evidence in the Melvin case.[95] But most newspapers across the country would report such details, particularly if they were part of a murder case, such was the public's appetite for crime stories by this time.[96]

Newspaper reports also drew a clear line between the description of injuries, however intimate, and the description of sexual acts. Reporters had to use what amounted to a code to signal to newspaper readers when sexual penetration had taken place during a crime. Restrictions on what it was 'proper' to say about sexual assaults and rapes could make prosecuting them difficult too. The problem was that a woman would be 'shamed' by being the victim of an attack and might even no longer be marriageable. Lawyers would collude to 'protect' a woman's reputation, to the extent that perpetrators might be convicted of lesser offences of assault rather than rape. Some women also lacked a vocabulary with which to describe what had happened to them and, for example, said that they had 'fainted' when in fact they had been violated.[97] In the accounts of Sarah Melvin's murder there is a blank space at the heart of the reporting where the journalists could not go. When describing the 'outrage' to which Sarah had been subjected, ellipses indicate a trailing off from verbatim reports, but it has been possible to fill in lacunae by going beyond newspaper reports to the original court records.

How accurate and fair was the reporting of Sarah's murder? By corroborating details using other sources, such as census returns, it's possible to say, for instance, that the *Dundee Courier* got the details of the Melvin family wrong. Their report said that there were four children – two boys and two girls – of whom Sarah was the youngest, whereas in fact there were six children of whom only the eldest was male. In other reports, the Melvins were said to be living together again at the time of the murder after a brief period of separation.[98] (Perhaps this was a self-protective lie by the Melvins, in the light of the unwanted publicity they suddenly received, although they *did* co-habit again, and perhaps got back together very soon after the murder.) Michael Melvin was also reported to live at Blue Quarries (another nearby village) rather than the Felling, but this is a minor detail.[99] In one report PC Kemp was said to have retrieved Sarah's body from where it lay on the path and brought it to the Gardeners' Arms.[100] Mistakes could enter newspaper reports when journalists spoke to members of the public who might betray their own bias (perhaps against the Irish) or who had already made up their minds that Sarah had been murdered by her mother, but on the whole the reportage is measured and surprisingly accurate.

At this time, everything that needed to be recorded was written down verbatim and mistakes – mishearings – were inevitably made. I have identified a number of these both in newspaper reports and in the official record of the case. In the transcription of Dr Benjamin Barkus's evidence at the inquest, for instance, when he goes through his autopsy of Sarah Melvin, the 'flora' of the vagina is (or perhaps are) referred to, but in fact this should have been the 'floor'. Similarly, a later statement refers to a 'lump' in Sarah's neck when in fact it was a 'loop' in the rope around Sarah's neck that was being alluded to. If the person transcribing a speaker's words was not familiar with the vocabulary being used or did not know what was being described, they would simply write down what they thought they had heard. But by comparing newspaper reports with official documents it's usually possible to pin down what was actually said. At least one newspaper referred to an injury to Sarah's 'uvulva',[101] an error that may have been caused by subconscious discomfort at having to use such words at all. 'Uvulva' should be 'vulva' (as it was in the official record) but is trying to become 'uvula', which is not nearly so disturbing a part of the body. However, I have discovered one particular instance of misreporting that is more serious.

Two weeks after the murder, at the end of April 1866, the *Leeds Mercury* reported a case of sexual assault on a little girl that was chillingly similar to that of Hannah Bell (see Chapter 2).[102] On Thursday 26 April a man named Robert Wilson who worked at Lee Pattinson's chemical factory at Felling was brought before Gateshead Borough Magistrates. He was accused of having attacked a 6-year-old girl named Ann Brown, back in early March. Ann lived with her parents on Coldwell Street (now Coldwell Lane), between the Felling and Windy Nook. In front of the magistrates, Ann, described as 'a most intelligent child of her years', was sworn in. Giving her evidence 'in a straightforward manner',[103] she told how she had been sent by her mother to fetch milk from Carr's Hill. Having passed two strange men on the way to the farm, the same men were still there on her return and one of them snatched her up, took her into the plantation, knocked her head against a tree and then violated her.

More details were given in the *Newcastle Courant*.[104] Ann's attacker had put his hand over her mouth, but she bit him and then tried to shout for help. After that he had beaten her head upon the ground until she passed out. Ann's mother eventually found her after becoming worried and coming to look for her.

Ann's attacker may have been 'inspired' by another sexual attack in the Gateshead area at the end of the previous year. On 14 December 1865 John Stark attacked Sarah Herring near Winlaton, to the west of Gateshead. He had already assaulted Mary Ann Trotter a year earlier. Sarah, aged 12, was going to fetch milk for her mother at three in the afternoon. Stark jumped out over a hedge, grabbed Sarah and threw his legs around her, then 'belaboured' her about the head with her milkcan.[105]

Robert Wilson had been picked out by Ann from amongst five other men at the police station after he had been apprehended a day earlier (no explanation was given as to why he had become a suspect) and during the hearing she referred to him more than once as the man who had attacked her. Now he was remanded in custody so that police could investigate not only the alleged attack on Ann Brown but also the possibility that Robert Wilson was responsible for the murder of Sarah Melvin, less than a quarter of a mile away from where Ann had been attacked. Things looked grave for Wilson.

In fact, I have established that the two attacks on Hannah Bell and

Ann Brown were one and the same. A number of papers got their facts wrong (including the details of the child's name, her father's name and where the family lived). Hannah Bell was an incorrect version of Ann Brown and only Ann Brown actually existed (she was born in Felling in 1860, her father was John Brown, her mother Elizabeth). This error seems not to have been discovered at the time. Because so many newspapers copied stories from each other, a mistake only needed to be made once and it would be picked up and repeated by several other papers. It was impossible for each newspaper to check all the facts independently, given the constraints of distance and timing.

The 'doubling up' of an assault on a little girl just a month before Sarah Melvin was murdered may reflect the growing sense that the Gateshead area was lawless and unsafe. Scare stories proliferate in such an atmosphere. In this instance, although one source had got their facts wrong, the story was essentially true. When Mary Melvin told the inquest that she had moved to Carr's Hill because her young daughters were scared of walking home through the quarries and plantations on the hill, it was because of attacks such as the one on Ann Brown. Carr's Hill felt dangerous.

6

Edgeland

On 31 May 1866, six weeks after the murder, a young man of 20, Joseph Adamson Curry, was walking home from his job as an assistant with Mr Waller, draper, of Grey Street, Newcastle (a smart job to have and one that was perhaps intended to set him up to take over his father's own tailoring business eventually). Curry had been to Mount Pleasant to drop off a parcel and was on his way home up Split Crow Lane at about 8 p.m. Home was Robson House in High Felling and he didn't have much further to go when he saw a man coming towards him, staring at him threateningly. This man then pulled a lump of lead attached to a length of cord out of his pocket and said he was going to kill Curry.

Joseph Curry decided to make a run for it and the thug gave chase. When he realised that he couldn't outpace the other man Curry stopped and grabbed a stone. He shouted at the man that if he came any nearer he would 'fell him'. The would-be assailant immediately put his weapon back in his pocket and said, 'If you don't touch me, I won't hurt you,' but Curry jumped on him, wrestled him to the ground and managed to take the lump of lead off him. Curry then went to the police (who weighed the lead at 1¾ pounds) and pressed charges – for he knew who the other man was.[106]

He was Cuthbert Carr, the 18-year-old son of another Cuthbert Carr. Cuthbert Sr was the respectable middle-class owner of Carr's Villa on Carr's Hill and a retired customs officer. As well as sharing a first name, father and son both also had the middle name Rodham, in honour of Cuthbert Sr's mother Ann Rodham (which incidentally makes them related to Hillary Rodham Clinton, though obscurely).

Cuthbert Carr Sr had married Sarah Robson in Newcastle in 1839 when he was 30 years old and she was 22; they lived with Cuthbert's recently widowed mother in the industrial Ouseburn district of the city. Like so many people in England during this period, they were not urban by birth but had moved to a city from a rural birthplace. Both Cuthbert's and Sarah's families' roots were in Northumberland.

The Carrs left Ouseburn soon after their marriage and moved to Sheriff Hill (close by Carr Hill). Perhaps Mr Carr wanted to bring up his growing family in the healthier environment of Gateshead Fell. His job as a customs officer in Newcastle must have tied him to the Customs House and the teeming Newcastle quaysides, so it might seem odd that he would remove himself to the relative backwaters of Gateshead, but many people commuted to work in Newcastle from there, mostly making the journey on foot, and the Customs House was just across the old Tyne Bridge from Gateshead. By the 1861 census Mr Carr, aged 52, was describing himself as a 'retired custom house officer'.

Cuthbert Rodham Carr Sr bought the freehold to the land up on Carr Hill in 1840 when it was advertised for sale by auction. The property included a windmill then used for grinding corn, a stone quarry, a seam of fire-brick clay, houses, cottages, a stable and around fifteen acres of land. Mr Carr then built Carr's Villa at the highest point of his land, between the quarry and the windmill. The building of the house from scratch took a considerable amount of time but they were building the house they wanted in the place where they wanted to establish themselves for good.

Mr Carr lost his wife Sarah to bronchitis in December 1865 but his eldest daughter, Jane, acted as his housekeeper (and was described as such in the 1871 census). Cuthbert's first-born son, Matthew, had died (of the rather vague-sounding 'debility') in 1857, aged 17 and in the first year of his being articled as a solicitor's clerk. All Cuthbert Sr's other children still lived at home with him: as well as Jane and Cuthbert Jr there were Ann, Sarah, Richard, Elizabeth and the youngest, John, aged just 9.

The social status of the family is rather unclear. Cuthbert Sr doesn't seem to have participated much in public life – his name doesn't occur in the newspapers as a jury member or on any committees (his neighbour Matthew Laws, in contrast, served as a local guardian of the poor). It's notable, as well, that they don't seem to have employed any servants, at least not any who lived in. They were hovering on the edges of the middle class. There would have been income, either directly or indirectly (i.e. from rent on leases), from the quarry, mill, land and houses, but it doesn't seem as though there was a great deal of inherited money. Perhaps any accumulated wealth had been sunk into buying the freehold on Carr Hill and building the Villa. The men of the family needed to work for a living but at the same time they were respectable and respected in the neighbourhood. And also liked: Cuthbert Sr was known to his neighbours as Squire 'Cuddy' Carr, surely a shortening made with some affection (although a 'cuddy' is also a donkey or a dolt in old northern slang). They don't seem to have been related to the enormously rich Carr-Ellison family of Newcastle and Northumberland, aristocrats who made their fortunes from coal

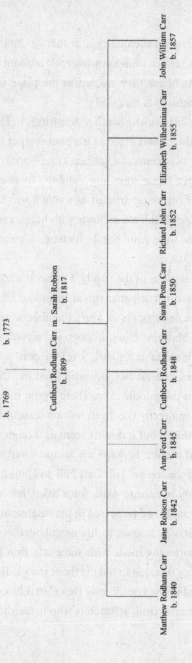

The Carr family

Matthew Carr m. Ann Rodham
b. 1769   b. 1773

Cuthbert Rodham Carr m. Sarah Robson
b. 1809   b. 1817

Matthew Rodham Carr — Jane Robson Carr — Ann Ford Carr — Cuthbert Rodham Carr — Sarah Potts Carr — Richard John Carr — Elizabeth Wilhelmina Carr — John William Carr
b. 1840   b. 1842   b. 1845   b. 1848   b. 1850   b. 1852   b. 1855   b. 1857

and trade, or if they were it was very distantly. Carr is a *very* common name in the north-east of England.

As already mentioned, there was no historic link between Cuthbert Carr and family and Carr Hill. The name of both the village and the surrounding area had been Carr Hill since at least the seventeenth century, but once the family were established there both became known as Carr's Hill by association with them. It's possible, though, that Cuthbert Sr was drawn to the area in the first place by the coincidence of the name. He must have derived a certain sense of kudos from residing in a house on a hill near a village all bearing his surname.

These few acres were liminal: the plot sat right on the boundary between the townships of Gateshead and Heworth and also straddled the boundary between Gateshead and Durham. Carr Hill floated between jurisdictions for decades and swapped between different enumeration districts in the census; no one seems to have been quite sure who controlled it. It was nowhere in particular, an edgeland. The strip of land was first defined as a single parcel when it was leased from local landowner Charles Brandling by a Charles Mills in 1800. Mr Mills built a windmill on the exposed rocky ground to grind corn. At some point the windmill was converted to grind sandstone into sand, to supply the glassworks at Warburton Place in Carr's Hill village. A waggonway was built to trundle 'chaldrons' of sand from the mill directly to the works. In *Ward's Directory of Newcastle and Gateshead* for 1865–66 John Robinson is listed as a sandgrinder at Carr's Hill, so that noisy, dirty work was going on whilst the Carr family were living in the Villa – in spite of the airy, holiday associations we have with 'villas', the setting wasn't as delightful as the name may make it sound. It was surrounded by rural entrepreneurs working hard for a living.

The sandstone quarries that fed the sand mill gave Carr's Hill an odd quality of impermanence. A quarry was nothing more sophisticated than a hole in the ground from which stone was presently being taken. They were small or large, more or less long-lived, depending on how easy it was to get the stone out of them. Over the course of the nineteenth century the location of the quarries changed regularly, as a study of maps from different decades shows. The footpaths that crossed Carr's Hill could thus never become absolutely fixed but went around the quarries, wherever they opened up. But although it was treacherous up there, especially after dark, it was also a highly convenient shortcut between Carr's Hill village and the Felling; another useful path cut through from Coldwell Street up to Laws' Farm (it was this path that Ann Brown was following to get milk for her mother when she was attacked).

Although Cuthbert Carr Sr owned the land there were rights of way across it, whether these were formal or informal, and people tramped at will up the drive to Carr's Villa and along the footpath that separated the house from its garden. It must have undermined the family's sense of ownership of their plot. Certainly this teenage boy, Cuthbert Rodham Carr Jr, seems to have felt a strong need to defend his patch. He behaved in a way that was aggressively territorial about the family's land up on Carr's Hill; this, in turn, seemed to encourage incursions that he experienced as hostile. It was a game of cat and mouse that had now got violently out of hand.

After Joseph Curry had complained to the police about Cuthbert Jr allegedly threatening him with a lump of lead, a warrant was issued for Cuthbert's arrest and the Chief Constable himself, John Elliott, went up to Carr's Villa and took the boy into custody. Cuthbert was slightly built, around 5ft 9in, with light brown hair, grey eyes and a fair complexion.[107] He did not appear threatening but, nonetheless, Chief Constable Elliott had taken four constables with him to make the arrest and they put the boy in chains before leading him away. Down at the police station in Gateshead he was charged with assault against Joseph Curry. Mr Elliott said that Cuthbert had 'talked a great deal of nonsense' when he was brought down to the station. What that 'nonsense' consisted of, we don't know.

The case came up before magistrates at Gateshead Police Court the following week, on 5 June. When Joseph Curry scrambled to his feet and ran away after wrestling the lead from Cuthbert's grasp, Cuthbert had allegedly said that he would be 'watching' him. In court Joseph insisted that he was 'really afraid of his life', as he frequently had to pass Carr's Villa on his way to and from work. But more details now emerged and suddenly the incident wasn't quite as clear cut as Joseph Curry had made out: Cuthbert claimed that Joseph had not been on his own (which was the way Joseph had told it) but that there had been five or six other young men with him and they had *all* been going to hit him. In other words, he had acted in self-defence.

However, Chief Constable Elliott said that he 'thought it was his duty to state to the bench that the prisoner was a terror to the neighbourhood, and the people had told him if he did not take steps to prevent the continuance of the prisoner's conduct they would draw up a petition. There was another young man besides the prosecutor,* who had been attacked by the prisoner, and who had avowed he would kill him, and a young girl and a man had also been threatened.'[108] There is an ambiguity in the way that Elliott's words have been set down: who had 'avowed he would kill' whom? I take the phrase to mean that the unnamed person who claimed that Cuthbert had attacked him had reported that Cuthbert had also threatened to kill him.

---

* A person bringing a case against another was referred to as the 'prosecutor', so here this means Curry.

Cuthbert was represented in court by a solicitor, George Brewis, and as Mr Brewis said that he had six witnesses he would like to call (but who were not present there and then) the bench agreed to adjourn the case until the following Friday.[109]

The court duly reconvened on Friday 15 June. The magistrates on the bench included Gateshead's Mayor, Edmund Crawshay Esq. Cuthbert had been remanded in custody since the first hearing, a period of ten days. Once again he was represented by Mr Brewis, who seems to have intensified his questioning of Joseph Curry:

> 'Curry repeated the evidence he had given at the former exam-
> ination, but positively asserted that he never was off the public
> highway until after the assault was committed. Mr Brewis
> cross-examined the witness very closely, and several times
> reminded him that he was on oath.'[110]

Next there was a witness for the prosecution. Thomas Lawson, a cooper, was sworn in and said that he remembered the night in question perfectly well. He and another young man were taking a walk up Split Crow Lane when they fell in with a third man, named Stephenson.* Lawson's friend climbed over the wall into the field (presumably either to urinate or defecate – all perfectly normal for the time), so Lawson sat down to wait for him on the bank at the side of the road. Stephenson sat on the wall. They were well placed to be an audience for what was about to happen.

Thomas Lawson recounted how he saw Joseph Curry coming down

---

* Several Stephensons crop up in the course of this book but none of them seem to be related to one another.

Split Crow Lane from Mount Pleasant. 'He passed me, and I then observed Carr coming in an opposite direction from Curry. When they met I saw Carr go up to him – they had some words, after which Curry turned back and ran up the road. Carr ran after him. I then followed, and when I came up to them Curry had a stone in his hand.' He added, 'I saw Curry take the lead from Carr, he took it from the right hand coat pocket.'

All of that chimed with Joseph's own account (as one would expect – they had had every opportunity to make sure their stories tallied). Lawson then said he had heard Cuthbert Carr say he would give Joseph the lead, if Joseph would return the string. He went on: 'Carr then went away up a footpath leading towards the quarry. Curry and myself with some others then went up the footpath that Carr had come down, when we saw him upon a bank.'

Here the lie of the land at Carr's Hill becomes a crucial element in events. Cuthbert had first appeared on the scene from one of the paths leading from Carr's Hill to Split Crow Lane (there were at least three). It seems likely to have been the path that ends at Woodbine Terrace. But having had his exchange with Joseph Curry he then went off up another path, probably the gravel drive leading directly up to the Villa. On the drive Cuthbert would feel the strongest sense of being in his own domain and of having a superior right to be there. Meanwhile, the other young men – Curry, Lawson and 'some others' (so perhaps even more had joined in by now) – went round the other way, up the same path that Cuthbert had come down: they were playing a dangerous game of cat and mouse. As all the footpaths converged on top of the hill, they found Cuthbert, by now in a defensive position up on a bank (there were many such banks of quarry spoil on the Hill).

Lawson said, 'He commenced pelting us with stones,' but then his account becomes rather confusing. He said, 'I took a stone up in each hand, and told Carr I would hit him if he did not give over. We were never off the road the whole time.' Footpaths were regularly referred to as 'roads' at this time; less distinction was made between unmade-up tracks and more significant routes. The issue, here, may have been one of potential trespass, but if the youths had not actually strayed off the paths which were legitimate rights of way, they could avoid getting into trouble for that.

Now Mr Brewis stood to make the case in Cuthbert's defence. He complained that Cuthbert had been very harshly treated by the authorities. When Cuthbert was arrested four policemen had accompanied Chief Constable Elliott and they had chained him and brought him down to the police station where he was locked up in a cell. In doing this, there may have been an element of giving the public what they wanted, as with the questioning of the Melvins at the inquest: Cuthbert was considered a holy terror, so Elliott could win some public relations points by demonstrating that he was taking a strong line with the boy. But Mr Brewis said his client was 'said to be of weak intellect, and such being the case it was the more necessary that he should have been more gently dealt with, and protected from the insults of a lot of lazy as well as cowardly fellows'.

Mr Brewis's version of events is slightly different from Lawson's and Curry's. He said that Cuthbert was

walking leisurely along the road, with his hands in his pocket, and after entering the gate into the road leading to his father's house, he was accosted by the prosecutor and [the] other three men, who said 'Cuthbert, you have no business here, we will not let you go.' Carr naturally drew the lead in his own defence. Curry then ran away up the road, Carr after him, with Lawson in the rear, so that his client was betwixt the two. When Curry stopped he picked up a stone, and Lawson took one in each hand.

The issue seems to have been that the Carr's Villa drive was actually private property, even though it was widely used as a right of way. If it could be proved that Curry and Lawson had chased Cuthbert up the drive, they would have been trespassing – according to their own account of events they had gone around by a different path (which seems less likely to be true). What's more, Mr Brewis said that he had 'numbers of witnesses in court that will prove that [Cuthbert was where Mr Brewis said he had been], and also show that there is a great deal of sympathy shown towards the prisoner in the vicinity of Carr's Hill. If Curry had not first interfered with Carr, there would have been no prosecution, but Carr merely defending himself had caused those proceedings to be taken.'

A very persuasive plank of Mr Brewis's defence was that 'If the young men had been afraid of the prisoner, they would not have followed him up the same footpath, but have kept out of his way.' Mr Brewis again repeated that he considered Cuthbert had been harshly dealt with, 'or otherwise he would have been brought there by a summons instead of a warrant, which was the usual way in cases of this sort'. He then called Elizabeth Dunn, Caroline Stobbs, William Dunn, John Mossman, Thomas Robinson, John Stephenson and Percival Robinson, all of whom swore that they had seen four men at or near the drive leading to Carr's Villa – two inside entrance and two outside. The witnesses all stated that Curry was the first one to insult the prisoner. John Robinson, sand grinder, and Francis Carrick were called to give character references for Cuthbert and they both declared that he was 'perfectly quiet and inoffensive'. Francis Carrick was a schoolteacher; perhaps he had taught Cuthbert at school. John Robinson ran the sand mill next to the Villa and must have known Cuthbert well. Thomas and Percival Robinson were his sons, Percival aged only 13 at the time of the court case.

After this the magistrates retired for a short time to discuss what they had heard and when they returned the Mayor said the bench had decided to dismiss the case. Joseph Curry had been foolish to try to pursue a case against Cuthbert when he himself was vulnerable to being accused of bullying the boy; it seemed he was not the innocent victim he had tried to make himself out to be. (In later life Curry became a successful grocer and, to judge by a family photograph, a rather mean-looking paterfamilias.)

After Cuthbert's appearance in court, his family sent him to the country to help on a farm, perhaps that of a relative (one of the farms where there had been a stackyard fire was owned by a Miss Carr but there's no way of knowing whether she was a relative of Cuthbert's). Feelings were running high and it was sensible to remove him from Carr's Hill until things calmed down.

Cuthbert was undoubtedly a misfit. At the age of 15, some three years earlier, he had been apprenticed at the nearby glassworks. This would have had the makings of a reasonable trade for him. Glass-workers were amongst the most highly paid (male) manual workers, earning on average 28–30 shillings a week in 1867 according to Baxter's *Hierarchy of Labour*.* If he did have some mental-health problems or learning difficulties (his 'weak intellect'), this could have settled him in a job for life and taken a lot of worry from his family's shoulders. Unfortunately Cuthbert absolutely hated going to the glassworks, to the point where it caused him severe distress. The apprenticeship

---

* Dudley Baxter, *National Income*, 1867. 28–30 shillings a week was on a par with printers, cabinetmakers, shipbuilders and others with specialist skills. They were in Baxter's second tier. Above them, earning on average 35 shillings a week, were the likes of surgical and optical-instrument makers, leather-case makers, engine-drivers and jewellery- and watchmakers.

would normally have lasted seven years but it had to be broken off after eighteen months as Cuthbert was suffering such acute anxiety. His work experience during the eighteen months seems to have been limited to packing the finished goods, so he was far from having learned the trade of glassmaking. The whole episode seems to have been a failure, succeeding only in rendering Cuthbert paranoid and defensive.[111]

Joseph Curry's older brother, Robert, had been apprenticed at the glassworks when he was 12 (in 1851). Now he was 27 and had very probably come across Cuthbert during his disastrous try-out at the works. It's easy to imagine the lads at the factory mercilessly bullying Cuthbert. Robert had probably regaled Joseph with accounts of the 'simpleton' at work and this may have spurred Joseph on to target Cuthbert later.

Cuthbert's older brother Matthew had died during the first year of his apprenticeship, when Cuthbert was just 9 years old. That loss must have been terrible for him. Could Cuthbert, still a child, have fostered a belief that it was the apprenticeship that had somehow 'killed' Matthew? When Cuthbert himself became an apprentice, perhaps he feared that it would be the death of him too?

After his indentures at the glassworks ended, Cuthbert tried bricklaying but only stuck at it for ten weeks, probably for similar reasons. If he had been apprenticed on his fifteenth birthday (in February 1863) and left the glassworks in August or September 1864, then, apart from his brief stint as a trainee brickie, he would have been ranging around Carr's Hill for a good two years with nothing to stop him getting into mischief. Cuthbert was a clever boy – one of his hobbies was the compiling of an Anglo-Saxon dictionary – but, as we have seen, many in Carr's Hill believed him to be 'of feeble intellect' and complained about his behaviour. As Deborah Cohen shows in her book *Family Secrets*, in Victorian England children who were mentally disabled were not generally hidden away in institutions (that came much later) but were usually accommodated and tolerated by their families (if not by local children and youths).[112] Cuthbert was not so mentally impaired that he couldn't be taken on as an apprentice but it seems he struggled to fit in. There is only so much information about Cuthbert that might allow a 'diagnosis' to be made (the only evidence ever given of the early onset of his mental-health problems was that as a child he refused to sit at the table for meals).[113] Perhaps he was on the autistic spectrum. Perhaps he was in the early stages of schizophrenia. There are other possible explanations too. Certainly his behaviour was becoming increasingly unpredictable.

7

'All About the Murder'

In the absence of a breakthrough in the search for Sarah Melvin's murderer, Chief Constable Elliott applied to the Home Secretary, Sir George Grey, for a reward to encourage anyone with information leading to the conviction of the perpetrator to come forward. The sum of £100* was duly put up on 13 June. And furthermore, if the informant should turn out to be an accomplice in the crime, they were promised a 'gracious pardon' as long as they weren't the actual murderer.[114]

Although it was relatively common for rewards to be offered, nonetheless it suggested that the police were not about to solve the murder without new information being injected into the case. They seemed to be showing their hand and that hand looked ineffectual.

No one hurried forward to stake a claim to the reward. Days passed with no apparent activity on the case. Another dead child had been found and Mr Favell, the coroner, held an inquest on 18 June. Nixon

---

* Equivalent to roughly £10,000 today, according to the Bank of England's inflation calculator.

Grey, a cartwright, had stumbled across a small body while mowing grass in a field near Catherine Street, on the west side of Gateshead. Dr Barkus carried out a post-mortem examination and said the body was that of a boy and that it must have been lying in the field for several weeks as it was quite badly decomposed. The age of the child was not given but it was probably an unwanted baby that had been disposed of by its mother. A verdict of 'found dead' was recorded.[115]

Another child killed, another inquest opened and concluded. The formal procedures were an effective way for communities to process terrible events. But as far as the Melvin murder was concerned, there was a sense of stagnation.

Then, on the evening of Wednesday 27 June at about 8 p.m., Cuthbert Carr, the boy who had so recently been acquitted of threatening Joseph Curry, walked into Gateshead Police Station. Police Constable Thomas Bryson was on duty in the charge room. Cuthbert came in and stood on the steps leading to the charge room. He asked to speak to Chief Constable Elliott. PC Bryson told Cuthbert the Chief Constable wasn't there and asked him if there was anything particular he wanted.

Cuthbert said, 'Yes, I want to see Mr Elliott to tell him all about the murder.'

PC Bryson replied, 'What murder?'

'The murder of the little girl at Carr's Hill.'

'You know something about it?'

'Yes. I will tell Mr Elliott but I'll not tell any other person.'

Bryson told Cuthbert he would have to detain him while he sent for Mr Elliott. It only took a few minutes for him to arrive. No doubt he wasted no time in coming to hear what this boy – who had already come to his attention such a short time ago – had to say. PC Bryson remained present (an important safeguard against any possible accusations of coercion or other malpractice) and Mr Elliott formally cautioned Cuthbert.[116]

The rule in place since 1848 was that a police officer could not question a suspect, which seems very strange today. The thinking behind this was complex and, to us, illogical, but boiled down to a fear that confessions would be rendered invalid if it could be proved they had been forced out of suspects, together with a belief that the proper place to test evidence was in court.[117] It was also felt necessary to avoid the risk of involuntary self-incrimination. PC Bryson bore witness to the fact that Mr Elliott did not question Cuthbert.

Cuthbert didn't need to be questioned. He was bursting to speak to Elliott. The Chief Constable had to write down whatever Cuthbert said, longhand, and Bryson noted that Cuthbert 'made the statement as fast as Mr Elliott could take it down in writing'.[118]

In reading Cuthbert's words, then, we need to bear in mind that they are as written down, firstly, by Elliott.[119] Then there is a further layer of transcription: John Elliott made his interview with Cuthbert public and at that point it was re-transcribed by an official. At two removes from Cuthbert himself, mistakes may have crept in (although Cuthbert himself confirmed on two separate occasions that Elliott's record of his words was 'every word the truth').[120] Nonetheless, Cuthbert's voice comes through powerfully and authentically, as though he were speaking directly to us. It makes for harrowing reading.

Elliott said, 'Now, Cuthbert . . .'

At once Cuthbert broke in. 'I wish to tell you all about the murder.'

'Well, you need not tell me anything unless you like.' Elliott gave Cuthbert the formal words of the caution, telling him, 'I will take down anything you have to say and it may be given in evidence against you.'

'I wish to speak the truth and to tell you all about it.' Cuthbert said that he had been 'sent to plough' over the past few days (since his release from custody after the Joseph Curry affair), adding enigmatically, 'and if it hadn't been for that I would have told you, but I would not have told you yet.' That doesn't make sense, logically, but it seems something had acted as a catalyst to strengthen Cuthbert's resolve. It must have taken some courage to come down and ask to see the Chief Constable. Yet in insisting on unburdening himself to the Chief Constable and no one else, there was an element of self-aggrandisement – only the top man would do to hear *this* story.

'I'm all wet with cold sweat,' he said, and rubbed his hands on his trousers.

Elliott took down the Occurrence Book where statements were written down. Immediately Cuthbert said, 'Now be sure and spell my name right,' and he spelled it out, saying that Elliott had spelled it wrongly on a previous occasion. 'It is Cuthbert Rodham Carr.' Elliott said he had not known they called him Rodham before that.

Then Cuthbert began.

On Friday afternoon the thirteenth of April – that is just the time – about half past two in the afternoon, I saw the little girl coming up the road – same road as the father and mother came up, after.

I took hold of her first and carried her away. She was over-frightened to cry, never spoke a word. I took her into the stable and up yon ladder, like, into the loft above, at the far end, like. She then said, 'Mother, Mother'. I just choked her then.

Before she was choked, I laid her down, then, you can understand, I laid on the top of her. She was choked after that.

I laid her underneath the hay to keep her warm. I can tell you the time when I think on. It was just half past six o'clock. I got one piece of string about a yard long. I split it with a pull. I tied the twine on her neck first. The neck had a loop in it, if I can mind right. She was dead long before that. I also tied her wrists together. That was at half past six, you know.

You know there is a door in yon stable. I opened yon door and just looked out at the door and I saw two women coming down – this Catherine Forster for one, the other one lives beside the Felling Station. I locked the door then – there is a lock in it you know – and come outside then.

I went into the house two or three minutes, like, and I saw Catherine Forster going up the road again. I could not see anyone else but her. Then I went up the road a bit myself, about thirty yards or so, to yon place where the gate posts is now. I went to look the distance where the gate posts had to be put in. It was a quarter to seven then. I stopped there about five minutes then came away again, came down again. I saw Catherine Forster coming down a second time, they were just singing, they did not speak to me.

I then went into the house for a bit. The stable door was locked at ten minutes to eight o'clock. My sister locked it with a key about quarter past eight and I went and opened it again. The key was on the chimney, it always lies there. I went upstairs into the loft after I had opened it and went to the corner where she was laying in under the hay. I carried her outside on to the road, you know. I was going to take her up the other way first, then there was some people came that way and passed us. I had her with me then. They went close past me and I put her onto the other side of the wall till they got past – close as you are to me. She was laying about three feet of[f]* some of the people

---

* The transcription says 'of' at this point but 'off' would make more sense.

when they went past on the other side of the wall. I was not a bit frightened, you know.

I then took her on to the road and picked the hay off her hair. Her hair was all wet with the water coming out of her mouth. The hay was all clagging onto it. I just carried her away to yon place. I had to wait a bit. There was some folks going down the road one after the other. I just let her drop over the wall out of our field at the corner, onto the footpath agin the wall. I was going over myself to take her into the quarry. There was someone come down, they were very noisy, but they did not come that way, they went into the Split Crow Lane by the back of our house. I then went into the house for about five minutes. I came out again to take her into the Quarry. I went round by the Split Crow Lane. I met the father and mother about ten yards below the gate. They were scolding one another very hard. I walked past them both. I then went up Williamson's Road to get to the other place, like. I heard them scolding themselves all the while. I waited a bit, maybe five minutes. They stopped about five minutes, very quiet, when they were up the other road beside our midden. I walked about twenty yards higher up the road. I was not as far up as where the bairn was lying. I had not got up to her when the father and mother went up the road again. I thought they were going to come down that road so I had to stop a bit. I waited till they got up the road a bit. They stopped talking when they got away.

There was the other two come down. They were speaking very low, they were walking sharp. I thought I could not get up to the bairn before they got down. I then went home the same road as I had come. I went into the house and went to bed maybe an hour after.

I never had a knife. She was torn with my finger. I tied her hands together just because the twine was there. It was our garden line. I burned it when you was there at a quarter past six o'clock the next morning, when you was down that road. I got up at four o'clock to see what was doing. I saw Kemp the Policeman there. There was the other two men there, sitting on the wall, Bob Bell and Dennis. They had only half their clothes on.

I knew the bairn was taken away. I saw the man and woman come down. I knew they could not pass it. I burned the garden line for fear it might be seen.

I think I have hardly anything else to say, but just I did not know who she was at the first. I knew her other sisters but I did not know her. When I was on the top of her that place was over small for me. I took my hand and tore it open. There was a lot of blood come out and I burned the hay that it come on to. I choked her until she was insensible. I then loosed my trousers down and lay on the top of her. Her heart was beating. She was breathing by gasps and died about ten minutes after that. After I pulled her open I got mine inside of hers. There was something come from mine. I never had a knife.

That was the end of what Cuthbert had come to say. Elliott read the statement over to him and Cuthbert agreed that it was accurate, saying, 'It is every word the truth now.'

The moment must have been extraordinarily potent. The Chief Constable would have been concentrating on taking down Cuthbert's confession as it poured out, focusing so hard that he probably couldn't actually take in the full import of the words. Then it was done, the confession made. And not just a flat admission of guilt but a horribly detailed account. How strange it must be for any detective who has failed to pin down the perpetrator of a crime to be handed all the answers in this way. Horror mixed with some sort of exultation.

At this point it's necessary to look closely at the substance of what Cuthbert told Chief Constable Elliott, to map the boy's account against those accounts of the day of the murder that had already been given by various actors in this awful drama. What new information was now available?

Most significant is Cuthbert's detailed memory of times. He says that he first saw Sarah at 'about half past two in the afternoon'. It will be recalled that the two teenagers Patrick Cain and James Mullen met Sarah just on the edge of the Felling at quarter to two. That time was confirmed as accurate by James Mullen having gone into a pub just after seeing Sarah to ask what the time was. So this now meshes with Cuthbert's account of seeing Sarah coming up the footpath from the Felling, back towards her mother's home in Carr's Hill village, at about half past two. A little girl of five, already tired from walking, would make slow progress up the steep hill path past Carr's Villa. Also, it seems that Sarah returned to the village by the slightly less direct route – the same route, as Cuthbert notes, that Mr and Mrs Melvin would take when they also returned to Carr's Hill from the Felling at around eight o'clock that evening: past the end of Woodbine Terrace, a little further westwards along Split Crow Lane, and then turning left into the Carr's Villa drive. The drive swept up from Split Crow Lane and round to the left into the stable-yard at the back of the Villa. Another path went round the side of the house to the front and at that same point several paths also branched off that all led back to Carr's Hill village.

Cuthbert Carr knew the lie of the land around his home intimately and moved around it quickly and efficiently. An important aspect of his personality was hypervigilance, probably fostered by his having been bullied since early childhood. He liked to keep on the move and to keep a keen eye out for threats.

He snatched Sarah at half past two in the afternoon and took her straight up to the loft in the stable at Carr's Villa. It was a standard loft at first-floor level for storing hay, and there was also a high opening to the outside with a pulley above it so that bales could be lowered down or lifted directly in.

Cuthbert said, 'I took her into the stable and up yon ladder, like, into the loft above, at the far end, like. She then said, "Mother, Mother". I just choked her then.' He was at pains to stress, later, that he was able to carry Sarah up the ladder under his arm with only one arm free to hold on to the ladder himself. He clearly felt slighted that doubt had been shed on his capacity to do this. It emerged later that, early in the investigation (on 18 April), the police had been following up the hayseeds found on Sarah's clothes and had searched the Carrs' stable, discounting the hayloft as a potential location for the murder on the grounds that no one would have been able to carry Sarah up or down the ladder. Cuthbert would have been aware of this search having been made. Another key characteristic of his personality becomes evident here: he could not bear anything he interpreted as a personal slight to be left unchallenged. His strength, having been demonstrated, must not be questioned.

It is surely significant that Cuthbert killed Sarah after she had spoken the only words he records her as having said. She cries out for her mother and that's when, impulsively, he chokes her. Cuthbert's mother had died just four months earlier, on 12 December 1865, and for a vulnerable boy who evidently had great trouble fitting in, that must have been a catastrophic loss. Sarah still had her mother and a lethal spike of envy and raw pain may have stabbed through Cuthbert's psyche at that moment.

Although Cuthbert's account of the murder may seem at first to be disturbingly controlled, in fact he jumps back and forth in time a good deal, perhaps indicating the difficulty of controlling what he said. In this somewhat confused timeline, Cuthbert now doubles back: 'Before she was choked, I laid her down, then, you can understand, I laid on the top of her. She was choked after that.' This is his admission of having sexually assaulted Sarah. His intention had been to rape her; he began to choke her to death after she called out for her mother.

Now Cuthbert jumps forward in time: 'I laid her underneath the hay to keep her warm.' Note that he says 'She was dead long before that' after he has described tying Sarah's wrists and neck with the garden twine. I believe he killed Sarah by choking her to death just as his sexual attack on her was ending (so not very long after half past two in the afternoon). Then he hid her in the hay with the deliberate intention of keeping her body warm to confuse those who would eventually find her body when he dumped it. In the meantime, he went out into the Carr's Villa garden, in full view of anyone who passed by on the footpath, and ostentatiously did gardening work in order to give himself an alibi. The *Dundee Courier & Argus* had mentioned this detail in its report of 17 April as an indication that the murder could not have taken place in the adjacent quarry (or this innocent gardener would have been sure to hear the child's cries), but the gardener was in fact Cuthbert.

Cuthbert left Sarah's body hidden in the hay for over three hours. Then, in the early evening, perhaps when the light was starting to fade, he went back to her and bound her wrists and neck: 'I can tell you the time when I think on. It was just half past six o'clock. I got one piece of string about a yard long. I split it with a pull. I tied the twine on her neck first. The neck had a loop in it, if I can mind right. I also tied her wrists together.' This preparation of the body before he took it away

96

from his own place was, it seems clear, to disguise in some way (perhaps only symbolically) what he had done to Sarah. Although entirely ineffectual, the tying of the twine around the neck that he had already strangled and the binding of the hands were both done to make it seem as though she had died a different death, not the death he had found himself compelled to inflict on her. It was done to mislead those who would investigate Sarah's death, but perhaps also to distance the awful thing he had done from himself, to make it more tolerable.

Now Cuthbert starts to work actively towards the disposal of the body. The time must be around twenty minutes to seven by now. He says, 'You know there is a door in yon stable. I opened yon door and just looked out at the door and I saw two women coming down – this Catherine Forster for one, the other one lives beside the Felling Station. I locked the door then – there is a lock in it you know – and come outside then.' Of course Cuthbert can't move Sarah out of the stable if Catherine Forster and her friend are going past. He opens the stable door and peeps out, sees the two women, so slips out of the stable and locks the door behind him (the sequence is slightly askew as he tells it – he couldn't lock the door before coming through it – but it's logical that he would lock the door behind him). He goes 'into the house two or three minutes, like,' no doubt watching what is going on outside from any window that affords him a view in the right direction, and then he sees Catherine Forster 'going up the road again. I could not see anyone else but her.'

This is key. He has seen Catherine Forster going past once, with a friend; now he sees her coming back again, on her own this time. (It is possible she was even seeing her friend safely home because the friend was nervous about the 'mad boy' who roamed around the Hill – the fact that Mrs Melvin had said her daughters were afraid to go home to the Felling from Carr's Hill adds further substance to this suggestion.)

It will be remembered that, at the inquest, Catherine Forster gave evidence under oath that she had met little Sarah 'in the narrow path between the garden wall and the rock'[121] at almost exactly this time, 'twenty minutes to seven'.[122] Catherine said, very touchingly, that Sarah had told her she couldn't find her way home and that, consequently, she herself went with the child back towards Carr's Hill as far as the Gardeners' Arms, in order to set her safely on her way. She told the inquest that she had said, 'You'll soon be at home, hinny.'[123]

Newspaper commentators had noted the apparent gap in the piecing together of Sarah's last day: 'From two o'clock she is not seen or heard of until twenty minutes to seven at night, and the minute investigations of the police have failed to elicit any fact by which a conjecture can be formed as to how or where she had spent the intervening five hours.'[124] No, they had not because, by Cuthbert's own account, she had been dead and hidden in the hay during that entire time. What was going on? There are possible clues in what Cuthbert says next:

'Then I went up the road a bit myself, about thirty yards or so, to yon place where the gate posts is now. I went to look the distance where the gate posts had to be put in.* It was a quarter to seven then. I stopped there about five minutes then came away again, came down again. I saw Catherine Forster coming down a second time, they were just singing, they did not speak to me.' Is an exchange between Cuthbert and Catherine concealed here? Did he threaten her, tell her to say she had seen a little girl on the path and taken her back to Carr's Hill or he would kill her – words to that effect? His ostensible reason for going up the road – to look at where the gate posts were going to be put in – is patently lame. He says he 'stopped there five minutes' – doing what?

---

* Mr Carr must have decided to erect a new gate to keep people off his drive after the unpleasant business with Joseph Curry and his mates.

Then he came back to the house again. He mentions seeing Catherine Forster 'a second time' but she has already come down a second time – this would be a *third* time – and suddenly she is with her friend again, now *singing*, and didn't speak to Cuthbert. It doesn't ring true, and why would Cuthbert say explicitly that they didn't speak to him if not to negate the fact that he actually did speak to Catherine? My supposition is that Cuthbert suborned Catherine to improve his alibi, thus relocating Sarah Melvin back in Carr's Hill village and still alive at twenty to seven in the evening.

Indeed, Catherine's statement at the inquest seemed to arouse the suspicions of the coroner: she was questioned much more closely than any of the other witnesses, including Michael and Mary Melvin, who, at the time, were suspects. Catherine made no mention of having been with another woman at any point – perhaps because that woman would not have corroborated her story.

Catherine had also said that she had seen a man up by Carr's Villa. First of all she said she had told Sarah to go home, 'for fear the bad man got hold of her'. But was this 'bad man' real or fictional? He seems to have been both. To begin with Catherine said that she had made him up, just to scare Sarah and ensure that the little girl didn't come back up on the Hill again. But then, when she was pressed by the inquest jurors, she added a few more flimsy details about the man, until finally she said that she had seen him defecating. Was this insubstantial figure a version of Cuthbert, who *had* been there but had told Catherine to keep him out of it? Had he crept into her account subconsciously, as things we're not supposed to say are wont to do? Or was the defecating man an invention intended to direct attention away from Cuthbert as a possible suspect?

Also at the inquest, a member of the jury remarked that it was 'a singular thing that the child should have gone down [towards the

Felling] again after the witness brought her up there, as she knew the road home well enough'.[125] This was a very pertinent point and again puts Catherine Forster's witness statement in doubt. As will be recalled, at the inquest it was felt to be crucial to determine the time of Sarah's death. This was estimated on the basis of how warm Sarah's body had been when found but was more firmly based on Catherine Forster's testimony. So between Cuthbert keeping Sarah's body warm in the hay and Catherine perhaps lying about seeing a child that had already been dead several hours, the authorities were sent down a false path that could have allowed the murderer to escape.

However, going *against* the likelihood of Cuthbert Carr having forced Catherine Forster to cover up his crime is his powerful urge to confess: one might reasonably ask why, if he was confessing to murder, he didn't also confess to this?

There was also the reward for anyone who led the police to Sarah's murderer: might Catherine not have been tempted to claim it by telling the authorities that Cuthbert had forced her to lie? Perhaps not, if he had put her in real fear of her life. When it's impossible to know what really happened, theories multiply like a hall of mirrors.

Returning to our close reading of Cuthbert's confession, we come to the disposal of the body. Cuthbert seems to have been putting on a nonchalant front: 'I then went into the house for a bit. The stable door was locked at ten minutes to eight o'clock.' It was part of the normal security routine of the household for Cuthbert's older sister to lock up the stable at around eight o'clock. (The sister was probably Jane, aged 23, who had the role of housekeeper.) On this particular evening she locked up at quarter past eight, whereupon Cuthbert took the key from its usual place and went back into the stable.

Now we can observe Cuthbert's powerful territoriality at work once again, along with the exploitation of his knowledge of all the ways around Carr's Hill, his domain. He brings Sarah's body out of the stable and onto one of the many 'roads' or paths near the Villa. This is a time of extreme jeopardy for him – he is carrying the body of the child that he has raped and murdered. He cannot afford to be discovered with her and yet these paths are well-used thoroughfares between villages and people go up and down them all the time. He shows a coolness (or perhaps a lack of affect) under this intense pressure that not many 18-year-olds would be able to call on:

'I was going to take her up the other way first, then there was some people came that way and passed us. I had her with me then. They went close past me and I put her onto the other side of the wall till they got past – close as you are to me. She was laying about three feet of[f] some of the people when they went past on the other side of the wall.' He hears people coming, so simply tips the body over the garden wall and waits until they have passed him. From his saying, 'I was not a bit frightened, you know,' one would perhaps infer that he was very frightened indeed.

Now he retrieves Sarah's body and takes it back to the footpath. He must be about to leave the body since he starts to think about cleaning it up: 'I then took her on to the road and picked the hay off her hair. Her hair was all wet with the water coming out of her mouth. The hay was all clagging onto it.' This 'water' is a horrible detail: saliva or mucus – fluids produced more copiously than normal as Sarah's body struggled in its final moments of terror and death, now running from her mouth.

It must have been a particularly busy time of day with people walking home from their work at the Carr's Hill glassworks and pottery: 'I had to wait a bit. There was some folks going down the road one after the other.' He must have had to hide Sarah's body on the other side of the wall a second time, and this time he climbed over the wall to hide himself as well. Finally he 'just let her drop over the wall out of our field at the corner, onto the footpath agin the wall.' No wonder Sarah's head had a number of quite severe contusions: these were most likely caused by her body being dropped several times on one or other side of the garden wall.

At this point Cuthbert still had to climb back over the wall to the path, so that he would again be on the same side of the wall as the body: 'I was going over myself to take her into the quarry.' But 'there was someone come down, they were very noisy, but they did not come that way, they went into the Split Crow Lane by the back of our house.' The paths were so closely intertwined that someone making noise on one path would be heard on another.

Cuthbert seems to lose his nerve somewhat now: 'I then went into the house for about five minutes.' There are probably just too many people about, but it is quite urgent that he should move Sarah's body from the path and hide it in the quarry: 'I came out again to take her into the quarry.' But instead of going straight to the body by the most direct route, he goes 'round by the Split Crow Lane'. Cuthbert moves around his territory at speed, using its network of informal pathways and cut-throughs to arrive at different points ahead of or behind people as he desires. He is always highly aware of everyone who intrudes on his patch.

Now the whole sequence of manoeuvres reaches its apogee: Cuthbert encounters the father and mother of the child he has killed on Split Crow Lane. Luckily for him, they are engrossed in arguing with each other: 'I met the father and mother about ten yards below the gate. They were scolding one another very hard.' And it will be remembered that both Michael and Mary Melvin mentioned having passed a man just by the entrance to the Carr's Villa drive – so they had in fact encountered their child's attacker unawares.

Cuthbert knew who they were by sight and he had to get away from them; no doubt the mental pressure on him was extreme at this point. 'I walked past them both. I then went up Williamson's Road to get to the other place, like.' Williamson's Road is the 'cart road' leading from the Gardeners' Arms past Matthew Laws' farm towards Carr's Villa and the Felling. Cuthbert plays cat and mouse with the Melvins, all the while aware that their daughter's corpse is lying on the footpath close by. He listens to their progress: 'I heard them scolding themselves all the while. I waited a bit, maybe five minutes. They stopped about five minutes, very quiet, when they were up the other road beside our midden.' The midden was the open-air rubbish heap where all the household waste from the Villa, including from the privies, was thrown. It was just on the other side of the stable-yard wall, beyond the coach house – so it was close to the drive which the Melvins, as we know, had taken to reach Carr's Hill village, thus narrowly avoiding stumbling across Sarah's body themselves.

Cuthbert still has the intention of retrieving Sarah's body from the footpath and moving it to the quarry (where, as the police and news-papers surmised, it would probably not have been found for at least a couple of days) but he has to manage his own movements in relation to those of the Melvins and anyone else who may appear: 'I walked about twenty yards higher up the road. I was not as far up as where the bairn was lying. I had not got up to her when the father and mother went up the road again. I thought they were going to come down that road so I had to stop a bit. I waited till they got up the road a bit. They stopped talking when they got away.'

But immediately, 'There was the other two come down.' This was Joseph and Ann Bourne: 'They were speaking very low, they were walking sharp. I thought I could not get up to the bairn before they got down.' This is the moment when Cuthbert abandons his plan to move Sarah to the quarry and simply runs away: 'I then went home the same road as I had come. I went into the house and went to bed maybe an hour after.' One can only imagine the thoughts running through the boy's head as he waited for those minutes to pass before he could escape to bed.

At this point in his confession, which is essentially over, Cuthbert backtracks and fills in a number of details regarding aspects of the crime where he is particularly concerned that the truth should be known. These relate notably to the accounts of the inquest that he had read in the local newspaper and on which he feels the need to set the record straight. Dr Barkus had said that the wounds inflicted on Sarah's genitals looked to him as though they had been 'caused by a knife'.[126] No, Cuthbert insists, 'I never had a knife. She was torn with my finger.' And as for why he bound her wrists, 'I tied her hands together just because the twine was there. It was our garden line. I burned it when you was there at a quarter past six o'clock the next morning, when you was down that road.'

Cuthbert reveals the intensity with which he kept watch over the site where the body was found: 'I got up at four o'clock to see what was doing. I saw Kemp the policeman there. There was the other two men there, sitting on the wall, Bob Bell and Dennis. They had only half their clothes on.' So when Alexander Kemp dragged himself out of bed at four in the morning on the day after the murder in order to carry out a close search as soon as there was light, Cuthbert was spying on him. He saw the two men who came along from the glassworks in their shirtsleeves – Robert Bell and Dennis McClure – whom he almost certainly knew from his own time at the glassworks. He must by now have been terrified that the murder would quickly be pinned on him: 'I knew the bairn was taken away. I saw the man and woman come down. I knew they could not pass it. I burned the garden line for fear it might be seen.'

Finally, and horribly, Cuthbert talked explicitly about the rape and murder of Sarah: 'I think I have hardly anything else to say, but just I did not know who she was at the first. I knew her other sisters but I did not know her.' He snatched the little girl he saw wandering past his house opportunistically, then realised, later, who her family were. Whether that realisation came before or after he killed her, we don't know.

He was determined to penetrate her vagina: 'When I was on the top of her that place was over small for me. I took my hand and tore it open. There was a lot of blood come out and I burned the hay that it come on to. I choked her until she was insensible. I then loosed my trousers down and lay on the top of her. Her heart was beating. She was breathing by gasps and died about ten minutes after that. After I pulled her open I got mine inside of hers. There was something come from mine. I never had a knife.'

Has a more terrible or frank statement of such a vile crime ever been made?

8

'Spoiled Entirely'

Immediately after making his confession, Cuthbert was held in custody and the legal machine began to work through its inexorable process.

Then, the next morning, after a night in the police-station cells, Cuthbert asked to speak to John Elliott again. Elliott had him brought up to the charge room. Cuthbert said, 'I wish to speak to you to tell more,' and, as on the previous day, Elliott wrote down Cuthbert's words as he spoke them, having again cautioned him. Elliott must have wondered what on earth Cuthbert was going to confess to now.

We can still hear Cuthbert's voice, coloured by the local dialect, in the transcribed words. He said:

I got the bad disorder at Berry Edge. That was what set us on, like. I was spoiled entirely. I thought the other way was the only way in getting clear – I imagined that at the time. I am better now. There is a difference between the old and young, do you see? You can understand it. I intended to kill her. That was the only way to keep it quiet. She did not know [me] at the first, the bairn did not know me, but she knew the place, like. That is all I have to say but, mind, I got better with that. A Staffordshire man told me that but I do not wish to name his name.[127]

When Cuthbert's statement, including this second part, was read out at a magistrates' hearing the next day and, naturally, transcribed by journalists for consumption by their readers, this section was variously censored. The *Dundee Courier & Argus*, which had heretofore given such a full account of every aspect of the murder, said that 'the prisoner' had given 'an account of his motive for committing the crime which is too horribly disgusting for publication'.[128] The *Carlisle Journal* said that Cuthbert had 'contracted a loathsome disease at Berry Edge. The violation and murder had undoubtedly been suggested to the mind of the wretched man by an unfounded belief unfortunately too common amongst grossly ignorant men.'[129]

It seems that the newspapermen understood Cuthbert's words perfectly well but deemed their meaning too horrible for publication. Certainly Cuthbert spoke much less plainly this second time than on the previous day. Although he does appear still to be in the grip of a powerful desire to confess his crime, even as he reveals more horror he obfuscates and blurs. The transcript, written in the smooth hand of the court transcriber, lacks punctuation. I have broken up the stream of words to make the best possible sense of them, but their meaning can't be entirely pinned down. This veiled language coupled with the fact that Cuthbert initially withheld his explanation of his reason for attacking Sarah indicates that it was difficult for him to admit to. But at the same time he still needed to 'come clean' to Elliott.

That phrase takes on a ghastly appropriateness in the context. The 'bad disorder' was a commonly used term for a sexually transmitted infection – syphilis or gonorrhoea. Cuthbert says he caught it at Berry

Edge – this is the town now known as Consett, which lies around fifteen miles south-west of Carr's Hill. Two years earlier, in 1864, the Consett Iron Company had been founded to make steel using the relatively new Bessemer process and the huge new works inevitably attracted not only workers and their families to the town, but also, as in any industrial hotspot, prostitutes in great numbers. It's relatively easy to find cases in the local papers of the time of young women being prosecuted for plying their trade at the entrance to the steelworks. It's quite likely that Berry Edge was one of the places young men went to from Gateshead to get their first experience of sex: far enough away to be discreet but where they were sure to find what they wanted. Cuthbert had picked up an STI (sexually transmitted infection), probably from a prostitute.

Cuthbert goes on to say that it was contracting the STI that 'set him on', by which he means started him on the path to murdering Sarah. His phrase 'spoiled entirely' speaks of his abhorrence at the symptoms of the infection. He says, 'I thought the other way was the only way in getting clear.' What does he mean by 'the other way'? He is referring to what was known as the 'virgin cure', the belief (entirely erroneous, it goes without saying) that sexual intercourse with a virgin girl, the younger the better, would cure a man of venereal disease. This horrible superstition had been prevalent in Britain since at least the eighteenth century and played on powerful (age-old) ideas of purity and its power to defend and heal.

Certainly Cuthbert seemed to be fully signed up to the idea: 'There is a difference between the old and young, do you see?' He even says, 'I am better now.' But one of the most disturbing aspects of the 'virgin cure' was the way that the primary symptoms of the sexual infection naturally diminished in any case as the secondary symptoms – which were much less visible but more serious – set in. So a man who raped a virgin child might believe, as Cuthbert seems to here, that his infection had 'cleared up', that he was better. And if the child then developed the primary symptoms of a sexual infection in turn, that would seem to confirm that the disease had been successfully 'passed on'.

Cuthbert ends this second session with the Chief Constable with the admission that he deliberately killed Sarah so that she could not identify Carr's Villa: 'I intended to kill her. That was the only way to keep it quiet.'

So Cuthbert Carr raped Sarah Melvin in an effort to rid himself of an STI.

The following Sunday, 1 July, Cuthbert requested a visit from John Elliott in his cell at the police station where he was on remand. When Elliott got there, Cuthbert told him that he was feeling unwell and needed a doctor (the word he used was that he was 'bad', meaning 'ill'). Elliott sent for Doctor Barkus. A few days later, as part of evidence he gave in court, Barkus said, 'I examined the Prisoner in the Police Station. I found him suffering from a gleet, the remains of a previous gonorrhoea. I have seen him twice since, he is still suffering . . . The Prisoner may have been suffering for some months from gonorrhoea – it might be more than twelve months.'[130]

Cuthbert, then, was still suffering from the suppuration of matter from his penis (the 'gleet'), a symptom of inflammation of the urethra and the classic sign of persistent or chronic gonorrheoa. Proof, if any were needed, that the 'virgin cure' did not work. Hopefully, Cuthbert understood that the cure had not worked and never could work. It's possible that he did understand this: when he says, 'I thought the other way was the only way in getting clear – I imagined that at the time,' he may be admitting that he has now realised he is still not 'clear' of the disease.

Sadly, belief in the entirely fallacious 'cure' accounts in part for the huge (and largely hidden) incidence of gonorrhoea in young girls in the nineteenth and early twentieth centuries (it was also of course often simply due to sexual abuse by infected men). In some parts of the world, principally in some African countries, belief in the 'virgin cure' is still prevalent (for example as a cure for AIDS).

The knowledge that Cuthbert attacked Sarah in order to apply the 'virgin cure' to himself strongly suggests that the sexual assault on 6-year-old Ann Brown in early March 1866 was probably also carried out by him – his first attempt to 'get clear'. The attack took place five weeks before Sarah's murder, no more than 'a quarter of a mile' from Carr's Villa, according to newspaper reports. Cuthbert didn't need to murder Ann because she didn't know him and therefore, according to his simplistic logic, she wouldn't be able to identify him.

It will be remembered from Chapter 5 that towards the end of April Ann had identified Robert Wilson, a chemical worker from the Felling, as the man who had raped her. Wilson was remanded in custody so that the police could investigate his alibi and also to see if they could link him to the then-unsolved murder of Sarah Melvin. Wilson claimed to have been at work at the time the assault on Ann was committed and said that he could produce witnesses to back him up.[131] Luckily for him, when Mr Hornsby, Wilson's foreman at Lee Pattinson's works, was called to a hearing in May he produced the factory's time-book which recorded that Wilson had worked 'a day and two hours' (from six in the morning until eight in the evening) on the day of the attack. Three of Wilson's workmates, Thomas Brown, Michael Kelly and John Wallace, also testified that he had not left the works until after 8 p.m. With this convincing alibi, Wilson was discharged.[132] No one else was ever accused of the attack on Ann Brown, not even Cuthbert, who, with hindsight, was very likely responsible.

*   *   *

Some time after he had made his confession, Cuthbert expanded upon it. Although we will come to the circumstances in which he did so in a later chapter, it's valuable to take this later account out of sequence and look at it here, because it refers so closely to Cuthbert's original confession and also because it further begs the question of why he had such an overwhelming need to lay bare his thoughts and motivations with regard to Sarah Melvin.

In reading the following paragraphs, it's important to note that they represent a boiled-down version of a dialogue, transcribed during an examination by psychiatrists. Their questions have been removed and only Cuthbert's responses remain, so that what he says seems to jump from sentence to sentence. However, it can be understood if it is read as his answers to the psychiatrists' prompts, intended to establish his moral outlook on various issues (his sense of right and wrong) and his mental capacity in various areas.

This revisiting of his original confession is even more harrowing than the original version. It's upsetting to read. He said:

I killed her because I thought if I didn't it might lead to bad consequences. I know what will out – murder will out. (*He laughed.*) If it hadn't come out for fourteen years they couldn't have touched me. Anybody that isn't found out is clear of murder in fourteen years. If you took that umbrella and didn't pay for it, it would be yours in six years. That is the law. If it had come out before that, I might have been out of the country. I have killed animals; vermin must be killed. It would be wrong to kill human beings. I never fight; I am very patient. I learned arithmetic; I can count pretty fair. Nine times nine are eighty-one. I was always considered quick at figures. I made this confession because I thought it would be best to tell all about it and get it off my mind, you know, and stand the consequences. I'm not afraid.[133]

With regard to the crime itself, as part of the same examination Cuthbert said:

I carried her up into the loft; I had my arm under her body. She was too frightened to cry. This is correct. She was too frightened to cry, I tell you, and, besides, I stapped my hand on her mouth. Yes, I carried her up a ladder with my right arm under her body, and my left hand on her mouth. Yes, I did it. It is possible, for I did it. I never carried a child before, but I have carried other things. She was pressed against my breast. She clung to me; I had no pity for her, at least not at the time. If she had cried out I would not have spared her, I would have done it all the same. So I would if she had begged for mercy. She did not speak at all except when I was choking her. She cried 'Mother! Mother!' It did not touch my heart a bit. I was determined to get quit of the disease because I couldn't bear it any longer. Doctors are no good. They do their best to protract disease, and when they can't protract it any longer they kill their patients; besides, if I had gone to a doctor it would have become known. They are dishonest, doctors. They poisoned the wells in the cholera time. It was to cure myself and keep it quiet I did this deed. It couldn't have come out in my case. I destroyed the proofs – the hay and the twine. I wasn't afraid of being found out. I was suspected. I laughed when they told me I was suspected; of course, I denied it then. The lassie was one of the proofs, that was why I destroyed her. She would have told on me. She didn't know me, but she knew the place, or she might have kenned me again. I took her into the hayloft because there were men working in the quarry. I choked her to make her insensible, and keep her from crying. I felt no sorrow. She wasn't dead, but gasping, when I had connection with her. I had the ordinary pleasure that a man has when having connection with a woman. After that I choked her again; I did it to kill her. She was still gasping; I had no pity (*smiling*). She was ten minutes in dying. I sat by and watched her till she was dead. Then I happed her up with the hay; it was to keep her warm. I did that because I was going to take away the body afterwards and lay it down somewhere, and I thought it would mislead them as to the time it was done if it was warm.[134]

This elaboration of his confession gives important insights into Cuthbert's personality, as well as into the crime itself and his reasons for confessing to it. As he must have realised, perhaps when the reward for information leading to the murderer was declared, the police were not closing in on him. He knew that they had searched the stable at his house, including the hayloft, and that had not led to the discovery of any evidence pointing to his being the perpetrator. Clearly this was playing on his mind when he talked about the statute of limitations and his belief that, if his crime was not pinned on him within fourteen years, then he could no longer be held to account for it: 'Anybody that isn't found out is clear of murder in fourteen years.' There is no statute of limitations on murder in English law and never has been, so Cuthbert was mistaken here. But, as Cuthbert said, it was very unlikely that he could have been held to account for the murder if he had left the country. So why, then, was he compelled to confess?

Given the level of suspicion and dislike directed towards him by many of the villagers of Carr's Hill, Cuthbert may have felt his arrest was imminent. If he could stay one step ahead of the people baying for his blood, he could control the narrative about himself, and dictate (literally) the terms on which his arrest was made. That seems to have mattered more to him than the loss of his freedom.

Cuthbert understood that actions had consequences. He said: 'I killed her because I thought if I didn't it might lead to bad consequences.' Then, very quickly, he adds, 'I made this confession because I thought it would be best to tell all about it and get it off my mind, you know, and stand the consequences.' In Victorian England the chief consequence of confessing to murder was usually hanging. Yet I think that Cuthbert's main motive for confessing was to rid himself of his secret, of the burden of having done something that he knew to be bad. He quotes Chaucer: 'murder will out' (the quotation goes on, 'that see we day by day. Murder is so wlatsom [loathsome] and abominable'), from *The Nun's Priest's Tale*. It's almost a joke, in this blackest of contexts, and I think that's why Cuthbert laughed when he said it, even though this may strike us as sinister or callous. The 'bad consequences' of not killing Sarah were that she would identify him as her attacker. But would the bad consequences of not confessing to the murder have been harder for Cuthbert to withstand than the possibility of being hanged: the torment of a guilty conscience?

His questioners must have begun by trying to determine whether he 'knows right from wrong', almost certainly a testing of the M'Naghten Rules on insanity in advance of a trial: *What can be killed?* Animals, vermin, can be killed. *Can humans be killed?* No, it would be wrong to kill human beings (and yet . . .). *Do you have a bad temper (would you kill in a rage)?* No, I'm very patient. *Are you an imbecile?* No, I know my times tables. I was always considered quick at figures.

When it comes to the crime itself, this is a retelling of the original confession. It's as if, before making his confession, Cuthbert wrote a script that he then memorised. Perhaps that's effectively what he did do, going over and over in his head the precise words he would use to inform Chief Constable Elliott of his bad deed. Now (a few months later) he is required to go over it again and so he returns to the script, which he can still remember pretty well.

It's impossible to tell for certain at this point whether the transcription indicates a sequence of separate answers given by Cuthbert to specific questions or a kind of dialogue with himself, checking the story against his memory as he goes through it yet again. Perhaps the former is more likely. 'I carried her up into the loft . . . She was too frightened to cry. This is correct. She was too frightened to cry, I tell you, and, besides, I stapped my hand on her mouth. Yes, I carried her up a ladder with my right arm under her body, and my left hand on her mouth. Yes, I did it. It is possible, for I did it.'

The reassurance of reality for him is palpable: people said that it was impossible to carry a child up a ladder but he doesn't have to prove that it is possible because he did it. It happened. For Cuthbert, I think that things that happened had a special quality of truth that mitigated their impact, however terrible. From the importance of having his name spelled correctly (and that middle name *was* quite frequently misspelled as Roddam, Rotham, Robert or even Lodham) to his need to prove his strength and his lack of fear, the 'truth' about himself was paramount. Truth had a special status for him and that is a large part of why he had to confess. The 'truth' of things anchored him in the world and gave him identity. It made his strange, embattled existence tolerable.

It was a single-string kind of morality – nothing more than honesty, really – that lacked almost every other resonance we think of as 'human': 'I had no pity for her, at least not at the time. If she had cried out I would not have spared her, I would have done it all the same. So

I would if she had begged for mercy . . . It did not touch my heart a bit.' He lacked any empathy for Sarah, and says as much.

By contrast, it's just possible that our hearts may be touched by Cuthbert's anguish at having caught venereal disease: 'I was determined to get quit of the disease because I couldn't bear it any longer.' He has a paranoid theory about doctors – or perhaps he had a fine understanding of the profit motive that underpinned nineteenth-century private medicine: 'Doctors are no good. They do their best to protract disease, and when they can't protract it any longer they kill their patients.' A little exaggerated, perhaps, but no doubt the more cynical commentators of the day would have agreed with Cuthbert. His opinion sounds like something he has picked up from reading outspoken newspaper columnists, or perhaps his father expounded such views at the dinner table. Had this jaundiced view been forged in the misery of Cuthbert's mother's final illness the previous Christmas?

There was a terrible stigma attached to sexually transmitted diseases, and the stigma, of course, stopped individuals from admitting they were infected, so that the bacteria, viruses and parasites that caused them were spread much more widely. Cuthbert felt the shame that silenced so many sufferers of STIs: 'if I had gone to a doctor it would have become known.' Cuthbert was able to confess to being a murderer more easily than to having caught gonorrhoea. No, *worse*, it was easier for him to commit murder than to face the shame of sexual infection: 'It was to cure myself and keep it quiet I did this deed.'

Once again Cuthbert demonstrates his profoundly disturbing capacity to talk about both his terrible acts and his feelings in an apparently affectless way, even with some apparent pleasure – if we're to believe the asides about his laughing and smiling. It's possible, though, that these are tics, signs of social awkwardness and not true indicators of a perverted sense of humour.

Cuthbert's use of the phrase 'ordinary pleasure' is the nadir of all that he says about what he did to Sarah Melvin. 'I felt no sorrow. She wasn't dead, but gasping, when I had connection with her. I had the ordinary pleasure that a man has when having connection with a woman. After that I choked her again; I did it to kill her. She was still gasping; I had no pity (*smiling*).' Yes, he is a monster here, by all the ways in which we judge people to be 'monsters'. A cold-blooded, cruel, cunning monster. But it's easy to call someone a monster.

9

Sensation

News of Cuthbert's arrest and the fact that he had made 'certain statements of a criminatory character' had already got into the local newspapers by the day after his second confession.[135] To judge by the newspapers' reactions, there was little sense of surprise. The *Newcastle Courant* reported that when the Curry assault case was being heard 'suspicions were rife as to the prisoner's innocence of the murder of the little girl'.[136] It went on, 'On that occasion the Chief Constable averred that Carr was a terror to the neighbourhood, and many people stood in fear of him.' One may wonder, then, why the police were not able to arrest Cuthbert on suspicion of murdering Sarah at some earlier point, but it seems that there had been no supporting evidence. The work of looking for that evidence 'went on very slowly',[137] said the *Newcastle Guardian*, with a hint of criticism (although, generally, the local newspapers were very supportive of Elliott and his men). Even now, after Cuthbert had made a full and graphic confession to the murder, it was reported that much would depend upon the corroborative evidence that could be produced.[138] There was also some doubt over whether the confession itself would stand: 'What weight can be attached to the statement – given, as it is, by a person of weak intellect – remains yet to be seen.'[139]

The confession itself was not made public immediately, but if people were eager to read the incriminating words themselves they did not have long to wait. Two days after he had turned up at Gateshead Police Station to speak to Chief Constable Elliott, Cuthbert Carr appeared before the Borough Magistrates for a remand hearing. The magistrates' court was crowded for the hearing with members of the public keen to see the boy who had confessed to the 'outrage' on Carr's Hill. Newspapers carried word of the murderer's appearance in court to their waiting readers:

> As he passed forward into the court the feelings of the specta-
> tors found expression in a manner to show that difference of
> opinion prevailed amongst them. Whilst some gave utterance to
> expressions of aversion aroused by the monstrous nature of the
> crime, others again, apparently struck with the unmistakeable
> mark of a weak intellect impressed upon the prisoner's features,
> were moved by feelings nearly allied to pity and commiseration.[140]

One hundred and fifty years on, given that we so readily view the Victorian era as a dark pantomime of harshness and cruelty, it's surprising that 'pity and commiseration' are the words chosen here. And heartening too. At the very least one wants this odd, evidently disturbed boy to have the benefit of a fair hearing. This, it seems, was going to be the case. The *Newcastle Guardian* said, 'Carr, while in the dock, appeared to be somewhat eccentric in his manner, but the question of his insanity or imbecility remains to be proved by the medical authorities.'[141] Most of the newspapers that covered the story took a similar stance: there was no frenzied baying for Cuthbert's blood.

Cuthbert's father attended the hearing and the *York Herald* reported that 'much sympathy is manifested for the relatives of the unfortunate young man.'[142] The *London Evening Standard*, which reported the case in detail, including a transcript of the full confession, said that Cuthbert 'did not betray any emotion in the dock, except occasionally smiling as portions of his statement were read.' It added, 'His parents occupy a respectable position.'[143] Apart from the fact that the paper was seemingly unaware that Cuthbert's mother had recently died, his father's respectability was probably the factor most in Cuthbert's favour as far as the likely outcome of the case was concerned (and, almost certainly, also explained the newspapers' circumspection, at least in part). In the nineteenth century the criminal courts were as class-ridden as every other area of society and you stood a much better chance of being acquitted of even the most terrible crimes if you came from a well-off family than if you were poor.[144] A straightforward equivalence was easily made between a 'better class of person' and moral decency.

Mr and Mrs Melvin were also in court. If anybody was aware of the vulnerability that being poor brought about it was the Melvins, who had been held by the police and interrogated over the death of their own child. No wonder they wished to see the alleged perpetrator with their own eyes, to reassure themselves that they were no longer suspects. And perhaps to express their grief and rage at the boy who had taken their child. If they saw that the crowd was minded to pity Cuthbert on account of his 'weak intellect', it surely would have deepened their sense of alienation from the entire society in which they had ended up.

The hearing cannot have lasted very long. It consisted of the reading out, by the Chief Constable, of the confession he had himself scribbled in the Occurrence Book ('as fast as he could take it down').[145] In itself this must have been strange to see, the solemn authority figure effectively performing a monologue by a deeply disturbed young criminal, allowing himself to 'become' Cuthbert for as long as the confession lasted. When it came to Cuthbert's description of how he had torn Sarah Melvin's flesh with his fingers, there was 'sensation' in the court – audible responses by those present to the distressing words.[146]

George Brewis, the solicitor who had defended Cuthbert in the Curry case, represented him again but had to admit that 'he could not raise any valid objection against the prisoner being remanded'.[147] His only hope, as far as defending his client went, was that Cuthbert's statement would not be proven: 'He had a strong hope that this was all fancy on the part of the weak-minded young man.'[148]

Cuthbert was formally remanded until Wednesday 4 July when committal proceedings would be held. That did not give the Chief Constable very long to substantiate the case against Cuthbert – less than a week – but he said he should have evidence enough prepared by then.

On the following Wednesday Cuthbert was duly brought before the Gateshead magistrates' bench again, now formally charged with the wilful murder of Sarah Melvin. It was the task of this hearing to consider the evidence in the case, including the statements of witnesses, in order to decide whether there was a sufficiently strong case for the accused to be tried. Since 1848, magistrates had been forbidden to interrogate the accused, though they were permitted to cross-examine prosecution witnesses.[149] The accused in the dock could not be questioned, but they or their representative were allowed to cross-examine witnesses.

In reconstructing the committal hearing, the detailed newspaper reports that are available have been stitched together with the official transcripts of the witnesses' statements from the National Archives. The documents were tied together with faded red ribbon in a box full of papers from court cases in 1860s Gateshead and Newcastle. A thick layer of gritty coal dust coated everything. The knots had never been undone before.

It is not so much that either record is biased or censored but rather that small details are missing from both. This must be the inevitable result of verbatim transcription, to which there was, of course, no alternative at the time (the typewriter would not be commercially available in England for some years). Read together, the missing details in one are often supplied by the other.

Before the proceedings got under way, Mr Brewis made an intervention. He said that he intended to file a plea of insanity on behalf of his client but that, if Cuthbert were to be committed for trial, there would be insufficient time for the necessary assessment of his mental state by qualified medical men before the next assizes, which were fast approaching (the Durham summer assizes were due to open on the following Monday, 9 July). Mr Brewis said that he had consulted with Dr Barkus and also with Mr Brickwell, a surgeon, and both agreed that it would be 'extremely difficult to examine the state of the prisoner's mind' before then.[150] Whatever the outcome of the committal proceedings, Mr Brewis asked that any trial be postponed until the following assizes (which would take place in December). But his request was in vain, or, rather, the Magistrates' Clerk felt that any decision regarding postponement would have to be taken by the judge at the assizes. So the case was heard as planned.

Now the witnesses who had previously given sworn statements at the inquest were required to appear again and go over their evidence a second time, together with any new witnesses whose parts in later stages of the affair were now germane. Taken together, the sequence of witness depositions entered into the record was intended to shape the case against the accused, in order that a legal case for trial might be made against him.[151] So poor Michael and Mary Melvin had, once more, to recount their movements on the fateful day of the murder. Mary, understandably, seems to have found taking the stand an ordeal. She was 'greatly moved' by having to speak publicly about Sarah, almost certainly weeping.[152]

This time it was notable that both the Melvins made more of the 'tallish man' they had passed close to the entrance to the Carr's Villa drive. (Mary also glided over the hour or so that she and Michael had spent in the Shakespeare pub at the Felling from 7 p.m., saying instead that she had got to Michael's house at 'about eight'.)[153] Mr Brewis, stepping up to cross-examine them in turn on Cuthbert's behalf, clearly tried to make something of their new focus on the tall man. Was this the only man Mr Melvin had seen? Michael replied that he might have passed other men without noticing but that he had already mentioned seeing this particular man, at the inquest.[154] Why hadn't Mrs Melvin mentioned this loitering man at the inquest if he was so significant? Mary's response, as recorded, makes it sound as though she was completely flustered: 'It was not very long that my Husband and I stopped in the Lane, it was not many minutes, it was just a few minutes – I don't know how many minutes make an hour. I don't know whether or not the Coroner asked me if I had seen a man. I was so confused at the time.'[155]

Almost inevitably, the Melvins were subtly slanting their accounts to incriminate Cuthbert, who was now widely thought (and correctly so) to have been the young man whom the Melvins had seen up on Carr's Hill while they were arguing. As we shall see, other witnesses also discreetly amended their statements to fit the new picture that had been revealed by Cuthbert's confession. Mr Brewis obliged Mr

Melvin to state that he had been questioned twice already about his movements on the day of the murder – no doubt in an effort to discredit him and revive the possibility that he might still be a suspect in the case. However, Brewis did not really seem to strike any meaningful blows for his client.

After the Melvins it was the turn of the boy James Mullen (who had met Sarah at the Felling at a quarter to two) and then Joseph Bourne to rehearse their stories once again. Mr Brewis did not have very searching questions for them but tried to pin down exactly where the Bournes had met Mr and Mrs Melvin. Perhaps he still had a vain hope that the murder might be pinned on them?

Next on the stand was Police Constable Kemp, who once again produced the pieces of garden twine that had been tied around Sarah's neck and wrists. When he came to describe the straw and hayseeds that had been caught in Sarah's hair and on her clothes (including in the pocket of her dress), he produced a packet containing them. He also produced a second packet of seeds which he had collected from the Carr's Villa hayloft. This was new. Kemp said that he had searched the 'cow byre' (that is, the stable) and outbuildings of Mr Carr on 18 April and 'brought away some hay seeds that were lying on the floor' – it was these he was now producing. He said that there had been some hay 'lying in a corner of the loft' and that to 'get to the hayloft you have to go up a ladder'. No one was now questioning whether it would have been possible for someone – anyone – to climb up the ladder to the hayloft carrying a child (even with one hand over their mouth to stop them from crying out). Thus, again, the 'official' narrative can be seen to be moulding itself to Cuthbert's confession.

Mr Brewis's cross-examination of Kemp seems to have been entirely ineffectual. He asked Kemp where he first saw hayseeds on Sarah's clothes (Kemp said it was at the Gardeners' Arms when he first saw the body) and about how much hay had been in the hayloft – Kemp said 'about three trusses'. Kemp described the hayseeds found on Sarah's body as 'quite fresh' and said they 'had been under cover all winter at some place'. He then said that he had been back to Mr Carr's loft since 18 April. Mr Brewis wanted to know if Kemp knew for certain where the hay found on Sarah's clothes had been grown. Of course Kemp could not say that he did. Brewis tried to land a blow against Kemp's hayseed evidence by asking him whether he knew Matthew Laws' farm. Kemp said that he did (indeed, that was the farm where he had fallen ill trying to protect it from the firestarter). Asked how far it was from Carr's Villa, Kemp said that it was about 300 or 400 yards distant. Had Kemp compared the hayseeds from Sarah's clothes with those from Mr Laws' stack? Kemp had not.[156] The inference was that the seed might have come from any farm, particularly the farm closest to the Villa, and so could not be used as a reliable means of tying Cuthbert to Sarah.

At that point, perhaps fearing that the validity of the police's only physical evidence that could link Cuthbert to Sarah Melvin was being undermined, the Chief Constable broke in to say that Mr Laws' hay-stack had been sold at the end of April and was no longer available (which, of course, did not refute Brewis's point that the seeds might have come from there rather than from Carr's Villa but nonetheless put an end to Brewis's line of questioning).[157] Kemp's evidence was completed and he stood down.

Now Dr Barkus was called to give the details of his post-mortem examination again. It must have been particularly awkward for Dr Barkus to take the witness stand that day. It was largely on the basis of his evidence at the inquest (together with Catherine Forster's alleged meeting with Sarah) that the time of the murder had been estimated. He had said then that 'It was quite possible that the limbs might be cold in almost an hour: scarcely less than an hour.'[158] This had tended to corroborate Catherine Forster's story and had caused general acceptance of the idea that Sarah had been killed not much more than an hour before her body was found. Now, having heard Cuthbert's confession, he altered his interpretation of events, the better to fit with the boy's: 'I was of opinion that the child had been dead some hours when I first saw her.'[159]

Similarly, with regard to the injuries to Sarah's genitals, at the inquest Dr Barkus had said they 'had been done by a sharp instrument' and that 'the instrument had been drawn upwards'.[160] It was clear he believed a knife had been used. He had also said, back in April, that he believed the cause of Sarah's death was strangulation with the cord that had been tied around her neck. But now, having heard Cuthbert's insistence, firstly, that he had not used a knife and, secondly, that he had choked Sarah to death with his bare hands (and tied the cord around her neck and wrists several hours later), the doctor said, 'I thought one wound in the vagina had been inflicted with a knife. I told the coroner that I thought the wound might have been inflicted with a sharp-pointed knife. On reconsideration, I am disposed to think that the marks on the child's neck above the mark of the cord on the left side might have been done by fingers. I now think that both the fingers and the cord may have contributed to the death.'[161] This was not a complete volte-face, but it was still a significant move away from his initial interpretation of the post-mortem evidence.

Most seriously of all, at the committal hearing Dr Barkus altered his statement (from what he had said quite categorically at the inquest) with regard to whether or not Sarah had been raped. It will be recalled that at the inquest he had concluded that there had been no rape but that wounds he thought *suggestive* of rape had been inflicted on Sarah's body *after* her death. Barkus had said then, in an exchange with the coroner:

> The Coroner: 'You did not discover that she had been violated?'
> Barkus: 'There was no trace of it.'
> 'You could not make out that she had?'
> 'No.'
> 'Could there have been any attempt without your discovering it?'
> 'It is possible, but I think I should have found traces if there had.'
> 'And a more bruised appearance?'
> 'Not a more bruised appearance. The wound had been caused by a knife.'
> 'Either at or after death?'
> 'Shortly after death. I am pretty strongly of opinion that it was after death.'[162]

This conclusion had been reached largely on the basis of the amount of blood that Sarah had lost (based on the blood on her body and clothes) and the strength with which it seemed to have been pumped out of her cut veins. It was also based on the fact that he had not discovered any semen in Sarah's vagina (that was what trace/traces referred to). But after the doctor had heard or read Cuthbert's confession, he subtly altered his reading of Sarah's wounds in *this* regard as well. He now said: 'The vagina was so much torn and destroyed, I cannot say whether or not she had been violated. I found no trace of semen.'[163] This was a different – and more honest – account of what it had been possible to infer from an examination of Sarah's body. Yet by making an assertion (more of an over-interpretation) about the circumstances surrounding the sexual attack on Sarah, Dr Barkus had caused her own mother to be suspected of killing her and faking the rape of her own child in order to divert suspicion away from herself. The fact that he had not found any semen in Sarah may have been due simply to the rudimentary pathology techniques available at the time. Cuthbert, in his confession, had talked graphically about his having intercourse with Sarah and said, 'There was something come from mine,' suggesting he did ejaculate.

Some of the contradictions in Dr Barkus's different versions of events emerged under questioning from Mr Brewis (it was the practice of the newspapers to report only evidence given and not the questions asked, so we don't know exactly how Mr Brewis went after Barkus). But beyond undermining the doctor's apparent expertise to a certain degree, there was nothing that was going to help his client in any practical way. Indeed, Dr Barkus had altered his account to fit more closely with Cuthbert's confession, so that tended to give it a more powerful sense of truthfulness.

After Dr Barkus had finished, it was the turn of Sergeant Bryson to describe what had happened when Cuthbert had turned up at the police station seven days earlier. The *Newcastle Journal* had a detail that was missing from every other account – perhaps whichever sharp-eared reporter the paper had present was able to write more quickly (or accurately) than the others. Cross-examined by Mr Brewis, Sergeant Bryson said that Cuthbert had said he would have confessed to the murder sooner 'but he did not wish to put his father about,'[164] meaning (in a very northern turn of phrase) that he didn't want to upset or trouble his father. This was an early glimpse of Cuthbert's relationship with his father.

Chief Constable Elliott now took the stand and went over his part in the investigation from the very beginning. He made a great deal of the hayseed evidence (it was all he had, after all). He also (like Kemp) said that the seeds found on Sarah's clothes were 'quite fresh'. Then he said that on the day after the murder, he had gone to the place 'where the body had been found. I searched field over field and hedge over hedge but could not find any hayseeds.'[165]

Perhaps Elliott was relying on the power of the hayseeds to tie up the case conclusively as a result of reading about a case in Alfred Swaine Taylor's recent book, *The Principles and Practice of Medical Jurisprudence*, which hinged on hayseeds being found on the body of a victim:

> In Reg. v. Hazell (Taunton Lent Assizes, 1848), the body of the deceased was found in a well. When examined, there were on the head several severe wounds quite sufficient to account for death. There was much blood on the clothes and face, and in the blood were sticking a quantity of hayseeds, which led the medical witnesses to consider that the wound must have been inflicted in a stable, or in some place where there was hay. On examining a neighbouring stable, the spot where the murder was committed was rendered evident by the discovery of marks of blood.[166]

To that end, as soon as Mr Elliott had finished reading out Cuthbert's confession, a brand-new witness was called. This was one William Stephenson, who worked as foreman to Mr Finney, seedsman. He had been in the seed trade forty-eight years, he said. He had scrutinised the two packets of hayseeds produced by PC Kemp (one from Sarah's clothes and hair, the other from the Carr's Villa hayloft). At first Stephenson said, 'I have examined the two packets of hay seeds, and, as far as my judgement goes, they are both of one kind. There are many varieties of hay seeds, all having distinctive marks.' So far so good, as far as corroborating Cuthbert's confession went, but then Mr Brewis came forward to cross-examine the seed expert. In answer to what may have been a very well-informed question or perhaps a lucky one,

Stephenson said, 'There are two varieties of seeds in the larger packet [the seeds from the hayloft]. But I will not swear there are two varieties in the smaller. I will not swear they are both from the same field or the same stack.'[167] This evidently very down-to-earth man had just contradicted himself utterly and thrown away any chance of linking Cuthbert to Sarah through the seeds.

That was it. One might question why Catherine Forster was not called to give a statement at these proceedings. Of all the witnesses at the inquest, her evidence was most at odds with what was now known as a result of Cuthbert's confession. Surely she should have been questioned on this? However, it's possible that she was not called by Mr Brewis because Cuthbert had let him know that her testimony was untrustworthy. After all, if she had been coerced by Cuthbert into covering up certain aspects of the murder, it wouldn't help him if she revealed this on the stand. As for the prosecution, they had Cuthbert's confession and hardly needed to do very much other than present it for the murderer to be committed for trial on his own say-so.

Cuthbert was remanded for a further two days so that the written records of all the witness statements (the depositions) could be prepared and signed as accurate. Once this process was complete, Cuthbert would be committed for trial at Durham Assizes. He himself had played no active role in these committal proceedings – as mentioned, he was not allowed to be questioned and Mr Brewis had asked questions on his behalf. As has so often been noted in the trials of very young or immature people accused of serious crimes (for example, Mary Bell or Robert Thompson and Jon Venables), he seems to have been disengaged from the process, perhaps not fully understanding what was happening: 'The prisoner, during the proceedings, did not seem to mind what went on, but simply looked as a disinterested party, occasionally looking wildly around the court.'[168]

As the hearing drew to a formal close, Mr Brewis made an application for a Dr Alexander and other 'medical men who had had experience in cases of insanity' to examine Cuthbert in his cell 'as frequently as they think fit'. The bench had no objections.

10

'We Use "Imbecile" in the Legal Sense'[169]

The timing of Cuthbert's committal hearing in relation to the next Durham Assizes was most unfortunate. The assizes were held in Durham every six months, in July and December, and were referred to as the Summer and Winter Assizes (there were occasionally Spring and Autumn Assizes too). Serious crimes were fed through to the assizes from all over the county to be tried before a judge and grand jury. The Durham Summer Assizes were due to open on Monday 9 July, only three days (and that was including a weekend) after the depositions made at Cuthbert's committal had been drawn up. The depositions were a vital part of the formal process of indictment, which preceded a trial: the indictment was a written document drawn up for each case by the Clerk of Court, bound together with the depositions, and then considered by the jury.

The indictment read: 'The Jurors for our Lady the Queen upon their oath present That Cuthbert Rodham Carr on the thirteenth day of April in the year of our Lord one thousand eight hundred and sixty six feloniously wilfully and of his malice aforethought did kill and murder one Sarah Melvin. Against the Peace of our said Lady the Queen, her Crown and Dignity.' Below this charge was written the single word, 'Murder'. [170]

It was for the jury to decide whether the indictment constituted a 'true bill', in which case the accused would be tried; if, on the other hand, they deemed the case 'not found', it would be dropped and the accused discharged. George Brewis (who would not actually defend Cuthbert in court – he had retained a barrister, Mr Blackwell, for that purpose) was working tirelessly to have Cuthbert discharged by means of an insanity plea, but there had not been sufficient time for a full assessment of his mental state to be carried out. The proper working through of justice was at stake.

The assizes were a legal juggernaut, trundling into Durham city every few months with a long-established protocol. Where once the judge would have ridden into town on horseback or in a carriage, these days he caught the express train from London and was met at the station by county officials and accompanied to the courts. The judge at this time was Sir Robert Lush, a well-known member of the Queen's Bench who had been knighted the previous year.*

It was a regular aspect of the assizes for the judge to pass a commentary on the range of cases that were about to be considered, a kind of editorial. Justice Lush's overview of the court's business sought to score a political point, first of all, then focused on the Carr's Hill murder: 'his lordship said there was nothing in the calendar [of cases] to congratulate [the jury] upon, and nothing particular to find fault

---

* On Sir Robert's death in 1881, the *Spectator* wrote a fulsome obituary of which this is a brief excerpt: 'He was a strong Judge, without the least tincture of arrogance or self-assertion; a quick Judge, and yet in the highest degree cautious and painstaking; and a universally popular Judge, who never "played to the gallery", or deviated by a hair's-breadth from the line of strict impartiality.'

with. He found eight cases of stabbing and wounding, and these had been committed in that state when the men were neither drunk nor sober – and it appeared that so long as the high rate of wages prevailed in the county, such crimes would be repeated. There were two cases of murder, and one was a most horrible case indeed. As to the prisoner Carr, from Carr's Hill, who was committed last week, in all probability there would be an application to postpone the trial, on the ground that he was of unsound mind. This was an element for [the jury] to consider, but he had a strong opinion as to the law of the matter.'[171] What that opinion was remained to be seen.

As could perhaps have been anticipated, the jury, after considering all the documents in the indictment, found it to be a true bill – meaning that Cuthbert must stand trial for murder. Cuthbert was now locked into the criminal justice system, having confessed to a crime for which the statutory punishment was death. It was time for his legal representatives to play the only card in their hand.

Mr Blackwell handed a document to the Clerk of the Court. It was an affidavit (written in beautiful copperplate handwriting) that had been sworn by George Brewis at Newcastle the previous day before Joseph Shipley, a 'Commissioner for taking affidavits'. This is the wording in full:

In the Prosecution of

The Queen against Cuthbert Rodham Carr

I George Brewis of the Borough and County of Newcastle upon Tyne Attorney at Law make oath and say

1. That the Prisoner was on Friday the sixth instant committed to take his trial for wilful murder at the present Durham Assizes.

2. That I have been retained to defend the Prisoner by his friends and only obtained a copy of the Depositions on the afternoon

of Saturday the seventh instant.

3. That the evidence against the Prisoner is a confession made by him to Mr Elliott the Superintendent of the Police for the Borough of Gateshead after voluntarily surrendering himself into custody.

4. That the main ground of defence will be Insanity.

5. That shortly before the Prisoner's surrender I heard the above mentioned Superintendent Elliott declare in open Court that the Prisoner was believed to be a dangerous Lunatic and that the Inhabitants of the locality of the Prisoner's home were about to petition the Magistrates to take steps to restrain the Prisoner or words to that effect.

6. That I have had the Prisoner examined by several Medical Practitioners who require larger opportunities of examining the Prisoner before they can arrive at a definite conclusion as to his sanity.

7. That I require time for the purpose of collecting the Evidence alluded to in Number '5'.

Sworn at the Borough of Newcastle upon Tyne aforesaid this ninth day of July – One thousand eight hundred and sixty six [signed] Geo. Brewis[172]

It was a bold move to use Chief Constable Elliott's own words about Cuthbert (during the Joseph Curry assault case) in a desperate bid to have him declared insane. Mr Brewis was also trying to buy time by saying he would need to collect statements from the inhabitants of Carr's Hill as to their views on Cuthbert. Where previously local opinion had been prejudicial to Cuthbert's chances of fair treatment (when his name was bandied about as a possible suspect in the murder investigation) it now became a straw to be clutched at.

Responding for the prosecution, Mr Meynell said he was willing to leave the decision in the judge's hands and had not received any instructions to oppose a postponement of the trial. Justice Lush said that the prisoner had only been committed the Friday before and upon his own confession: 'That confession, of itself, was sufficient to show to anyone that it was not made by a perfectly sane man. It was quite reasonable to allow an opportunity for having his state of mind examined by competent persons. He therefore put the trial back till the next assizes.'[173] He added that he 'felt no doubt in the matter.'[174]

Brewis's gambit had been successful. Cuthbert was duly remanded until the Winter Assizes in December and sent to Durham Gaol where his mental health was assessed by the medical staff. He was also occasionally visited by doctors from the County Lunatic Asylum at Sedgefield.

The report that was subsequently prepared by Robert Smith MD, the Medical Superintendent of the asylum, is a fascinating document and provides a vivid snapshot of mid-Victorian psychiatry:

Report as to Mental Condition of Cuthbert Rodham Carr, a prisoner confined in Durham Gaol, examined by me on the 1st, 3rd and 6th days of December of the present year.
I am of opinion,
1. That Cuthbert Rodham Carr is a person of unsound mind and I have formed this opinion on the following grounds.
A. From his postural appearances. He sits in a listless idle manner indicative of imbecility. His gait is awkward and incoherent.
B. From his Physionomical [sic] Appearances. He has a simple, weak or imbecile expression of countenance. His mouth is

small and the lips thin. The pupils of his eyes are dilated. His ears are misshapen and improperly developed. His shoulders are high and awkward looking. There is considerable curvature of the spinal vertebrae which throws the head back and the neck forward. He has a vacant, unmeaning laugh in which he frequently indulges without provocation.

C. From his mental constitution. He is suspicious and irritable. The suspicions which he entertains regarding his father amount almost to delusions. With the exception of Memory and Imagination his Intellectual faculties are of a low order. His Memory is almost abnormally acute. Though he can in some measure distinguish between right and wrong his views on complex cases are clouded and uncertain.

2. That he labours under that form of insanity known as partial imbecility.

3. That it is possible that the disease may be owing to congenital defect but it is more probable that it is the result of a retardation of development during the early years of childhood.

4. That his disease is liable to be increased by any disturbance of the cerebral circulation such as fear, intemperance, disease, exhausting discharges (seminal emissions).

5. That his disease will probably terminate in Dementia.

6. That he is irresponsible for his acts and a proper person to be under care and treatment in some Asylum.

With regard to subdivision C in the above report I may state that it is a recognised fact that where Memory and Imagination are unduly developed or where they are not kept in check by other Intellectual faculties the unfortunate possessor is apt to be Eccentric and to become Insane.

I beg further to state that after my first interview with the Prisoner I made enquiry into his family history and discovered several instances of Insanity among his immediate relatives both on his father's and mother's side – of Paralysis – of Epilepsy – of Eccentricity and of Talent. I also discovered that the Prisoner himself had been when teething the subject of convulsions.

Robert Smith M.D.

Superintendent

Durham County Asylum

Sedgefield

7th September 1866 [175]

Robert Smith's signature and the few lines that come after it look to be in different handwriting from the rest of the document – not so odd if the report were dictated to a secretary and then signed off. But the dates pose more of a conundrum: why is the report dated 7 September 1866 if Dr Smith did not see Cuthbert until those three days in December mentioned at the very beginning? Cuthbert was in the asylum for six months, from the second week in July until 10 December 1866 when his trial began. Perhaps Dr Smith saw him in September, then hurriedly updated the report just before Cuthbert was due to leave the asylum – though the document does not appear to have had an addition shoehorned in. Perhaps the doctor was absentminded and wrote 7 September instead of 7 December? Or perhaps it was routine for the doctors to sign blank reports which were then filled in by other members of staff (which would seem rather irresponsible). We cannot know at this distance in time.

On first reading the report, one has the sense that Cuthbert is springing to life through its descriptions. Yet can we say this is the 'real' Cuthbert with any certainty? No doubt there is something of the real boy here, and we can choose to imagine him as he is described: lanky (we know from the earlier descriptions of him that he was tall and thin, though 5ft 9in might not seem particularly tall by today's standards), physically awkward as though he was uncomfortable in his frame, the facial features suggesting a degree of cognitive impairment, the unpredictable laugh that seemed to be much more a way of nervously filling a silence than anything relating to humour. But, in truth, Dr Smith's verbal portrait of Cuthbert clearly conforms to the *idées fixes* of the nascent science of psychiatry. There may be some aspects of Cuthbert recorded here (perhaps he really did epitomise the 'type' of a 'partial imbecile'), but the report reads much more as a tick-list of traits which would firmly fix Cuthbert as 'insane'. The report may even have been written in this way for humane reasons (within a system that required its insane people to conform to a certain stereotype), so that he could avoid the death penalty.

In the 1860s psychiatry was still in its infancy. The term 'psychiatry' had only been coined in 1808 and ideas regarding the diagnosis and treatment of mental disorders were evolving rapidly amid much debate. Early psychiatry had been greatly influenced by phrenology, the supposed science of 'reading' the specific characteristics of individual brains via the bumps and indentations on the surface of the skull. The theories of the German doctor Franz Joseph Gall and his followers had gained a huge following in the first half of the nineteenth century, among all strata of society from Queen Victoria down.* And although Gall's ideas had been taken up by many others and had evolved into more sophisticated and nuanced theories by the 1860s, the idea survived that by careful evaluation of the outer characteristics

---

* In 1842 Prince Albert invited the eminent Edinburgh phrenologist George Combe to 'read' the skulls of the Princess Royal and the Prince of Wales.

of an individual, one could discern their inner state with a meaningful degree of accuracy. We see this to be very much the case in Dr Smith's 'reading' of Cuthbert.

On each re-reading of the report, it seems more ambiguous: while it clearly doesn't meet present-day standards of psychiatric assessment (we would not expect to judge a person's mental capacity on the basis of the shape of their ears or the thinness of their lips) at the same time the picture that is painted is of someone who, in layman's terms, we might recognise as 'impaired'. Does the report give an honest description of a disturbed person with long-term physical and neurological problems or is it an unthinking caricature? John Hutton Balfour Browne, in his *Medical Jurisprudence of Insanity* (first published in 1871), wrote callously of 'idiots':

> They almost always agree in these things: they have misshapen heads, large gaping mouths, and their other features are not unfrequently ill-formed and distorted. As for expression! Expression is only thought become external to itself in the flesh, and therefore idiots' faces are marked by an utter want of all expression, and there is little or no power of speech . . . Their limbs and trunk are imperfectly developed, their complexion is generally sallow and unhealthy. Very often one or more of the senses is defective, sometimes one of them is entirely wanting. Only in the rarest cases is the head of full size and well formed. They usually die before the age of thirty.[176]

Smith's language has clear echoes in that of Balfour Browne, suggesting that a lazy, cliché-ridden shorthand might have evolved quite widely for describing 'idiots' and 'imbeciles'. As for the description of Cuthbert's mood, no wonder he was 'listless', 'suspicious' and 'irritable':

he was shut away in a prison cell being assessed by doctors who would decide whether or not he was hanged for murder.

In many ways, Dr Smith wrote a textbook diagnosis of Cuthbert and there is little doubt that it would have been regarded as soundly scientific by contemporaries who read it (even if he or his secretary misspelled 'physiognomical'). He proceeded in steps from a reading of posture (the whole person), to a reading of the facial features ('physiognomy'*,) to a reading of Cuthbert's mental state. He sees signs of 'imbecility' in Cuthbert's physical stance and in his face, though not explicitly in his 'mental constitution', of which more in a moment. The diagnosis is 'partial imbecility'.

'Partial imbecility' was not widely used as a diagnostic label. It's a conflation of 'imbecility' and 'partial insanity', the latter being the diagnosis which was liberally applied to individuals who were deemed to have a 'monomania', that is to say a dangerous obsession in one area of their life but that otherwise left them functioning normally. Whether or not monomania was a valid psychiatric concept, it is readily understood in a lay context: the condition of a person who obsessively believes someone is in love with him or who becomes fixated on a single pursuit, with damaging effects on their wider existence. 'Partial insanity' or monomania was widely depicted in nineteenth-century literature, from Heathcliff's obsession with the dead Catherine Earnshaw in *Wuthering Heights* to Raskolnikov's obsessive desire to commit murder in *Crime and Punishment*.

The term partial insanity was established in the psychiatric spectrum by Jean-Étienne Esquirol (1772–1840), a key figure in European psychiatry and someone of whom Dr Smith was no doubt aware. How-

---

* Physiognomy means both the facial characteristics and the 'art' of reading character from them. The slang word for face, 'fizzog', is derived from it.

ever, most English psychiatrists would have used English-language texts to learn their profession, and chief among these was James Cowles Prichard's *Treatise on Insanity and Other Disorders Affecting the Mind*, first published in 1835 (and dedicated to M. Esquirol, as well as quoting liberally from his works). In attempting to pin down the infinite degrees and many types of madness, Prichard and others almost always began their thick volumes with detailed taxonomies of derangement. Treatises of all types have been structured in this way since the ancient Greeks, but the strenuous discipline of categorising and labelling perhaps reached its apotheosis in the Victorian age. Everything – everyone – must be made to fit. Thus Balfour Browne, encountered above, included the following table in his *Medical Jurisprudence of Insanity*, based on M. Esquirol's fundamental divisions of madness:[177]

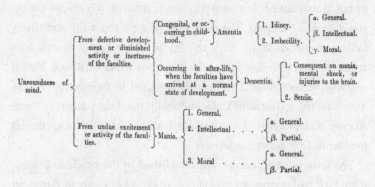

Table showing how 'unsoundness of mind' can be broken down, from J. H. Balfour Browne's The Medical Jurisprudence of Insanity.

From this it will be seen that madness was understood to be the result of an imbalance in the function of the faculties – either too little activity (amentia or dementia) or too much (mania). Mania was further broken down into general over-activity of the mind ('raving madness') or over-stimulation of either the intellect or the emotions (confusingly referred to in Victorian literature as 'moral insanity': the word 'moral', here, did not have precisely the same ethical overtones the term has today but also referred to mood, temperament, disposition). Intellectual insanity or moral insanity could both, it was believed, be either general or partial.

However, on the other branch of the chart, where Cuthbert's diagnosis is to be found, there was deemed to be no possibility of a 'partial' condition. The family of conditions that include imbecility occur as a result of defective development or just simply because of 'slowness'. They were understood to be congenital or to occur very early in childhood (amentia – the 'a' implying an absence or lack of mind), or to set in at a later stage after a number of years of 'normal' development (dementia – the 'de' implying deterioration or loss of the faculties).

On the amentia branch, 'idiocy' and 'imbecility' were really degrees of the same kind of mental incapacity and writers of the period struggle to differentiate between them – idiocy was the more severe of the two. Both could be 'general', 'intellectual' or 'moral'. 'Partial imbecility' is not found on the chart (or in the literature more widely) and is really a contradiction in terms – on the whole, congenital 'stupidity' (which is basically what imbecility came down to) is usually something that affects every aspect of a person's mind. However, the chart includes the concepts of 'intellectual' and 'moral' imbecility. And these do, logically, imply the possibility of an imbecility that does not affect all aspects of someone's mind and which is therefore 'partial'.

Taking into account all the details of Robert Smith's report on Cuthbert, I assume he identified Cuthbert's particular mental state as 'moral imbecility' but referred to it as 'partial imbecility'. J.H. Balfour Browne expounds at some length upon a particular type of imbecile whom he identifies as being 'moral [for which we may read partial] imbeciles'. This is the type that Cuthbert was thought to be:

> There is another class [of imbeciles], however, in which, together with very considerable capacity for the acquisition of knowledge, and for the retention of memories, there seems to be an entire absence of that power which is used for the determination of the moral qualities of acts ... there is no reason to think that nature has deviated from her ordinary procedure when she has given a man real intellectual capacity in regard to several sets of circumstances, and has still left him a fool with regard to other matters of relation quite as simple and comprehensible ... Now this affords another class of imbeciles. As we have general imbecility so we have moral imbecility, and, in rare cases, we find simple intellectual imbecility. In this latter class we do not find a perfect moral nature, but there is not the same utter incapacity to appreciate all moral distinctions that we find in those of the second class.[178]

Somewhere in this taxonomy Victorian psychiatry had found a niche for Cuthbert.

Dr Smith acknowledges that, intellectually, Cuthbert is a mixed bag. His intellectual faculties are 'of a low order' but he has an abnormally acute memory and it is implied that he has a lively imagination as well. He can distinguish between right and wrong to a degree but struggles to do so when the circumstances are more complex. Clearly he is not, in lay terms, a complete idiot. Smith goes on to say, 'it is a recognised fact that where Memory and Imagination are unduly developed or where they are not kept in check by other Intellectual faculties the unfortunate possessor is apt to be Eccentric and to become Insane.' This view is almost certainly part of the legacy of phrenology, in which the brain was believed to consist of a host of different 'organs', each responsible for a different area of personality, with the ideal being a balance between the 'higher faculties'. In his 1835 book, *On the Functions of the Brain and of Each of its Parts*, Gall himself wrote: 'Extraordinary memory and a talent for satire are found in individuals who lack judgment and kindliness of feeling.'[179] Partial imbecility would have been the most appropriate label available at the time to describe someone with exaggerated skills in some areas of life and severe deficits in others.

Between the early nineteenth century, when 'alienists'* such as Philippe Pinel began to identify certain types of insanity that were different from classic 'raving madness' in that some aspects of personality seemed impaired whilst others were unaffected, and the complex array of personality disorders available as diagnoses to today's specialists lies a key period in the history of psychiatry. It has been an increasingly complex process of unfolding as understanding of the mind has increased exponentially. Where in the mid-nineteenth century the concept of 'moral insanity' was an acceptable diagnosis, seeming a meaningful fit with the symptoms of those so labelled, by the first decades of the twentieth century, new subdivisions of mental illness were beginning to be delineated. At the very end of the nineteenth century, Emil Kraepelin formulated schizophrenia as a specific type of illness, distinct from mood disorders (such as mania

---

* 'Alienist' is an old word for a psychiatrist.

and depression). It was originally referred to as 'dementia praecox' (having been understood as a form of dementia that appeared at an unusually young age) but Kraepelin refined his understanding of this kind of mental illness to describe three separate delusional disorders. The process of refinement continued, mostly based on close observation of patients, so that newly labelled disorders were descriptive of clusters of symptoms as actually observed. There are currently more than a dozen different personality disorders which can be given as a diagnosis (the number varying according to different diagnostic manuals). These are separate from the autism spectrum disorders, first defined in the early twentieth century.

What would be the twenty-first-century diagnosis for Cuthbert Carr? Could he have had Asperger's? (Even if there was no concept of 'autism' or 'schizophrenia' or any number of other disorders in the 1860s, people still had them; their symptoms were simply shoehorned into the existing taxonomic framework.) Cuthbert does seem to exhibit the impaired social interaction that is a key marker of the autism spectrum. His rather narrow interest in compiling a dictionary of Anglo-Saxon words could fit our understanding of Asperger's syndrome: Aspies are well known for developing 'splinter skills' that seem far in advance of their other abilities. They are pedantic, verbose even, and very often have great difficulty making friends as they lack the ability to 'read' other people. All of this seems a good fit for Cuthbert.

The defining of autism as a separate set of characteristics grew out of the nascent understanding of schizophrenia and the distinction between the two was often blurred. Schizophrenia typically becomes apparent in adolescence or young adulthood and, in crude terms, is characterised by a failure to understand 'reality' correctly. Schizophrenics suffer from false beliefs about the world, often in the form of paranoid delusions, and they frequently feel persecuted. Social isolation and a failure to form relationships are both symptoms and consequences of the illness. Again, Cuthbert could be understood in these terms.

But none of this knowledge was available to Dr Smith. Having diagnosed Cuthbert as a 'partial imbecile', Dr Smith went on to consider what might have caused his mental illness. He believed it was likely to have been brought about by convulsions suffered when Cuthbert was teething as a baby (convulsions probably caused by a high temperature). In this Smith was conforming to a current medical belief. Balfour Browne wrote:

> Children become insane. Wherever there is a mind at all, it may become liable to mental disorder. All the diseases which occur in adults, with the exception of general paralysis, have been observed in children. Idiocy, however, is the most common form of insanity in early life; and not unfrequently, where unusual manifestations of mental activity have occurred at birth, after the convulsions caused by dentition or gastro-intestinal irritation, imbecility has taken the place of the undue excitement of the faculties.[180]

The importance of heredity in psychiatric disorders was understood in a rudimentary way at this time and Dr Smith notes that other members of the family suffered from madness of various kinds (including paralysis, epilepsy, eccentricity and talent, none of which we would consider mental illnesses today, with the possible exception of psychosomatic paralysis); this is taken as indicative of a predisposition to insanity. A later report on Cuthbert which seems to have been based, at least in part, on Dr Smith's report, adds the following details:

Cuthbert's great aunt had two sons who were described as insane and one of his uncles on his mother's side was also insane, but there are no clues as to the truth or otherwise of these assertions. In this same report, the death of Cuthbert's older brother, Matthew, officially the result of 'debility', was put down to 'brain disease' – but as he had been articled to a solicitor prior to his death, I don't feel that his insanity can have been very apparent, if it existed at all.[181] It was an easy 'proof' of madness to state that it ran in the family – and there may well have been a temptation to exaggerate.

An extraordinary example from a few years earlier will illustrate the extent to which heredity could be used (or abused) in order to persuade juries that an accused person was congenitally insane. In 1858 24-year-old James Atkinson was accused of murdering his 'sweetheart', Mary Jane Skaife, near Darley in Yorkshire. Reading accounts of the crime, it seems clear that Atkinson was consumed with jealousy because Mary Jane's parents disapproved of him as a possible husband and she had been seen talking to another young man at a fair. But at his trial Atkinson's lawyer, Mr Bliss, went all out for an insanity plea:

> [Atkinson] had unhappily come by this [insanity] from heredi-
> tary taint of his family. They would find that family conspicuous
> for idiocy and lunacy; that his brother was an idiot; his aunts
> were lunatics; that his father's brother was a furious lunatic;
> that his grandmother had brought lunacy into the family; that
> this malady was traceable to even more remote generations, and
> they would find six or seven lunatics in the family, in every gen-
> eration – in the prisoner's own generation, in his father's, in his
> grandfather's, and even in his great grandfather's generation . . .

an effete and worn-out stock affected with idiocy and lunacy on both sides of the house.[182]

Dr Smith states that Cuthbert's 'disease' was 'liable to be increased by any disturbance of the cerebral circulation such as fear, intemperance, disease, exhausting discharges (seminal emissions)'. This was an expression of a widely shared idea that one's health was an economy (both metaphorical and literal): overspending of one's energies was associated with increased risk of mental illness. In particular masturbation was seen as a dangerous waste of a man's physical capital (women's masturbation, if acknowledged, was pathologised as an aspect of hysteria and was not seen to represent a literal waste as no precious fluid was spilt in the course of orgasm). A calm, ordered life was the prescription for all – but the inexorable repercussions of such a culture of self-control and self-limitation were repression and neurosis.

Dr Smith expected Cuthbert's imbecility to lead to increasing mental impairment so that he would eventually succumb to dementia. Although the term dementia was used to refer to a more generic condition than nowadays, the symptoms of intellectual, emotional and physical decline would have been broadly similar. However, whether there was any evidence that imbecility led inevitably to dementia is another question.

Ultimately, Dr Smith declared unequivocally that Cuthbert lacked the mental capacity to be responsible for his acts and should be treated in an asylum. As Balfour Browne forthrightly declared, 'if this want of the common forethought and prudence of mankind is due to mental disease, or that congenital defect which we have described [i.e. imbecility], then it would be as absurd to punish such an individual as it would be to punish a stone because it cut a man's head open. In every sense, and for every reason, it would be the height of injustice and inexpediency to punish such an individual.'[183] This was the best that Mr Brewis, as Cuthbert's legal representative, could have hoped for. Dr Smith's report now stood between Cuthbert and the gallows.

11

'Who Does it, Then? His Madness . . .'[184]

At 10 a.m. on Monday 10 December 1866 the Durham Winter Assizes opened for business with Sir Robert Lush presiding, as during the previous session in July. The assizes had been convened the previous Thursday, when Sir Robert gave his habitual overview of the cases to be brought before the grand jury of 23 local men of independent means.

Sir Robert, as in July, had said that he 'could not congratulate' the jury on the 'character' of the cases they were to oversee (it is hard to imagine any circumstances in which a jury might be congratulated for the nature of the crimes brought before them – unless perhaps they were of a very trivial nature – but this seems to have been part of the rhetoric of the assizes). The jury were to understand that they were representatives of the wider community, and that *all* citizens were collectively responsible for the moral probity, or otherwise, of the community. In this session, the cases included charges of rape, wounding, an 'unnatural act' (probably sodomy) and five murders, including the murder of Sarah Melvin.

Cuthbert Carr's case was the first to be heard that Monday and the court was densely crowded for the sensational murder trial. After all the newspaper coverage of the crime and of Cuthbert's confession, there was intense curiosity about him, as well as a prurient desire to see in the flesh this boy who had confessed to such an abhorrent crime. Every person in the court would judge Cuthbert on the basis of his appearance, his facial expression, his posture, the shape of his head, the way he spoke. To do so was instinctive human behaviour and, as we have seen, also coincided with the rather simplistic level of psychiatric assessment of the time.

Cuthbert had been held in Durham Gaol for the previous six months while he underwent psychiatric evaluation and waited for the next assizes to come round. One or two newspapers commented that he seemed to have withstood this ordeal surprisingly well, to judge by his demeanour, and even to be in a better state than when he had last been seen in public, at the committal proceedings in July.

The *Newcastle Guardian* said, 'The improvement in the appearance of the prisoner since his committal at Gateshead was very marked. The only sign of nervousness he displayed was the constant twitching of his mouth.'[185]

The *Courant* seemed to be looking to demonise Cuthbert to a greater extent, although it conceded that he was not bad looking (a factor which, given the human propensity to judge by appearances, almost certainly helped his cause considerably):

When placed in the dock this morning he had the same strange and eccentric appearance as when before the magistrates. His head leaned to one side, and his eyes were exceeding restless. He entered the dock with an air of careless indifference, and, as formerly, there was a peculiar and suggestive smile on his countenance . . . The long confinement does not seem to have affected his health in the least. He is a strong built young man, and he possesses a rather pleasant appearance, while his head is fully developed in every region.[186]

Cuthbert's smile, which seems to have been something of a constant tic, disconcerted those who observed it. No doubt it seemed highly inappropriate in the context and, the shape of his head notwithstanding, it is the chief trait which marked Cuthbert as 'peculiar'. It perhaps indicated his lack of understanding of the process to which he was being subjected and his inability to engage with it in any real sense. Yet, as we shall see, although there was no alternative mechanism by which society could process Cuthbert's actions, the court did its utmost to deal with him humanely: in spite of the curious crowds pressing into the courtroom, this was not a grotesque parading of a 'monster'.

It was widely assumed that Cuthbert's counsel would attempt to prove he was not of sound mind and the newspapers reported that the trial was expected to be lengthy. However, it was not a given that he could be considered insane: 'The prisoner appears to have been regarded of weak intellect since his infancy. He had never been treated as an insane person, however, and he had been apprenticed to serve his time in a large glass manufactory in Gateshead.'[187] The fact that Cuthbert had to all appearances been sufficiently 'normal' to be taken on as an apprentice might make it difficult for the defence to convince the jury that he was genuinely lacking in mental capacity when it came to knowing right from wrong.

The M'Naghten Rules, a set of principles upon which a defence of insanity might lawfully be based, had been in place since 1843, when Daniel M'Naghten* had been acquitted of murdering Edward

---

* The correct spelling of M'Naghten's name is actually a more conventional McNaughtan, but in relation to the rules on insanity, M'Naghten has more or less become the standard version of the name.

Drummond, Personal Secretary to Prime Minister Robert Peel, for whom M'Naghten had mistaken him. The House of Lords explored the question of insanity as a defence by asking a number of hypothetical questions about a perpetrator's state of mind at the time the alleged crime was committed and the Rules were then formulated: 'to establish a defence on the ground of insanity, it must be clearly proved that, at the time of the committing of the act, the party accused was labouring under such a defect of reason, from disease of the mind, as not to know the nature and quality of the act he was doing; or, if he did know it, that he did not know he was doing what was wrong.' Ironically, M'Naghten himself would have been found guilty, had the Rules been applied to his own crime, but they have been applied as a standard test for insanity in cases ever since. If a defendant was found either 'not guilty by reason of insanity' or 'guilty but insane' the sentence was usually a period of treatment of indeterminate length in a secure asylum ('at Her Majesty's pleasure').

If Cuthbert had been labelled an 'imbecile' from an early age then it would have been more of a formality to have him declared insane on the grounds that he was incapable of knowing right from wrong. As things stood, it would fall to the 'medical men' who had been assessing Cuthbert during his time in Durham Gaol to deliver their opinions on him and decide his fate.

Cuthbert's father was in court to support his son: 'Among those present was the prisoner's father, who is a gentleman occupying a good position in Gateshead, and highly respected by those who know him.'[188] Ever since the murder had been committed, the Carr family had been largely left out of newspaper reports, even though the crime had been committed on their land and in close proximity to their home. When local people began voicing their suspicions about Cuthbert more and more explicitly (for example when Cuthbert was accused of attacking

Joseph Adamson Curry in June 1866), their concerns were still kept out of most newspaper reports. Cuthbert Sr's middle-class respectability (he had been a customs officer and was now retired, but he was also referred to at least once as a schoolmaster) and the affection which his neighbours seemed to feel for him both appear to have insulated the family against hostile exposure in the press. While dreadful insinuations might have been made about poor Mrs Melvin, there was a notable absence of curiosity on the part of reporters about life in Carr's Villa, even when Cuthbert had confessed to this most horrible of sex attacks.

The barristers assembled for the case (and at this date defendants did not always have legal representation in court – the cost was prohibitive for many) were Mr Meynell and Mr Wright for the prosecution and Mr Blackwell and Mr Campbell Foster for Cuthbert. The latter pair had been instructed by George Brewis, Cuthbert's solicitor.

In the record of the case, Cuthbert was described as a 'labourer', because his last formal period of work had been as a trainee bricklayer, but, like his apprenticeship at the glassworks, he had hated it and had dropped out of that trade after ten weeks. It had been many months, if not a couple of years, in fact, since he had done any 'labour' at all. Had this situation perhaps been a sore point in the Carr household, with Mr Carr criticising his layabout son for refusing to stick at any kind of occupation and bringing no money into the home? These six months in prison, away from his father, might explain why Cuthbert now seemed in a better frame of mind. Mr Carr was here in the court for Cuthbert, but did Cuthbert welcome his support?

The case began with the formal charge of the wilful murder of Sarah Melvin being read. This was the indictment, to which Cuthbert was required to plead either guilty or not guilty. Cuthbert said, in a clear voice, 'Guilty.'[189]

This caused consternation, and not only amongst Cuthbert's representatives and supporters. That was not what he was supposed to say. Even the judge intervened to induce Cuthbert to change his plea.

Justice Lush said, 'Do you understand what you are pleading to?'

Cuthbert's barrister, Mr Blackwell, raised his hand. 'My Lord . . .'

Justice Lush: 'Speak to him.'

Mr Blackwell then conferred in whispers with Cuthbert, who every now and then could be heard saying, 'I don't wish to change my mind.'

After doing his best to persuade Cuthbert to change his plea, Mr Blackwell said, 'My Lord, he says he would have pleaded not guilty if the conditions had been complied with, and the conditions are that his father and brother will make him an apology for having bound him apprentice at the glassworks.'

This is quite extraordinary (and surely unique in the history of British justice). It shows the extent to which Cuthbert was bound up in his own world, with little awareness or understanding of the real world or how it might treat him. Whether or not Cuthbert was guilty of Sarah Melvin's murder seems to have had no bearing on his thinking; he was entirely caught up in his obsession about the apprenticeship that he had hated so intensely.

Justice Lush insisted. 'He had better plead not guilty.'

But Cuthbert was implacable. 'I will plead guilty.'

'Are you aware what you are pleading guilty to? Are you aware that if you insist in that plea of guilty, I must sentence you to be hanged?'

The length to which a senior judge would go in order to spare someone who had confessed in callous detail to the most horrible murder of a little child is striking and quite counter to the commonly held view that the Victorian legal system was cruelly draconian.

Cuthbert could not be persuaded, and his next words make him sound as though he is in control of the situation: 'I still plead guilty, taking all the consequences there are.'

The judge changed tack. 'What is the prisoner's state of mind?'

Mr Blackwell replied, 'There is Dr Shaw, the surgeon to the gaol, here, who has attended the prisoner since his confinement.'

Justice Lush then asked Cuthbert again, 'Do you know that you will be hanged if you persist in the plea of guilty?'

Cuthbert replied, 'I cannot act against my conscience, however it may be.'

Now Cuthbert's father came up to the dock and exchanged urgent words with him. Mr Blackwell then announced, 'My Lord, he now says he will plead not guilty if the conditions are the same.' Yet immediately Cuthbert spoke up again: 'My lord, I still plead guilty.' Was this said purely to aggravate his father?

Cuthbert's relationship with his father is absolutely key to understanding him. Robert Smith, the Sedgefield doctor, had said in his report, 'The suspicions which he entertains regarding his father amount almost to delusions.' What were these suspicions and could it be that they were actually rooted in the reality of a poisonous relationship? We should bear in mind that an attitude of unquestioning obedience towards one's parents was expected during the period, so that any resistance to parental discipline might seem like disturbed behaviour – 'delusions', even. Coloured by our present thinking, we may be more likely to wonder whether Cuthbert's father abused him in some way, perhaps bullying or humiliating him. The normal robust manner in which a father expected to handle his son might, for a boy like Cuthbert, amount to harm. Did he torment Cuthbert with the failed apprenticeship, or relentlessly nag him to get a job? Had he even blamed the boy for driving Sarah Carr into an early grave with his carryings-on? Alternatively, is it too outlandish to imagine that

Cuthbert's father might have encouraged his lad to seek out a prostitute for his first experience of sex as he came of an age to be curious – and that Cuthbert therefore blamed his father for the sexual infection that was at the root of all his present woes? There is certainly a long-standing tradition of well-to-do fathers orchestrating their sons' first sexual experience in this way.

Now the long-suffering Mr Blackwell said only, 'He has changed his mind again. We had better have medical evidence.'

Justice Lush: 'Yes, we had better take medical evidence as to whether the prisoner "be or be not at this time in a fit state of mind to plead" to the indictment.'

If all this bizarre and mercurial chopping and changing was exasperating for the judge and lawyers, outwardly they remained remarkably calm, saying nothing to betray their frustration. When the judge decided to hear the medical evidence, he quoted the formal wording of the legal situation they were now in, that of deciding whether or not Cuthbert was even fit to plead, let alone face trial.

Robert Smith was called. He said that he was the surgeon at the Sedgefield Lunatic Asylum and that there were about four hundred 'inmates' there. He reported that he had seen the prisoner three times. 'I have seen him this morning. In my opinion he is certainly not able to plead to this indictment from unsoundness of mind.'

Justice Lush was clearly aware that he must tread carefully. His language continued to be absolutely formal: 'I understand you to say that by reason of unsoundness of mind he is not in a condition to plead.'

'He is not.'

The judge directed the jury to say whether, from this evidence, the prisoner was able to plead or not. If they agreed that the prisoner was not able to plead he would be kept in custody until Her Majesty's pleasure was known (that's to say, indefinitely). There was no question of Cuthbert regaining his freedom, but by being declared unfit to plead he might be spared the death penalty.

Perhaps sensing some doubts on the part of the jury, Mr Blackwell then said, 'I have also got the gaol surgeon here if the jury desire any further evidence, and he has attended the prisoner during his confinement in gaol since June last.'

The jury members were asked whether they felt the need to hear the surgeon's opinion.

A juryman said, 'It will be more satisfactory,' so Dr Shaw was called.

'I am surgeon to the gaol in this city. Since June last I have, in the course of my duty, visited the prisoner, and formed an opinion as to his state. I have visited him very frequently, sometimes every day, and I formed the opinion that he was an imbecile. That opinion I still retain and I am inclined to think that imbecility is on the increase. He is not in a fit state to be able to plead.'

Mr Meynell, for the prosecution, apparently making his first intervention in the proceedings, asked Dr Shaw, 'How long have you been of opinion that he was an imbecile, and also that imbecility was on the increase?'

'I have seen more of the lowness of his intellect within the last week than I saw before.'

Mr Meynell then asked Dr Shaw whether he had ever given an opinion until today that Cuthbert Carr was not fit to plead.

Dr Shaw said that he had.

'When?'

Dr Shaw couldn't remember exactly.

'To whom?'

'I think I told Mr Brewis, Mr Blackwell, Dr Smith and also the prisoner's father.'

Mr Meynell then tried to play his trump card. 'Are you aware that there has been an examination by medical men from lunatic asylums and they are of different opinions?'

Dr Shaw said that he was unaware of this. It was not really any concern of Dr Shaw's whether there were other doctors who held a view that contradicted his, but it is strange how there are always experts available to give the opinion that 'helps' both sides of a legal argument. This seems always to have been the case and is rather damaging to the very concept of the 'expert'. In any case, no opposing expert appeared at the trial – one wonders why not.

'Have you any reason to think that he knew the nature of the crime with which he is charged?'

At this point the judge interrupted, saying that he didn't think this was a proper question to ask: their sole concern was the state of the prisoner's mind at the present time.

Dr Shaw repeated that he believed Cuthbert was an 'imbecile' and unable to plead.

Justice Lush: 'And that he is unable to understand the consequences?'

Dr Shaw: 'He does not appreciate the consequences.'

The jury had been given clear assurances, now, that Cuthbert was unfit to plead. Judge Lush had swiftly headed off the topic of whether or not Cuthbert understood the nature of his crime; he was firmly orchestrating the outcome of this strange legal drama. With so many cases to get through, the pace at which juries came to their verdicts was much faster than we are used to today. Having directed the jury to find Cuthbert unfit to plead, they 'consulted for a moment', without retiring, and duly declared that the prisoner was not in a position to plead, owing to unsoundness of mind.

That was all the judge needed to hear. He declared, 'Let him be kept in strict custody until Her Majesty's pleasure is known.'

Cuthbert was taken down from the dock and returned to Durham Gaol. His journey through the legal system was over.

Justice Lush had gone to great lengths to spare Cuthbert's life. It is possible that he had personal doubts about the morality of capital punishment. Certainly there was a strong current of reform regarding the death penalty flowing right through the nineteenth century, beginning with Sir Samuel Romilly's success in removing the death penalty for the crime of pickpocketing in 1808. The legal debate was wide-ranging and profound and as recently as December 1865, a year before Cuthbert's trial, the Royal Commission on Capital Punishment had published its report. While their inquiry had been very thorough, the main question they were required to consider was whether the death penalty should be abolished altogether, and the commissioners had not been able to come to a unanimous view on this. Since 1861 the death penalty had been applicable to only four crimes (as far as civilian courts were concerned): murder, high treason, arson in royal dockyards, and piracy with violence. It was only mandatory for murder and treason. The 1865 commission did put a formal end to public executions, which were widely felt to be inappropriate, and it was clear that informed opinion was heading inexorably towards abolition, however long the process might take. (In the event the death penalty was effectively abolished in 1965 when it was 'suspended', but it was only finally removed as a possible punishment in 1998.) So it seems perfectly possible that Robert Lush was not in favour of this 18-year-old boy being hanged, however vile his crime.

Just one week later, Justice Robert Lush had moved on to the next stop on his circuit and was presiding over the Winter Assizes at Leeds Crown Court. On Tuesday 18 December he heard a case that bears some comparison with that of Cuthbert Carr and which sheds further light on the use of the insanity plea and Justice Lush's attitude to the death penalty.

A month earlier, on Tuesday 20 November, a Mr Edmund Draper (whose eponymous trade as a draper would have been amusing if the circumstances under which he came into the spotlight had not been so dreadful) was woken at half past seven in the morning by one of his apprentices. Mr Draper had several apprentices working for him at his shop in Barker's Pool in the centre of Sheffield and they also lived in with him at his home, which adjoined the shop. On this particular morning, Henry Gabbites, who, at 16 years old, was one of the more senior apprentices and had been working for Mr Draper for nearly three years, knocked on Mr Draper's bedroom door and called out, 'I have killed Arthur.'[190]

Arthur Allen was just 15 and shared a bed with Gabbites in an attic room in the house. The oldest apprentice, Stephen Moss, had the room next to theirs.

Mr Draper, fuddled with sleep, could hardly make sense of what he was hearing.

'What?'

'I have killed Arthur – I have done it for revenge.'

'What can you mean?' asked Mr Draper.

Gabbites replied, 'I have hammered him with the hammer and stabbed him with a knife.'

Mr Draper hurried upstairs and found Allen lying unconscious on his back on the bed in a pool of blood. Despite the best efforts of doctors, within a few days Arthur would be dead. His skull had been badly damaged with the hammer that Henry had taken from downstairs (which now lay, covered in blood, on the dressing table) and the large knife that he had also taken from the house was embedded in Arthur's ribs, where the blade had broken off.

Henry told Mr Draper that he had attacked Arthur at around five thirty in the morning, just as the nightwatchmen were going off their beat. He said he had gone to the police station to give himself up but in the event had not gone inside – he said he thought his story would not be believed – so he had come home again and told his employer instead.

Now Mr Draper sent Henry back to the police station, this time accompanied by the senior apprentice, Stephen Moss. Moss reported that Henry had 'talked freely and with apparent composure' on the way. He told Moss that he had struck Allen with the hammer several times and then stabbed him. Moss asked him why he had done it and Henry replied, 'I did it for revenge.' Apparently Moss also asked Henry, 'Do you know what you have been doing?', which was an extremely pertinent question, considering the M'Naghten Rules, but Henry's response was not recorded. At the police station he began to make a confession but was unable to go through with it, so Moss completed the statement. Like Cuthbert, he was immediately detained and, once poor Arthur Allen had died, was remanded before the magistrates on a charge of murder.

Why did Henry kill his close companion Arthur? Mr Draper said that Henry was a 'good, industrious apprentice, and clever at his business'.[191] By all appearances, the pair were good friends right up until Henry's savage attack, but they had both recently been grounded by Mr Draper. The two boys had been in the habit of going out after their day's work was over until around ten o'clock, but that privilege had been stopped because of what *The Times* called a 'trifling scrape':[192] Arthur had gone into a confectioner's shop and had a glass of wine and a tart, though he had no money with which to pay. Henry had waited outside while this was going on, but Mr Draper had punished both of them equally. The newspapers reported that Henry hadn't appeared to bear a grudge against Arthur but on the Saturday before the murder he had appealed to Mr Draper against what he saw as an unjust punishment and Mr Draper had refused to change his mind (he told Henry he considered them both equally to blame). It was this unfair treatment that seems to have rankled, leading eventually to Henry's dreadful attack on his friend.

There was no delay in bringing the case before a judge and jury and so Henry was indicted for murder before Justice Lush one week before Christmas, 1866. In a parallel with Cuthbert's case, Henry initially pleaded guilty but then, on the advice of his counsel, changed his plea to one of not guilty. Coincidentally, one of the barristers who had been in court for Cuthbert's aborted trial, Mr Campbell Foster, also appeared in Henry's trial, but this time he led for the prosecution.

Mr Campbell Foster ran through the details of the crime itself. Then he began to shape the prosecution's case:

> The knife and the hammer must have been carried up to the bedroom the night before by the prisoner, for the hammer was in constant use downstairs, and the knife belonged to the shop, so that . . . it had required some degree of contrivance on the part of the prisoner to secrete those weapons in that way. He asked if they did not show a degree of premeditation, indicating contemplation of the deed in question, and proving that the murder was wilfully and intentionally done.

Just as Doctors Smith and Shaw had been called to give their opinion of Cuthbert's mental capacity, so in this case a respected psychiatrist, Dr George Pyemont Smith, was asked to visit Henry Gabbites in his cell that morning and to assess his state of mind. Dr Pyemont Smith said that Henry had 'talked rationally, calmly, but with a slight degree of reserve. He answered all questions but volunteered none.' Their conversation had 'turned upon the present accusation'. Dr Smith added that Henry's 'appearance altogether is defective, but there was nothing about the head indicating disease of the brain. His face was the worst part, the lower part being very receding.' As in Cuthbert's assessment, the emphasis on physical appearance is very evident. The lingering influence of phrenology means that the shape of the head was considered informative – a receding jaw would indicate overall weakness of character. *The Times*' reporting of Dr Smith's contribution to the trial sounded a rather acid tone:

> Dr Pyemont Smith, a physician who had paid considerable attention to mental disease, was called by the prosecution, and said that he had examined the prisoner on the morning of the trial, and as the result of 20 minutes' conversation with him gave it as his opinion that he was perfectly competent to distinguish between right and wrong, and to appreciate the consequences of his acts. He stated that his *physique* seemed to be badly nourished, but he was unable to say that this would have any effect upon his mind.[193]

This may simply be a straightforward statement of the facts, but the inclusion of the detail that the conversation lasted a mere twenty minutes could suggest that the reporter thought this a rather paltry amount of time in which to decide a boy's fitness to hang.

Next to be called for the prosecution was Mr W.N. Price, surgeon to the Leeds gaol, who stated that he had talked with and observed Henry on several occasions and in his opinion, too, Henry knew right from wrong and was able to understand the consequences of any act he might do.

Both doctors were then cross-examined by Mr Waddy, Henry's barrister, but said nothing to undermine their opinions.

Mr Waddy now embarked on the case for the boy's defence. He said that he would be calling several witnesses who had known the boy from birth. He said that Henry was the child of a very 'fond, affectionate and devoted mother' who was consumptive and who had died when Henry was only about 5 years of age. There were further echoes of Cuthbert's case when Mr Waddy said that he would be bringing forward witnesses who would swear that Henry had suffered from severe fits as a child – 'these afflictions extending over some length of time, and drawing from his own mother at one time the expression of the wish that the Lord would take him first, inasmuch as she considered he was mentally and physically ruined by this ailment.' These fits had very much shaken him, and after suffering them 'he appeared to be dull and obtuse in intellect'.[194]

After Henry's mother died, his father – 'unfortunately for the lad' – remarried and at that point 'the whole course and history of the lad's life was changed. He was treated with great cruelty and made to undergo considerable hardships. The stepmother systematically ill-treated him, and soured his life.' A female witness was called who described several acts of cruelty on the part of Henry's stepmother 'but her evidence neither showed insanity nor any act by the stepmother likely to produce it'.[195] This comment by *The Times*' reporter (who was almost certainly a legal professional moonlighting for the paper)* indi-

---

* Where today we would expect trained court reporters to attend such hearings, in the mid-nineteenth century it was much more likely that legal professionals would transcribe the proceedings for the newspapers. Trainee and newly qualified barristers, in particular, would cover the costs of their training or supplement their meagre incomes as anonymous reporters. The effect was to raise the standard of legal reporting in British newspapers considerably over the nineteenth century. See Judith Rowbotham and Kim Stevenson, eds, *Behaving Badly: Social panic and moral outrage – Victorian and modern parallels*, p.34, Ashgate, 2003.

cates that the courts were not necessarily inclined to accept evidence of childhood abuse as mitigation for crimes committed by its victims later in life.

But Mr Waddy elaborated on his theme: Henry himself, he said, 'had declared, in unguarded moments, and when he was suffering from this shameful treatment, that his stepmother had told him that she knew he was doomed to the gallows. From his early days, that appalling vision had haunted and darkened his life until it had culminated in the horrible thing about which they had that day to enquire.'

Witnesses were called who spoke of Henry's having been 'subject to convulsive fits or epileptic fits, as they were variously called, of unusual severity, which left him deaf, and, as one of the witnesses said, with a "daft and simple appearance".'[196] A schoolmaster who had taught Henry as a child spoke of him as 'a dull lad, whose imitative faculties were good enough, but whose powers of reasoning were small'[197] (this contrasted with Mr Draper's calling Henry 'clever at his business', but it was, after all, only the rather dull business of drapery, so perhaps Henry had simply managed to find a suitable niche for his capabilities).

Mr Waddy also called two well-known doctors, Dr Caleb Williams and Dr John Kitching, both from York, as witnesses. He said he hoped the jury would give their testimony careful consideration. Both medical men gave it as their opinion that the prisoner was 'labouring under homicidal monomania, and was in other respects of unsound mind. Dr Williams said he thought the prisoner had some imperfect notion of the difference between right and wrong, but that this notion would be obliterated at the time of the commission of the crime with which he was charged by the influence of the mania under which he laboured.'[198]

Homicidal monomania had become a key diagnosis in the array of diagnoses available to mid-nineteenth-century psychiatrists ever since it was first defined by leading French alienists.[199] A person suffering from a monomania might be sane in all respects apart from one distinct obsession. If that particular fixation were triggered, then the person would not be able to control their actions (the phrase used was 'a lesion of the will') and if their particular monomania was 'homicidal', then they would commit murder. The problem with this, particularly in a legal context, was that the label could only be given to someone as a result of their actions and, to that extent, it was more a description of behaviour than a meaningful diagnosis. In a forensic context, the term was seen by many as particularly dangerous as it absolved the perpetrator of responsibility for his or her actions – was it fair to argue that someone incapable of controlling their impulses (murderous or otherwise) should not be punished? Many thought not. Still, Mr Waddy clearly felt it was worth trying the argument in the rather hopeless case of Henry Gabbites.

Dr Kitching, the Superintendent of the York Retreat (very well known for its humane, not to say radical, approach to the treatment of the insane), confirmed Dr Williams' evidence. He said Henry had told him he 'always had a belief he should kill someone or himself, and finding himself in a bedroom with a fellow-apprentice, he thought his opportunity had come, and he seized it . . . He said his stepmother had so instilled the idea into his mind that he would come to the gallows, that he felt that it was indisputable that he must kill someone.'

Dr Kitching's testimony concluded the case and the jury retired. After deliberating for eighteen minutes (a typical length of time for the period) they returned a verdict of guilty, but 'strongly recommended the prisoner to mercy, on account of his youth'. Judge Lush then put on his black cap, saying he could not trust himself to comment on the awfulness of having to pass sentence of death on a boy so young. He promised to convey the jury's recommendation of mercy to the Home Secretary. His duty was simply to pronounce the sentence of the law, which he duly did, his voice 'broken by emotion'.[200] Many of the women spectators wept as he spoke, and the judge himself appeared deeply moved. Henry, though, 'maintained to the end an impassive and stolid bearing, betraying not the least emotion.'[201] According to the *Newcastle Courant*, he 'descended the steps from the court into the cell below as lightly and freely as if he were passing out into the outer world instead of into the gloomy and fearful recess of a condemned cell.'[202]

Judge Lush's apparent grief at having no choice but to pass a death sentence on a 16-year-old boy may be an indication of his opposition to capital punishment or, at the very least, of his desire to have more discretion in its application (judges had none – only the Home Secretary could commute a mandatory death sentence). In Henry Gabbites' case, before the year was out his sentence was commuted to transportation for life and consequently Henry was shipped to Australia in October of the following year. Henry died of 'fever' in Perth Colonial Hospital on 17 May 1868.[203] Given the length of the journey out to the colony, he cannot have lasted very long once he arrived. It was a sad end for a boy who was abused and in whom the idea of his 'badness' was so thoroughly implanted by those who were supposed to care for him. He fulfilled his 'destiny' with the inevitability that obsession brings and ruined his own life along with that of poor Arthur Allen.

Henry's case shows that it was not easy to predict whether a jury would accept expert opinions in support of an insanity plea. A jury might be inclined to mercy, as here, and there might be extenuating circumstances that could paint a pitiful picture of an alleged perpetrator, as here, but the jury nonetheless took what might be called a 'common-sense view' and decided that, whatever miseries he had suffered as a child, he could not be absolved of all responsibility for the premeditated murder he had committed. In this case we do not see

Justice Lush intervening as he did when trying to persuade Cuthbert Carr not to plead guilty. Granted, Henry Gabbites had already withdrawn his guilty plea and perhaps the judge felt he could go no further to influence the outcome of the trial. Perhaps Henry did not present as clear cut a case of 'imbecility' as Cuthbert. Regardless of the formal process each had undergone, both boys found themselves deprived of their liberty as 1866 drew to a close.

12

Patient No. 388

By 1866, Christmas was well established as the time of family-centred good cheer that still pertains today, thanks to the efforts of Charles Dickens, Prince Albert and others to foster the warm Yuletide fantasy. But for Cuthbert Carr and his family, Christmas 1866 offered little comfort. Since 10 December Cuthbert had been in Durham Gaol awaiting news of where he was to be sent 'at Her Majesty's pleasure', and, as the wheels of government did not pause for very long, even during the Christmas season, a warrant was duly issued, on 20 December, for 'the reception of Cuthbert Rodham Carr into the Broadmoor Criminal Lunatic Asylum in the County of Berks'.[204] The warrant was signed by Spencer Horatio Walpole, the Home Secretary, and arrangements were swiftly made for the secure transfer of Cuthbert down to the great asylum for the criminally insane in Berkshire, most likely by train. He arrived on 27 December and was processed for admission.[205] It was noted that the left side of his neck was slightly swollen – perhaps he had caught an infection on the long journey.[206]

Cuthbert was numbered patient 388 in the asylum register, which identifier was to stay with him for the rest of his life. It was a relatively low number, reflecting the fact that Broadmoor had only been open for three years when Cuthbert arrived and had not yet reached full capacity. At the end of the year in which Cuthbert was admitted to the asylum, there were approximately 340 male and 100 female patients being held there. The ratio of patients to attendants was roughly five to one.

In Cuthbert's slender file in the Broadmoor archives (held at Berkshire Record Office), the first sheet of paper is his admission record.[207] This form, written in a rather ignorant hand and with a good number of spelling mistakes (the asylum did not yet have pre-printed admission forms so everything is in an uneven copperplate), records all the details of the patient:

Reg. 388

Name: Cuthbert Roddam Carr

Age: Born 21st February 1848, 18 Years & 10 Mths

Date of Admission: the 7th of July 1866

Former Occupation: apprenticed to Glassworks but indentures cancelled at the end of 18 months, a short time at Bricklaying viz. 10 weeks; afterwards and up to the time of his apprehension with his parents and did no work.

From whence brought: Gateshead County of Durham

Married, single or widowed: Single

How many children: Nil

Age of youngest: Nil

Wh[e]ther first attack: Not first attack

When previous attack occured: Symtoms more or less from childhood

Duration of existing attack: decidedly increased from Feb'y 1863 when apprenticed

State of Bodily health: good

Wh[e]ther Suicidal or dangerous to others: Neither

Supposed cause: Hereditary

Chief delusions or indications of Insanity: Chief delusions on religious subjects

Whether subject to epilepsy: Convulsions during teething in infancy

Whether of temperate habits: of temperate habits

Degree of Education: above mediocrity

Religious Persuasion: Protestant

Crime: Charged with wilful murder

When and where tried: Tried at the assizes held at Durham on Thursday the 6th day of December 1866

Verdict of Jury: That the Prisoner is of unsound mind and not capable of pleading and taking his trial.

Sentence: To be kept in safe custody untill Her Majesty's pleasure respecting him be known.

Parish with which he was chargeable: Goverment

Weekly amount paid: [*bracketed together with above answer, no sum given*]

Name & address of the person to whom payable: [*bracketed together with above two answers*]

There is much to be teased out from this form even though it smacks of box-ticking to a certain extent. Cuthbert would have been very put out if he had known they misspelled his middle name.

The date given for his 'admission' is backdated to 7 July 1866, the day after the committal proceedings in Gateshead which sent Cuthbert to Durham Gaol. It does not record the date of his arrival at Broadmoor.

It was standard for a person (particularly a man) to be defined by their trade or profession (and if you were a married woman who did not work you would be defined by your husband's occupation) and it was also standard practice for inmates in lunatic asylums to be recorded as having had an occupation, even if, like Cuthbert, they had not been able to cope with the world of work. So, Cuthbert's abortive eighteen months as an apprentice glassworker are recorded here, as well as his even more pitiful stab at bricklaying.

The form then asks whether the patient is being admitted to Broadmoor as the result of the 'first attack' from which they have suffered. This implies that a defined and specific period of disturbance has taken place which is not in keeping with the person's 'normal' demeanour or behaviour. Although the form records that the period of disturbance which culminated in the murder was not Cuthbert's 'first attack', his mental illness, if such it was, does not seem to have taken the form of 'attacks'. There is nothing to suggest that his personality altered from time to time, becoming more or less difficult to control. The response on the form is more appropriately worded when it says that he presented more or less the same 'symptoms' throughout his life. The onset of the current 'attack' is pinned to the date when Cuthbert's apprenticeship began, on or soon after his fifteenth birthday, and it's fair to say that this moment, when Cuthbert was supposed to enter the world of men and work and to conform to the prevailing ways of men (or face their ridicule or bullying), was indeed a moment of profound crisis for him. The strategies he may have used during his childhood and adolescence were no longer enough. The failed apprenticeship lies at the very heart of Cuthbert's pathology.

The form states that Cuthbert was not a risk to himself or others – that he was neither suicidal nor likely to attack other people. In the patient case book, which includes several date-specific entries about Cuthbert, there is another copy of this same admission form, containing mostly identical information, but leaving some things out and adding other details. Where the form states that Cuthbert was not a risk to himself or others, a second person has written underneath 'Probably both, certainly dangerous to others'. This strongly suggests that Cuthbert's mental state deteriorated after he arrived at Broadmoor. In the period during which he was held in custody after his confession he had given every appearance of placidity and the improvement in his overall health had even been remarked upon, perhaps suggesting that he did better away from his family in a very contained setting (even that of a prison cell). But now, released (relatively speaking) into the world of the asylum, in the company of a great many other disturbed men, there were many provocations and frustrations which may have led to him lashing out. And there was ample evidence that Cuthbert soon began to pose a very real threat to others.

Where did the information recorded on the admission form come from? It doesn't seem to have been supplied by Cuthbert himself, or even to be someone's interpretations of answers given by Cuthbert – the picture that is painted of him is too formal and too inaccurate (because it is limited to a formal set of data). It was perhaps based in part on Dr Robert Smith's report on Cuthbert's mental condition.

There had been no previous hint that Cuthbert suffered from 'delusions on religious subjects': he did not seem particularly interested in religion. His chief focus was himself, his detested apprenticeship and his obsession with his father (and, to a certain extent, his brother). Perhaps he was questioned about his beliefs and said something cynical or atheistic, which might have counted as a 'delusion' to a good Victorian Christian; or perhaps 'religious delusions' were so common that the staff at Broadmoor put them down on the form when no other delusions presented themselves.

So what exactly were the 'indications' of Cuthbert's insanity? He had committed a violent rape on a very young child and then murdered her, he had been labelled 'of weak intellect' and had a reputation for terrorising the neighbourhood – but none of that necessarily indicated insanity. On the contrary, he carried out the rape in the belief (mistaken, but sincerely held) that it would cure him of gonorrhoea; he then killed the child in order to avoid her identifying him. A cool, if diabolical, logic was behind both acts. His 'weak intellect' had not prevented him from compiling a dictionary of Anglo-Saxon words (indeed, the admission form's judgement that his education was 'above mediocrity' was rather ungenerous, as we shall see), and his bad behaviour around his home patch might well be understood as a defence against bullying because he was 'different'. Cuthbert certainly did not conform to the Victorian ideal for a young man, and he had committed terrible crimes, but that is not to say that he was actually mad – though of course lunatic asylums had long been places where social misfits were conveniently put out of sight (and mind). But if he had not been found insane he would have faced the death penalty.

Dr John Meyer was the first Medical Superintendent of Broadmoor; his deputy was William Orange. When Meyer died in 1870 (partly as a result of head injuries received when various patients attacked him),[208] Orange took over as superintendent. The asylum had been built in the wake of the Lunacy Act of 1845, which reflected a widespread change of approach towards the treatment of the mentally ill, away from physical restraint and punishment and towards a more benign containment. The buildings and extensive grounds that made up the asylum were intended to be secure, but within their walls the regime was to be relatively kind and paternalistic.

There had been passionate advocates for reform of the treatment of the insane throughout most of the nineteenth century, with a strong headwind of public opinion behind them. Perhaps the greatest driver for this was the report by Edward Wakefield published in 1815. Wakefield had visited the Bethlem Hospital in London – widely known as Bedlam – and seen both men and women, sometimes naked, chained to poles and strapped inside harnesses that inhibited almost all movement. The priorities, as set out in 1841 by Thomas Wakley, a leading reformer, were to introduce a 'Humane System' for treatment that could be rolled out right across the country, to open up asylums to the scrutiny of official visitors,* to stop the indiscriminate mingling together of quiescent and violent patients, and to end the practice of restraint. The solution, according to Wakley, was more staff:

> It has been shown within a brief period, that an enormous number of patients in one asylum may exist almost without restraint – that the chains and manacles that used to be hung about upon the limbs of these unfortunate persons might be entirely laid aside, merely by the appointment of an additional number of keepers and intelligent and humane superintendents.[209]

By 1863, when Broadmoor first opened its doors, Wakley's new system was well established throughout the country. The new asylum was set in a 53-acre site at Crowthorne near Bracknell and the original design by Sir Joshua Jebb was for five blocks for male patients and one for women. Whilst the first patients had started arriving in 1863 and 1864 (female and male respectively), the buildings were not actually completed until 1868, which must have posed something of a security nightmare. Broadmoor was conceived of as a secure asylum

---

* It was when the much criticised public visiting at the Bethlem Hospital was stopped in 1770 that the most inhumane treatment was meted out to patients, away from the public gaze.

for the criminally insane, but it nonetheless strove to conform to the enlightened new model of treatment for its patients, at least in its first decades. This 'moral treatment' (which had little to do with 'morality' as we think of it today, and much more to do with 'morale', that is to say the mood of the patients) was built around simple concepts of creating a calm, pleasant environment, with fresh air and healthy outdoor work for those who were able to undertake it. Inmates were to be given the opportunity to recover their wits in these therapeutic surroundings, and a period in Broadmoor could even come to an end if an individual was considered safe and pliable enough to be released into the care of family or friends. This however happened only rarely, particularly following one or two cases where patients thought to have been 'cured' committed murders after being freed.[210]

While the first major proponents of *traitement moral* were the French psychiatrists Pinel and Esquirol at the end of the eighteenth century and into the early nineteenth, their ideas were taken up by the Quaker doctor, William Tuke, at the York Retreat (where Dr Kitching, who spoke up for Henry Gabbites, was the superintendent in 1866). Tuke's take on 'moral treatment' had more of a religious element, but its emphasis was on a rational community of patients and attendants living and working together. His work, and particularly that of his grandson Samuel Tuke (author of the highly influential *Description of the Retreat, an institution near York, for insane persons of the Society of Friends* published in 1813), helped to set the benchmark for the treatment of the insane, and Broadmoor Asylum was opened in a spirit of optimism and transparency.

Even so, early visitors to Broadmoor entered its buildings with a powerful sense of fear and awe. It was if they were entering Hades: the idea that those held within the asylum's walls would never leave and would in all likelihood die there was particularly chilling. A long article in *The Times* in January 1865 illustrates this very well: 'The criminal lunatic . . . is, when once acquitted of murder on the ground of insanity, as dead to the world as if the earth had already closed over him . . . A committal to Broadmoor for murderous madness is as final as regards the chances of return to the world as death itself.'[211]

When Cuthbert Carr arrived there in the dying days of 1866, Broadmoor was still finding its feet. Six months earlier, in May 1866, Dr Meyer had had to report to the monthly meeting of the Broadmoor Council that a patient named Peter O'Donnell had 'escaped from the Airing Court on the 5th instant, but was followed and retaken immediately'.[212] Dr Meyer went on to say that the patients were aware how easily they could escape by climbing over the subdividing walls, and he requested, for additional security, that the Council authorise these walls to be raised by an extra three feet. This work was approved, at a cost of £50. As the very concept of a national asylum for insane criminals was in its infancy ideas of security could only really be tested in situ.

The 'airing courts' were a key component of the regime at all state-funded asylums built in England during this period. They were large grassed areas surrounded by secure walls or fences where patients would spend a large part of most days walking and talking and perhaps watching staff play a cricket match or listening to a band made up of staff members playing for their entertainment. Other patients might work in the asylum gardens or help with services, in the laundry or cobbler's workshop, for example. Large asylums aimed to be as self-sufficient as possible and were run on the lines of small communities. At Broadmoor, though, there was less emphasis on the need for patients to work hard, partly because their homicidal tendencies meant that tools could too easily be used as weapons.

Visitors could find the contrast between the rather charming scenes of patients at their leisure and the horror of the deeds that had brought them to Broadmoor disturbing: 'Here one may occasionally see a female croquet party on the lawn, the players in which have been guilty in the aggregate of some 30 murders; or, on the men's side, playing at bagatelle, a little group, with each of whose crimes all England at one time rung.'[213] But in the case of *The Times* journalist who visited Broadmoor in January 1865, once his prurience had been overcome, he marvelled at the abundance and tolerance that underpinned the asylum's regime (whilst perhaps also offering readers a pleasing opportunity to criticise its profligacy): 'All ... observe the same rules of early rising, at 6 o'clock in summer and 7 o'clock in winter. Their diet is nourishing and abundant. The men who smoke are, under the doctor's orders, allowed tobacco in moderation.'[214] Much later, newspapers would become more overtly critical of the high cost of keeping so many criminal lunatics in relative luxury: 'the cost of management [seems] beyond all reasonable bounds in every single item – food, clothing, salaries, laundry expenses, recreation, and indulgences. The dietary is far better and more ample than that of county lunatic asylums or of convict prisons, though convicts do hard work and the Broadmoor lunatics do little or none.'[215] The same article singled out the money spent on tobacco for censure. In fact 'treats' such as tea, tobacco and beer were part of the reward system of the asylum: although they were routinely provided, they could also be withheld as a punishment for unacceptable behaviour.

Improvements that would aid the smooth running of the asylum were still being made as the staff discovered flaws in the design of the building that made their job more difficult or devised new systems that would improve on existing ones. In January 1867, the asylum council granted permission to fix speaking tubes from the Steward's offices to the stores (provided the cost did not exceed two pounds and ten shillings).[216] Even if there was still some work to be done on the buildings, the relatively enlightened regime that was the cornerstone of mid-Victorian approaches to asylum culture was in place by the time Cuthbert arrived at Broadmoor. Superintendent Meyer's report for 1866 included the following paragraph on 'Amusements':

There is a good library – books, periodicals, and newspapers are distributed throughout the wards to all capable of using them. The billiard table is fully appreciated by the better class of male patients. There is a bagatelle board in each of the five blocks occupied by men. Cards, dominoes and draughts are likewise provided. Theatrical performances have taken place in the central hall eight times during the year. In the summer the male patients play at croquet and bowls. Classes for elementary instruction and singing have been formed by the schoolmaster. The band has played regularly twice in the week.[217]

A billiard ball or two slipped inside a sock makes a highly effective cosh, so it is surprising that the asylum staff were happy to allow the billiard table (not to mention the potential harm that could be caused with bowling balls). A 2014 television documentary on the present-day regime in Broadmoor high-security hospital showed an alarming panoply of confiscated weaponry made from just about anything the patients could lay hands on: even CDs and plastic spoons had had to be banned as they could be snapped and sharpened into blades. Perhaps during the first years the asylum staff had not yet become fully aware of the potential risks posed to them by some of the patients. Indeed, a long section in *The Times* article of 1865 described how one patient had fashioned a knife 'sharpened to the keenness of a razor' and had ingeniously hidden it in the space beneath the floorboards in his bedroom, accessing the hiding place through a removable knot in one of the planks and pulling the secret weapon up on a thread. The culprit, suspected of having a knife, only disclosed its whereabouts after being deprived of tobacco for a fortnight.[218]

In Dr Meyer's annual report, the patients' 'dietary' was also itemised. Each day, the patients had three meals, two of which – breakfast and tea – consisted of 'tea with bread and butter'. However, the midday meal was lavish by comparison, if rather dull. Each day, the male patients received 5 ounces of meat (off the bone and weighed after cooking rather than before) – beef (sometimes corned), mutton, bacon or pork, depending on the day of the week – accompanied by 12 ounces of potatoes and a weekly treat of pease pudding. Dessert seems to have been raisin pudding most days, varied occasionally with fruit pie or suet pudding. Sometimes there was a pint of soup instead of pudding. Each patient was given three quarters of a pint of beer with this main meal, no doubt brewed on site. There were additional snacks of bread and cheese for working patients and oatmeal gruel at bedtime 'for those who wish for it'. Overall, it seems like a decent if extremely repetitive diet. Fish, eggs and green vegetables are noticeably absent, but of course this was the sort of diet most ordinary people lived on during this period.

Cuthbert Carr had now entered this closed world where, although he would not be abused, his liberty would be severely curtailed. He had done terrible wrong and, even though he had not had to take legal responsibility for his actions, he was now facing the consequences. Whether or not he was glad to have been spared the gallows, Cuthbert's future now lay at Broadmoor, indefinitely. He was 18 years of age and had no idea if he would ever leave. He would find out whether life in the asylum for the criminally insane was worth living.

13

'Every Species of Mischief'*

The first sign of trouble came on 30 January 1867, little more than a month after Cuthbert had arrived at Broadmoor. A disturbing note was written in the patient case book:

> Yesterday he [Cuthbert] secreted a knife while working in the shoemakers shop which he hid in a boot and was subsequently seen by another patient (H. Edwards) to place the knife in the roof of the porch, outside a window. He confessed to another patient (D. James) that he intended to kill someone with it.

* 'Some insane persons display their condition by a propensity to commit every species of mischief, though devoid of any feeling of malevolence. A case of this description, strongly marked, was lately pointed out to me in the York Lunatic Asylum, by Dr. Wake, the able and intelligent physician to that institution. The individual is a youth of good temper, cheerful and active, having no defect of understanding that could be discovered, even after long observation. He is continually prone to commit every kind of mischief in his power, and not long ago escaped from his confinement and made his way to Bishopthorpe Palace, with the design to set it on fire.' From J.C. Prichard, *A Treatise on Insanity and Other Disorders Affecting the Mind*, p.22, Sherwood, Gilbert and Piper, 1835.

Placed in a single room for security. He gave to the latter patient a minute account of the crime which he had committed. He has stated that his purpose with the knife was to kill a patient (G. Clark) who he says committed an unnatural offence upon him in 1860. It is certainly true that the patient indicated comes from the same neighbourhood as Carr.[219]

Could Cuthbert really have come face to face with a man who had committed a sexual assault on him when he was a child?

From this brief entry in the case book we gain a vivid sense of the mesh of relationships that inevitably grew up between the patients: alliances and animosities, enemies made and secrets confided. How could this not be the case? But it is George Clark who emerges as the focus of Cuthbert's animus, just a month into his new life in the asylum. Who was he?

In 1867 Clark was aged around 50. In February 1862 he had been found guilty of murdering Mark Frater, a tax collector, outside Frater's office in Newcastle city centre just after Frater had got off the bus bringing him to work one morning in October 1861. Clark held a grudge against Frater because he had sent bailiffs to seize his woodworking tools – Clark owed six shillings' dog tax. He stabbed Frater in the neck as he stood talking to an acquaintance. Frater managed to walk up to his office but within ten minutes had died from the wound.

At his trial, Clark seemed very disturbed (the *Newcastle Journal* described his efforts to defend himself as 'like those of Shakespeare's poor mad Prince').[220] He was described as 'a slender, active man with a rather repulsive countenance'.[221] While he still had his freedom, he had been in the habit of consuming large quantities of olive oil, which he believed would sustain his spirit in his 'mansion in the sky' – he believed he was 'Christ no. 17'. The jury at his trial initially found him guilty of murder, but the Home Secretary subsequently declared him insane and he was sent to Broadmoor. Did Cuthbert ever encounter George Clark back in Newcastle? And, if so, did George Clark sexually assault him? Cuthbert would have been 12 years old in 1860, when the alleged assault by Clark was said to have happened. Was Clark homosexual? Clark was unmarried but his fantasies of being Christ included having been married with two children in Jerusalem (in a previous incarnation).[222] Nothing further is known.

Could it be, rather, that Cuthbert identified the Geordie Clark with his own father (Clark was just a few years younger than Cuthbert Sr) and one reason for Cuthbert's animus against his father could perhaps be that he had been sexually abused by him? By all available evidence, Cuthbert's father was a decent, caring man. There is nothing concrete to suggest that he ever abused any of his children, apart from Cuthbert's potent hostility towards him. But one can nonetheless speculate about the roots of Cuthbert's difficulty with his father. One thing to consider is that we now know a history of childhood abuse is associated with the development of personality disorders in adulthood: neglect, physical or verbal abuse, and above all the sexual abuse of children all correlate with a pattern of psychopathology.[223] So, although it is a circular argument, we might possibly extrapolate a history of abuse of some sort from Cuthbert's mental state itself.

It seems clear that, as a result of being held in Broadmoor, Cuthbert's madness effloresced. The note about George Clark suggests that specific circumstances, however extraordinary, may have contributed to a worsening of his mental health. But whether or not George Clark had once attacked and (as the phrase 'unnatural offence' suggests) sodomised Cuthbert, certainly Cuthbert was more disturbed and aggressive now than he had been during his time in Durham Gaol.

It seems unbelievable that a knife could have been so easily removed from the cobbler's workshop – and inevitable that a patient such as Cuthbert, believing himself to be locked up with someone who had once attacked him, should arm himself with such a weapon.

The traces of Cuthbert's existence inside Broadmoor are to be found in his slim personal file; there are also one or two mentions of his name in the Superintendent's journal (an official diary) and in the reports to the asylum council; he also appears at intervals in the patient case book. Notes were only taken sporadically and kept in a large collective register rather than in separate patient files. These glimpses of Cuthbert are fascinating and paint a vivid, not to say frightening, picture of an increasingly disturbed young man.

There is something completely unexpected early in the notes. In the very first record of the basic information about him – essentially a copy of his admission form – there is a note in the margin in someone else's handwriting, at the place where his crime is recorded as 'wilful murder':

He accused himself of murdering and violating a little girl. The evidence against him is far from conclusive and at his trial he insisted on pleading guilty. The jury was therefore desired to pronounce on his state of mind.

This is quite a shock. When Cuthbert first made his confession, his solicitor, George Brewis, declared that he hoped it would prove to be 'fancy on the part of a weak-minded young man',[224] and several newspapers were careful not to rush to judgement, with one writing, 'What weight can be attached to the [confession], given, as it is, by a person of weak intellect, remains yet to be seen and will depend much upon the corroborative evidence which can be produced.'[225] As it turned out, the only corroborative evidence put forward by the police was the hayseeds, which Mr Brewis was able to undermine. But such was the impact of Cuthbert's confession that it seemed to carry all who read it to the unshakeable conclusion that he had committed the rape and murder of Sarah. This is the only post-trial instance where his guilt is questioned. Who wrote this note and on what basis did they believe that the evidence against Cuthbert was inconclusive? This is basically to reject the veracity of his confession for, apart from that and the circumstantial evidence of the location of the murder and Cuthbert's record of being a 'terror', there was little to tie him to the crime (forensic science not yet having progressed to the point of being able to analyse blood types or semen). That he was in fact guilty of this, as well as of other misdemeanours, does not seem in doubt, but it is of great interest to see that a member of the asylum staff did question his guilt. And if his guilt was in doubt, why did he remain a patient in a criminal lunatic asylum? There is no hint of any steps having been taken to reconsider his situation at any point.

Three weeks after Cuthbert had been admitted to Broadmoor, in mid January 1867, and just before the trouble with George Clark kicked off, the first record of an examination by asylum staff appears in his notes:

Mental State – memory appears very good. Sleeps well. Takes his food well. Is quiet, appears to have no delusions. He will not give information about his crime in any way but says that as the authorities here have all information about it he need say no more. He is perfectly coherent in his answers to questions and exhibits a certain degree of intellectual acuteness. He works in the shoemakers shop and appears to be anxious to learn a trade. He is rather irritable.

How interesting that the boy who was compelled to confess his crime in such detail to Chief Constable Elliott had decided that he would not talk about it to the asylum authorities. Withholding the details of his crime may have been a way for Cuthbert to show his resistance to the regime in which he had been placed. It wasn't the case that he refused to tell *anyone* what he had done. Only a week later, it would be noted in the case book that Cuthbert had given fellow patient David James 'a minute account' of his crime (the same patient to whom Cuthbert had confessed his intention to kill George Clark). It would be fascinating to know what factors determined whether Cuthbert confided in or, conversely, distrusted fellow patients. David James was a canal boatman from Talybont-on-Usk in what is now Powys, Wales. In August 1849, when he was 16, James was leading a horse along the canal towpath near Brecon, towing a boat. Three young brothers standing on a bridge over the canal started to pelt James and the boat with stones. Incensed, he ran up and grabbed the smallest boy, Richard Warner, aged 4. He ran with the child for a distance along the path, then threw him into the canal, where he drowned. At his trial James was acquitted on the grounds of insanity and had been held in asylums 'at Her Majesty's pleasure' ever since. Something in the 34-year-old Welshman must have spoken to Cuthbert.

Cuthbert had gone from being a loner, up on Carr's Hill, to the strangest of communities, where he was amongst men who had all been labelled as insane criminals. He was a proud young man – he had even been compelled to boast of his prowess and strength in committing his crime – and he was intelligent. He might well have thought himself superior to many of the other sick and deranged men in the wards of the asylum. If he needed to feel a cut above, Cuthbert would find himself following a dangerous trajectory.

*   *   *

The next few entries about Cuthbert in the patient case book show him testing the boundaries of his freedom within the asylum: on 20 February he hit a fellow patient for no apparent reason; a few weeks later he broke two thermometers by throwing them out of a window. His disposition was described as 'spiteful' and 'unsociable' and he refused to speak. He tore a shirt and would stand 'with his back to the wall leaning down from the plaster with his nails' – a kind of self-crucifixion, perhaps? It is not a picture of someone who has docilely accepted that the asylum is now their place. He must have missed his territory up on Carr's Hill and his mastery of its network of paths and quarries. All now was walls and doors.

Then, in June 1867, six months after he had arrived, whether opportunistically or as a result of planning, Cuthbert seized his moment. Dr Meyer wrote in his journal:

> Cuthbert Carr . . . attempted to escape from the Asylum in the morning of Saturday 22nd Inst. He was on his way with other patients to the Chapel and escaped through the window on the stairs, crossed the roof of the Steward's Stores and dropped off outside – he was retaken by a labourer named Smith – pursued by the Gate Porter and several others – No blame appears to attach to any attendant or servant of the Asylum.[226]

The previous evening Cuthbert had broken two window sashes, perhaps in the hope of creating an escape route. When Smith caught up with him, Cuthbert was making for the stables and was posssibly planning to jump on a horse and ride to freedom.

The council minute book also noted a formal report of the incident. This added little by way of detail except to say that Cuthbert had been retaken 'within a few yards of the building'[227] and that Smith had been rewarded to the sum of five shillings (the maximum reward allowed was five pounds but clearly the council felt this had not been earned – perhaps because Smith had not had to run very far after Cuthbert; nor had Cuthbert been armed).

Although the walls around the asylum airing courts had now been built up an extra three feet to prevent patients escaping, the newness of Broadmoor and the relatively easygoing regime meant that not all possible means of escape had been anticipated (for which we may perhaps substitute 'tried') and blocked by the time Cuthbert arrived there. Peter O'Donnell, whose escape six months previously had prompted the raising of the walls, was not the first patient to make a bid for freedom. A female patient, 51-year-old Mary McBride, had been the very first, jumping out of the chapel window in June 1864 and making it as far as Reading before she was spotted by a policeman.[228] After that, a few others had tried their luck, usually opportunistically when they noticed a door or gate left open in error or during the building work when security was harder to maintain.

The first male patient to escape, George Hage, managed to abscond for a few weeks in the autumn of 1864 before he was picked up in Sheffield and readmitted to the asylum. It emerged that one of the attendants had been complicit in Hage's escape, exposing the other major weak spot in any secure institution: the trustworthiness of the staff.[229]

Although breakouts (particularly of more than one patient at a time) were something the asylum very much wanted to avoid, the fear that this engendered in the early years does not seem to have been as intense as it would become later, when a doleful siren warned locals of an escape so that they could lock their doors and windows (this was instituted in 1952 following the escape of John Straffen, who murdered a child while at large). At the very beginning there does not seem to have been such a powerful sense of division between benign and dangerous 'lunatics' – such was perhaps the strength of belief in the restorative power of fresh air and calm pursuits: all might be returned to 'normality', however serious their aberration. The mid-nineteenth-century asylum movement was certainly characterised by a reforming zeal.

More practically, Broadmoor had been deliberately located in open country, to minimise the risk to locals from potential escapees, and it was generally assumed that anyone jumping over the walls was almost certain to be picked up before very long. With a system of financial rewards in place for those who brought back runaways, the superintendent's reports of incidents in his journal and, more formally, in his reports to the asylum council, have an almost offhand tone, though this may have been in order to play down the seriousness of escape attempts.

We don't know how ardently Broadmoor's early patients desired to escape. Some must have accepted their incarceration meekly, finding relief in the stability of the regime – the regular meals, a place to sleep; perhaps they enjoyed the amusements laid on for them. Institutionalisation must have been inevitable for many. Others, we can imagine, must have longed to get away, and studied the locks and windows, learned the staff routines and kept a keen eye out for a chance to make a run for it.

After his escape attempt, Cuthbert is likely to have been 'secluded' as a punishment for attempting to escape, that is to say kept away from other patients in his block, though not continuously.[230] Or if he was thought to be particularly difficult to control he might even have been moved to the 'refractory block' for a spell, where the regime was harsher and the arrangements for protecting attendants and patients alike from violence more draconian. Yet the next two entries in the case book sound slightly more tolerant, as if there had been some sort of accommodation between Cuthbert and the asylum staff – perhaps such an adjustment is almost bound to happen as time passes and strange new surroundings inevitably begin to seem mundane. In truth, the picture is mixed. On 17 August 1867 Cuthbert 'secreted himself in the coal cellar under the stair case' in Block 4B but was discovered. The report said that his mental state 'appears to be improved' and that he was now 'willing to be employed in writing'. However, 'his manner is still restless and peculiar'. 'Peculiar' seems an odd choice of word in this context, as presumably most of the patients were, by definition, somewhat 'peculiar' in the common parlance of the day. Does this mean that Cuthbert's madness was more pronounced than that of other patients?

It's hard to know why a note was recorded in the case book at a particular moment when they are so far apart and irregular. Clearly notes were made when there had been an incident, but the next note in the sequence, made on 27 January 1868, said that Cuthbert 'talks sensibly and quietly today. Has gained 9 lbs in weight during last three months.' One is led to believe that Cuthbert might have been 'settling down' and yet the entry finishes with 'Attendant states that he is very mischievous, tearing and breaking furniture.'

That one bid for freedom, so swiftly thwarted, does not seem to have snuffed out Cuthbert's belief that he could get away. A year after his first attempt, on 6 May 1868, he was once again the subject of Dr Meyer's journal. This escapade was more serious:

At about 6.45 p.m. yesterday an alarm was given that two patients had escaped from a window in No. 4 dormitory in 4 Block. C. Carr and Thomas Douglas were missed. These men made their way from the window on to the roof of the Main Store. So short a time had elapsed [before they were missed] that escape seemed impossible. Men were placed on the road round the Asylum. Garland, Gregg and Peters got on the roof to search for the men whom they found behind the chimney. Carr had armed himself with a Holdfast which had been sharpened forming a formidable weapon. With it he stabbed Garland in the forearm – near the joint. Douglas struggled when taken but he was unarmed. The Bolts in this Block had been examined by the P.Att. [Principal Attendant] on 24th April. There is an entry to that effect in his Book. Carr had managed to provide himself with a bent Bolt which formed a perfect wrench, and with which he could have removed any Bolt. Mr Orange was in No. 4 Block at the time of the first alarm and took the management of attendants and others employed upon the occasion.[231]

It is virtually impossible not to feel a sense of Cuthbert's derring-do in reading this account and even to root for his escape to be successful, but such events must have been frightening for the asylum staff. A 'holdfast' was a cast-iron tool, used to hold woodwork steady on the workbenches in the asylum workshops. A sharpened holdfast would indeed make a terrifyingly effective weapon, akin to an axe.

A note in the case book signed by Mr Orange himself (Mr Meyer's deputy) gives a very similar account, describing Cuthbert as being found 'crouching in one of the valleys' (of the roof). The three members of staff, Garland (a carpenter), Gregg and Peters, seem to have selflessly rushed to the roof in pursuit of the two men. Neither Cuthbert nor Douglas got very far. Thomas Douglas was 'taken in the road' by the wonderfully named Henry Hazard (who at 20 was the same age as Cuthbert). From the absence of further details about Cuthbert, it seems that he did not manage to jump down from the roof and was manhandled back inside the asylum by the trio of attendants.

Mr Orange added that 'Carr made a very spiteful resistance and did all he could to injure the man who found him. He is removed to No. 6 Block. He says that he is unlawfully confined and that he should have no hesitation in injuring anyone who interrupted him whilst he was trying to escape.' No. 6 Block was the refractory block for difficult and disruptive patients. The idea that Cuthbert believed he was wrongly held in Broadmoor is aired for the first (and last) time here. No doubt it was a satisfying complaint to make and one that gave him a sense of righteousness, but it seems unlikely that he honestly believed that to be the case. Again, it doesn't square with the Cuthbert of two years previously, who made his detailed confession, in which telling the truth of it overrode all other considerations.

Later in 1868, the Commissioners in Lunacy, overseers of the asylum system, would write a report following one of their regular inspections of Broadmoor. They expressed disquiet that seven men were being kept in isolation in the refractory block. The commissioners argued forcefully for all patients, even the most difficult, to be treated equally, saying that only 'moral treatment' had been shown to help such individuals. They were critical of the fact that violent patients were increasingly being kept in solitary confinement, even taking their limited exercise alone. At the time of their inspection, they reported, seven men were being held in 'cages' which they rarely left. Their meals were pushed in to them through hatches in the wall. One man did not even have a table or chair in his room.

Stung by the criticisms, the Council of Supervision at Broadmoor wrote an angry rebuttal in which they countered each point (giving, for example, the dimensions of the isolation cells 'which the Commissioners are pleased to designate as "cages"') and argued that bringing those particularly violent men 'into association with the quiet and well-conducted would be like putting a patient suffering from confluent small-pox . . . into a ward with other sick persons.' They also gave short personal histories of the seven men in solitary confinement. Six of these were given in an appendix where the men were identified by their initials. The seventh, for some reason, was described in the main part of the letter and no initials were given for him. He was the man referred to as not having even a chair or table in his room:

He is afflicted at times with the most destructive propensities, and tears and breaks in pieces everything within his reach and power. During the year 1868 he destroyed:

18 sheets
8 pillows
3 pillow cases
8 mattresses
31 blankets
1 shirt
8 counterpanes

and broke:

3 plates
3 mugs
8 jugs
112 panes of glass
1 birdcage
5 window sashes
4 iron bars
1 door

He further, more or less, injured two fellow patients, as also an attendant; upon two occasions he escaped from the asylum; his habits and language are of the most disgusting description. On first admission he was placed in one of the better blocks; within the last 8 months every effort has been made to improve his condition; he has been allowed to keep pigeons, to cultivate a small garden; he has been provided at different times with a concertina, with book and pictures, paints, carpenters' tools, etc, etc; at this moment he is not in seclusion, though not allowed, for obvious reasons, to associate with other patients. At the present time he is quiet, but as little to be trusted as ever; he is undoubtedly insane, though very cunning and capable of combining with others, which he does whenever an opportunity occurs. In such cases a small trapdoor in the wall of a single room has been found a great convenience; through it a single attendant can pass anything the patient may require, and by this means the chance of collision between the attendant and the patient is avoided.[232]

Could this possibly be Cuthbert? He was one of very few patients who had made more than one attempt at escape, and he also had a tendency to 'combine with others'. The torn shirt is mentioned in the list of items destroyed but not the two thermometers. If this *is* Cuthbert (and I think it is), the passage affords us fascinating details of the lengths to which the asylum staff had gone to find him pleasurable ways to occupy his time, but the treatment didn't seem to be working. The broken birdcage is particularly poignant.

At their meeting in June the council approved the following rewards for the men who had foiled Cuthbert's escape bid: [233]

Garland £5
Gregg £1.15.0
Peters £1.5.0
Hazard £2

Garland was awarded the maximum reward, having been wounded by Cuthbert. It would be interesting to know the reasoning behind the different amounts received by Gregg and Peters and whether it caused any disgruntlement. Clearly there was a very precise 'tariff' for these financial rewards, which perhaps encouraged attendants to take more risks when confronting escapees.

Thomas Douglas's involvement in the escape bid is interesting. Douglas, an ex-soldier from Cumberland, had already been involved in two escape attempts, both involving more than one patient, and he would be involved in at least one more, later in 1868, again with another patient.[234] His role was perhaps always to be the sidekick, never the ringleader, but as his attempts were notched up Douglas's savvy must also have been accumulating. The two men demonstrated their ability to use 'bolts' as tools – these were the bolts that fastened the windows. There was history associated with their use in escape attempts. All the window bolts had originally been made of cast iron, but these proved relatively easy to break off and had been used in one of Douglas's earlier escape attempts. Following that escapade, the bolts in Block 1 were replaced with stronger wrought-iron bolts, but the cost of replacing all the bolts throughout the asylum was felt to be too great.[235] Now that was looking like a serious error of judgement. Meyer's desire to cover his back is very apparent in his detailing of the checks that had been made on the window bolts just before the episode (but perhaps they should have been checked more frequently than every two weeks when there were wily old hands such as Douglas around).

In August 1869 the windows throughout all the blocks occupied by male patients were secured with wrought-iron bands at a cost of £1,100.00.[236] This seems to have put a stop to most escapes, judging by the statistics given in the Superintendent's annual reports: no male patient escaped from the asylum in the year following the installation of the new bands.[237]

That was also the end of Cuthbert's escape history. When Cuthbert made his second bid for freedom he was still only 20 years of age and, having weighed up the prospect of spending the rest of his life in Broadmoor, must have decided that escape was worth a try. But once the windows were rendered more secure, opportunities to abscond were minimised and the malign energy that had been given an outlet in adrenaline-fuelled leaps out of the windows was now focused on people and property within Broadmoor's walls.

14

Refusenik

Deprived of escape routes, Cuthbert's next form of protest turned on himself. On 19 September 1868 Dr Orange, the deputy superintendent, recorded that Cuthbert had refused his food, 'saying he had not enough to eat'.[238] 'He [Cuthbert] wrote a letter stating that he intended to starve himself to death in order that there might be a coroner's inquest.' A hunger strike is of course a classic means of resistance open to someone deprived of their freedom. The asylum staff don't sound too concerned in the case note: Cuthbert 'was weighed and found to be 12 stone'. As the average weight of a man aged between 25 and 49 in 1865 was roughly 10½ stone, Cuthbert was certainly not underweight (and as a young man one might expect him to weigh less than the average).[239] Dr Orange noted, rather laconically, that 'after a day and a half of abstinence he took his food again'. The asylum was rather proud of the decent quantity and quality of the food it fed its patients, detailing their 'dietary' in the Superintendent's annual report each year. No doubt many of the patients missed the freedom to eat their own choice of food, but there was little risk of them starving to death.

Perhaps if Cuthbert had put his back into some labour he would have been more satisfied, as there were extra snacks for working patients, but Dr Orange's entry in the case book ended, 'he is mischievous and not by any means industrious'.

To fail to be 'industrious' was perhaps a greater indication of non-cooperation and lack of response to the moral treatment on offer at Broadmoor than hunger strikes and breakouts. The curative regime in all state-run asylums of the time was founded on the idea that the patients would apply themselves to tasks necessary to the smooth running of the asylum community and, in contributing their labour to the common good, would themselves return to health and productiveness. Only then could they be considered as candidates for reintroduction into wider society.

For reasons already mentioned, work was not all that keenly enforced at Broadmoor, but clearly Cuthbert's lack of interest in work of any kind rankled. The next three notes in the case book all refer to it. On 17 November 1868 it was recorded that he 'does nothing to employ his time. Takes his food very well and sleeps well. So quiet. Says that this place does not agree with him.' A few months later, on 24 February 1869, he 'Is going on very quietly, still unemployed' and on 21 July he is 'Still unemployed, quiet, general health good.' It seems evident that patients were not coerced into employment and perhaps, realistically, this was the best way to deal with the problem: leave those who were unwilling to work to languish all day until, the staff must have hoped, boredom nudged them into doing something to fill the time.

Reading between the lines, perhaps Cuthbert was depressed: he was 'so quiet' and it seems significant that staff would record that he had said Broadmoor 'did not agree with him'. As a secure asylum for the criminal insane, that seems a statement of the obvious, but no doubt there were a good many patients who accepted the regime. The next note in the case book seems to indicate a deepening of Cuthbert's accidie: 'Is less inclined to read than formerly. Lies on the settees in a listless manner.' This dates from 30 November 1869. It goes on, 'His chief companion is Bisgrove who committed a murder last year in Somersetshire. These two then encourage one another in insubordination and the language they use and the principles they express show that they both of them are almost utterly regardless of any injury which they may inflict on other patients or attendants.'

'Bisgrove' was William Bisgrove, who was about two years younger than Cuthbert. He had initially been found guilty of the grim murder of George Cornish at Wells in early August 1868. Cornish was a navvy working on the extension of the Cheddar Valley railway to Wells. He was lodging with his wife at the Full Moon Inn in Southover, a street in Wells, when, at around one o'clock one night, he got out of bed and jumped out of the window. He crossed the road and the stream that ran alongside it and entered the field opposite the pub, something he had done before. Perhaps it was to defecate, or perhaps he liked to sleep out under the stars. His wife sat on the windowsill to wait for him but fell asleep there until five in the morning, when she awoke to discover that he had not returned. In fact a policeman had found him in the field at around two o'clock, suffering from terrible head injuries, and he had died just ten minutes later – but his wife had heard nothing to indicate an attack.

The policeman had first become aware that something untoward was happening in the field when he saw the silhouette of a man kneeling over another man and went to investigate. The kneeling man was William Bisgrove, who was then arrested. Bisgrove's story was that he had gone into the field to sleep off a drinking session and had lain down near Cornish, who was already asleep (Cornish had also been drinking heavily that night, so this was plausible). Then, Bisgrove said, he had woken to see a 'tall navvy' climbing over the stile into the field with a large rock held above his head. This man had come over to Cornish, smashed the rock three times into Cornish's skull, thrown the rock at Bisgrove's leg and then picked it up again and thrown it into the stream. A 40-pound rock covered in gore and hair was duly found by the police. Bisgrove was arrested and several other people were also detained, including Robert Sweet, an ostler, and his girlfriend, Elizabeth Drew, who sometimes worked as a prostitute. Sweet and Drew had been overheard talking that evening and it had sounded as though Drew was trying to dissuade Sweet from attacking someone. Bisgrove had been seen with the pair earlier in the evening and had paid Drew a shilling to go into the same field with him for sex (an event that she had tried and failed to keep from Sweet). It was assumed that Sweet had wanted to kill Bisgrove for going with Drew, but had killed Cornish in error.

Bisgrove was mostly described as a navvy in newspaper reports, but he had also been a sailor and a coalminer and some reports said that he was now working as a paper maker.[240] Sweet and Bisgrove were tried for the murder of Cornish and were both found guilty. Awaiting hanging, Bisgrove confessed to having murdered Cornish alone but insisted that he had no idea why he had done it. It had been merely an impulse that he was unable to withstand. Sweet was thus exonerated and reprieved, but procedures were also set in motion to reconsider the death sentence passed against Bisgrove. It was discovered that when he was working as a miner he had witnessed the death of a fellow worker who was crushed by a falling rock; after this incident he had developed epilepsy (which was put down to the trauma he had experienced). Indeed, Bisgrove had had an epileptic fit during a court hearing on 10 August 1868. The belief that Bisgrove's crime was genuinely motiveless took hold and became a powerful driver behind a campaign to have him declared insane (it certainly helped Bisgrove's cause that he behaved most piously in prison and constantly asked the prison chaplain to pray with him). The drama of his repeating the same kind of death (crushing by rock) that had caused his own madness also made a powerful impression. Inspectors were sent to the county prison in Taunton where Bisgrove was being held in a condemned cell and he was soon declared insane. On 26 January 1869 Bisgrove was transferred to Broadmoor.

William Bisgrove had been in the asylum for ten months when his alliance with Cuthbert was mentioned in the patient case book, long enough for a close bond to have developed between them. During the first years that he was in Broadmoor, Bisgrove was said to have 'displayed a considerable amount of violence of conduct and language'.[241] The awareness that the two young men 'encourage[d] one another in insubordination' must have been a significant threat to the asylum authorities. The last thing they would want would be patients who plotted together – 'combining' – particularly if the plans were to hurt or even kill both patients and staff. If there was sufficient awareness of the threatening conversations that Cuthbert and Bisgrove indulged in for them to be commented on in the case book, then the men can't have been particularly discreet: perhaps it was more a case of enjoying frightening people with their violent talk than actually intending to carry out attacks. But the next note suggests the opposite: Cuthbert 'struck attendant Palmer, causing a bruise and black eye on the 12th last. Secluded 58 hours: Excited and threatening.'

You sense, immediately, the charge between the two men, as they egged each other on to challenge the authorities. Together, Cuthbert and Bisgrove must have posed a real problem; it couldn't be allowed to escalate. After hitting Palmer, Cuthbert was kept in solitary confinement for two and a half days – and perhaps it was an effective punishment to deprive him of the company of his co-conspirator Bisgrove, for the next note in the case book dates from almost exactly a year later (25 January 1871) and begins, 'Tolerably well behaved lately and has not been secluded for a long time.'*

Unusually (as the notes are mostly separated by several months), the next day a further note was added:

At present is in No. 6 [refractory] Block and is quiet and orderly on the whole. But has a suspiciously cunning or hypocritical face and is always very carefully watched. Is a great deal given to masturbation. Lately has been complaining much of dyspeptic symptoms without diarrhoea or any great amount of feverishness. For this he occasionally keeps in bed for a day or two and for some time past has been under treatment. Has a pale anaemic appearance but in mean time is much improved.

This note is interesting because it doesn't seem to have been occasioned by any particular event but is more of a general review. One senses that Cuthbert was not well liked by the staff. His masturbation must have been rather difficult for them, given the social taboo surrounding it at the time, although the note does make it sound as though the staff were relatively unfazed by it. I doubt that he received much sympathy for his dyspepsia. The description of his face as 'cun-

---

* The case note of November 1869 is the sole mention of William Bisgrove in connection with Cuthbert, but he would go on to become notorious in his own right as the only murderer in the history of the asylum to escape and not be recaptured. According to Superintendent Orange's report, in July 1873, while he was walking in the asylum grounds with an attendant named Allan Mason, Bisgrove hit Mason on the head with a stone (seemingly his chief modus operandi), then tried to strangle him. Having incapacitated his guard, Bisgrove made a run for it and managed to slip through all the searches made for him, never to be heard of again.

ning or hypocritical' suggests that Cuthbert and the asylum staff were in a state of permanent opposition. Presumably, by its very nature the society of the asylum was not overbrimming with warmth and kindness on the part of either the staff or the patients and it would be foolish to wish that it were. Still, at least there were some friendships between the patients as well as enmities.

The relationship between Cuthbert and one patient in particular clearly veered from one state to the other. In October 1871 the need to watch Cuthbert closely proved to be justified. On Wednesday 21 October he 'broke 64 panes of glass in day room with a map roller. No change of condition had been primarily noticed to raise suspicion that he intended mischief.' Cuthbert wielded the map roller to maximum effect and must have been in full frenzy to break so many windowpanes (more to add to his previous tally of 112, perhaps). The breakages would have caused severe inconvenience at the asylum, with broken glass posing real risks if it fell into malign hands and the smashed panes letting in cold air and rain. Glaziers would have had to be brought in to do repairs, presenting security challenges (unless they had staff who could tackle the job). The case book went on, 'On being seen in his room soon after, he appeared quiet and as a reason for his conduct stated that he wished to be removed from the patient John Hughes who takes exercise in same airing court as Carr as he (Hughes) was an "unprincipled man" . . . Carr & Hughes used till very lately [to] be good friends. Was kept in seclusion Wednesday Evening and part of following day.' Again, the punishment for this really rather awful nuisance-making was very mild. It seems unlikely that Cuthbert achieved his aim of being separated from Hughes. Who was the focus of his dislike?

John Hughes had been a cabinetmaker before he was sent to Broadmoor. He was 49 when Cuthbert fell out with him, so twenty-six years older than Cuthbert. It seems that Cuthbert's relationships with older men, who might stand in psychologically for his father, were more volatile and more likely to end in hostility. His description of Hughes as 'an unprincipled man' could simply be a dismissive comment about someone with whom he had ceased to be friendly, but in fact Hughes had committed at least one seriously unprincipled act during his time at Broadmoor. In March 1866, already an inmate, Hughes had thrown a large stone which struck Superintendent Meyer on the temple, one of several attacks by patients and from which he never fully recovered (Meyer died in May 1870).[242] Hughes, who was in Broadmoor because he had vandalised a portrait of Queen Victoria in the National Gallery in 1859 (as well as damaging a statue of the Duke of Wellington),[243] believed that Meyer had accused him of 'murdering the Queen of Heaven', a calumny that he felt compelled to avenge.[244] Hughes lived a long life at Broadmoor, only dying in September 1893, at the age of about 71.

In June 1872 a brief case note recorded that Cuthbert had 'kept to his bed for some time past, complaining of great mental depression'. At least he was permitted to stay in bed when he felt depressed. It's possible that the immediate cause of this latest bout of low spirits was the failure to clear the first hurdle of a petition Cuthbert had recently tried to send to the government.

As early as 1865, only two years after the asylum had opened, a visiting journalist, on being shown the recreation rooms, noted that 'those writing so intensely are generally speaking preparing interminable memorials to the Home Secretary, or keeping the most insane of diaries to show the Commissioners in Lunacy as proofs of their cure and reasons for their discharge.'[245] Broadmoor patients had the right to petition the commissioners, those gentlemen appointed by the state to oversee the asylum system with a brief to consider the welfare of patients, as part of the Lunacy Act of 1845. The Seventh Earl of Shaftesbury was the head of the Lunacy Commission from 1845 until his death in 1885 and Lewis Carroll's uncle, Robert Skeffington Lutwidge,* was the first Secretary to the Commissioners. The commissioners consisted of three medical, three legal and five lay men. As well as being responsible for inspecting asylums, part of their brief was to hear petitions from individual patients. However, asylum inmates did not have a direct line to the commission and were obliged to submit any petition to the council of their own institution in the first instance. The councillors were thus in a powerful position to either allow a petition to go forward or to block it. One may therefore question how effective a channel this was for patients who wished to complain about the treatment they received.

In fact, not many petitions seem to have been submitted to the Broadmoor council for forwarding to the commissioners during the years that Cuthbert was a patient there. But Cuthbert was one of the few inmates who made a bid to be heard by the outside world. On 26 April 1872, the regular monthly meeting of the Broadmoor Council minuted that 'petitions from Cuthbert R. Carr, Thomas Garland and William H. Whitworth were considered'.[246] At this date, Cuthbert was 24 years old. We don't know the subject that Cuthbert wished to raise with the commissioners, but the council 'directed that C.R. Carr's petition should not be sent, and that those from T. Garland and W.H. Whitworth should be forwarded to the Home Office.'[247]

Was Cuthbert in the habit of writing petitions to the commissioners? Quite possibly. In his file there is an undated document which suggests that he had certainly honed his rhetorical skills to a fine degree. It's

---

* Lutwidge would die in May 1878 as a result of a head injury from a sharpened nail wielded by a patient during an asylum inspection.

an unfinished petition in Cuthbert's own handwriting and it may have ended up in his file precisely because it was unfinished, meaning that it was never presented to the Council for possible forwarding to the Commissioners in Lunacy.

It is a masterpiece of casuistry and paranoid logic and shows that, far from being of merely 'above mediocre' education (as his admission form had lazily claimed), Cuthbert had the classical grounding and mastery of grammar of the well educated. The petition, even unfinished, is a sustained blast of hot air, rather exhausting to read and leaving one little the wiser about the actual issue Cuthbert wished to raise with the commissioners. Here is the letter in full (including one or two spelling errors):

To Her Majesty's Commissioners in Lunacy.

In your forming an estimate as to the truthfulness of this concise statement relating to some of the injustice which has been done to me I beg of you to divest your minds of all bias that you may be possessed of, arising from any source: and to not harbour any opinion that is not warranted by sufficient premisses; but when these do appear to make inferences accordingly: although, without speaking personally, it is indeed customary to believe implicitly all that the conductors of these establishments choose to say. It must be admitted that the patients tell falsehoods in reference to their treatment; but for my own part, I not only do not make mistatements of what goes on here, but I have frequently reproved my fellow prisoners for doing so: knowing as I do that they who tell lies about the doctors would be ready to do the same about me; and that the truth about this place is bad enough: so you may rely upon what is here being actually true.

It may appear impropable, but it is nevertheless strictly true that espionage of patients upon one another is not only permitted here, but is encouraged and rewarded; so that it is universally prevalent: furthermore, the superintendent, head attendant and principal attendants take for granted whatsoever the patients may be inclined to secretly tell them of one another; although they know that those same men (if they are men) who are most willing to act as their spies and talebearers are the ones who are most of all given to telling lies about them: and they ought to know that they would speak falsely of other patients in like manner as they do of them.

I had been a long time, for what reason I know not, in no. 6 refractory block; and in the course of a conversation that I had with the superintendent, on the 27th of March last, about getting out of it, he distinctly made a promise that, on condition that I would refrain from what he called 'taking the law into my own hands', he would instantaneously remove any patient or attendant that might annoy me. Now Dr Orange had employed a lying scoundrel called George Rogers* (in reference to whom it is no exaggeration to say that anything bearing resemblance to truth seldom comes out of his mouth) as a spy upon me, although I had said or done nothing that was objectionable; so that all that was said about me must necessarily have been false: and I was therefore both under the discomfort of espionage and under the disadvantage of having lies reported of me; moreover, without the opportunity of defending myself: so on the 14th of May I, depending upon Dr Orange's solemn promise, asked him to remove the villain Rogers from me, on account of the secret work

* George Rogers was a fellow inmate, rather than a member of the asylum staff. I have been able to find out very little about him, beyond the fact that he was born in about 1842 and so was six years older than Cuthbert.

that he performed by Dr Orange's own authority, telling him at the same time that if he did not remove him that day, I would remove him myself the next day. As Dr Orange does not like to be told of his faults he was vexed at my telling him that he had employed Rogers; but I did not tell it him to vex him; but in order to shew him the reason why I wished the rascal to be taken from me: but (incredible though such baseness may appear) Dr Orange did not shift his myrmidon according to his promise; but he called him to a conference on the stairhead, with the door at the end of the gallery closed, of from 10 to 15 minutes duration; at the end of which conference, Dr Orange ordered the attendants to bring me downstairs, and have me locked up: and as I did not wish to hurt those attendants who were there (which I would have been justified in doing, on account of their obeying an iniquitous order) I went without resistance. Of course the next time that I saw Dr Orange I remonstrated with him for his unexampled perfidy in inveigling me to make a complaint, and then locking me up for making the same complaint; although it can only be considered that my moderation and forbearance were very great in consenting to the arrangement that he proposed: but he, with the shameless effrontery characteristic of him, evaded the direct question, and spoke as if there was nothing wrong: and he has kept me locked up ever since the 14th of May, without giving me any satisfaction whatever: and if I have destroyed any property since then it must be borne in mind that I have been driven to it, against my will, by such persecution [248]

The undated petition ends abruptly at this point and it seems it was never submitted to the council. It allows us to hear Cuthbert's voice and that voice is ferociously articulate. Going by its place in the sequence of documents in Cuthbert's file, it may have been written when Cuthbert had been in Broadmoor for over ten years and was in his thirties. His energies seem fully focused on besting the asylum staff and getting the latest of his paranoid gripes heard by the powers that be.

Taken together with all the incidents recorded in the patient case book, the petition suggests Cuthbert must have been a constant irritant within the asylum's routine. His ability to express himself surely came across as chippiness, alienating potential allies. And there is further clear evidence in the petition of his propensity for physical violence: he declares that he would have been justified in 'hurting' the attendants who went to move him to another room in the asylum but chose not to. If he has destroyed any property, then he is certainly not to blame as he has been driven to it. His manner is both threatening and arrogant. He must have been rather a nightmare for Superintendent Orange to deal with.*

It's interesting to note the difference in tone between the two chief documents we have that record Cuthbert's own voice: his confession, as transcribed by Chief Constable Elliott, and this petition. Of course the circumstances in which each was created were very different, and the act of confessing to a murder is singular, but whereas in the confession it was possible to hear the voice of a rough-edged north-east boy, with very little apparent awareness of the impression his terrible frankness would make, in the petition (which is purely a written text and not a transcript of spoken words), Cuthbert seems wholly in control of his words, a smooth and practised sophist, all traces of his regional roots expunged. It's almost as if his years in Broadmoor are the equivalent

---

* Orange had by now been promoted to superintendent after John Meyer's death in 1870.

of time spent at university. But he would be an eternal student, forever reading all the books he could lay hands on and honing his essay style. He would never graduate.

Going back to the patient case book, the note for 21 December 1872 gives the impression that Cuthbert has become more biddable: 'Has been behaving for some little time past and is allowed out for a walk occasionally with an attendant & to see the outdoor sports such as racing etc. Is after very depressed. Sometimes does a little ward work, reads a great deal.' One might feel that Cuthbert has established a melancholy but tolerable existence within the structures of asylum life. But then the next sequence of case notes overturns this completely. The entries are suddenly more frequent, revealing a heightened rate of recidivism on Cuthbert's part.

First, on 14 May 1873, the superintendent received a letter from Cuthbert ordering a certain patient to be removed at once from No. 6 Block, 'otherwise he (Carr) would await his opportunity and do the man a serious injury'.* The note continues, 'As he expressed himself determined to carry out his threat, he was placed in his room one hour before bed time.' This child's punishment doesn't seem to take Cuthbert's threat terribly seriously; it would be a further humiliation, adding to his sense of powerlessness.

One week later and Cuthbert is still ramping up the tension:

> Has continued in much the same dangerous state, necessitating
> his being kept in his room continually with the exception of an
> hour and a half's walking exercise in the court daily. He has

---

* The name of this patient is redacted by the Broadmoor Archives as he died less than a hundred years ago. Patient details are embargoed for a century after their deaths.

damaged nine rooms in the last few days, knocking down the plaster, cement and bricks. On the night of the 20th he tore up his bedding and on the 19th attempted to strike the Superintendent as he [was] talking to him in the airing court.

On 14 June there was 'Not much change since last report. Still threatens [patient X] and the Superintendent and has been kept in seclusion; in consequence has not torn up bedding etc since but almost every day destroys a portion of the arm seat in his room. Bodily health good.'

The next note was written six weeks later, which still represents a shorter than usual gap between entries: 'No change since last report – still in seclusion – gets very excited whenever he hears [patient X's] voice or sees the Superintendent. Threw a book at the last named on the 29th whilst he was visiting him.' Cuthbert seems to have become obsessed with this particular patient, and also with Superintendent Orange. The fixation feeds on itself and cannot be let go. If he did so there would be loss of face and, worse, a loss of part of his sense of himself.

The culmination of all this destructiveness came on 16 October:

This day he was airing as normal in the West court with att[endant] Hickens when suddenly he began to climb up the side of the building and before he could be stopped had got on top of the porch over the door leading into the block and when there refused to come down again – broke all the windows he could reach and began to pull the bricks out of the wall. After being up there about an hour he said he would come down quietly if we promised to remove him to B1; this promise was given and he came down and was removed accordingly.

Thus Cuthbert's porch-top protest won him something, perhaps allowing him to save face, and the asylum staff seem to have handled the incident fairly well, giving a certain amount of ground and, in the process, taking the heat out of the situation. Cuthbert had moved to Block 1 but he was still a Broadmoor lifer.

In the almost seven years that he had already spent in the asylum, Cuthbert had changed, and not for the better. The Geordie boy who breathlessly unburdened himself to the Chief Constable of Gateshead had grown into a disdainfully articulate adult, but whether one could say he had matured was another question. He was still prone to intense, almost obsessive hostility towards certain individuals and this seems to have been a consistent personality trait. He took against people, for who knows what slights, and was rigidly unforgiving: a remnant of his adolescence, perhaps, when he would defend himself against the bullies and teases who undermined his fragile sense of self. Cuthbert also became increasingly destructive over time: he seems to have tried to demolish Broadmoor one brick at a time. There is no sense that the quiet regularity of the regime was having the desired effect of calming him and restoring him to 'sanity'. On the contrary, being deprived of his freedom had focused his paranoia on those trapped in the wards with him and had also given him enforced leisure time in which to brood and plot. With no foreseeable chance of release, depression also seems to have descended on him, a numbing blanket that brought no comfort.

15

'The Most Dreadful Crime Ever Recorded'

On the morning of Thursday 30 March 1876, in a semi-rural district of Blackburn, Lancashire, a little girl ran to tell a woman, Alice White, that she had seen something wrapped in paper in a nearby field. When Mrs White went to see what the girl had found, she saw it was the body of a child, or, rather, just the torso, as the head and limbs were missing. A policeman was called at once and he took the body away for examination. It had been wrapped in two back copies of the *Preston Herald*, held in place with string, and inside the parcel there were a lot of short lengths of hair that didn't belong to the child, some dark and some white. The trunk showed signs of having been sexually assaulted.

James Holland, a mechanic, who lived with his family at 110 Moss Street, in the Daisyfield ward of Blackburn, tentatively identified the torso as that of his daughter Emily, aged 7, who had been missing for two days. Emily's mother, who had given birth to another child just seven weeks earlier, was prostrated by the discovery.

Emily had last been seen running an errand for a man who had asked her to buy half an ounce of tobacco for him from Cox's grocer's shop. The man was identified as a tramp who had been seen hanging around the area on the Tuesday when Emily disappeared. In the panic to find Emily's assailant, half a dozen tramps were picked up for questioning, whether or not they matched the description given by Emily's playmates.

Later that same day, Thursday, a farmhand found the amputated legs of a child in a ditch at Rishton, a few miles north-east of Blackburn. They were also wrapped in two recent back copies of the *Preston Herald*.

Although Emily's head and arms had still not been found, an inquest was opened into the murder the next day. Dr Maitland, the doctor who had examined the torso and legs, said that the right leg corresponded with the trunk. The body was 'smeared with blood and covered with hairs' (i.e. clippings).[249] He was satisfied that the child had been abused ('posteriorly ravished')[250] before the murder. The legs and arms had been cut off, and the thigh bones broken and smashed. A good-sized sharp knife had no doubt been used, he said.

The doctor carried out a post-mortem examination of the torso that same day and a firm identification was finally made, based on the remains of the meal found in the stomach: Emily had eaten ham and potatoes followed by figs for lunch on Tuesday, before going out to play. As the food was not yet digested, a time was fixed for the murder of within four hours of the meal.

A member of the jury remarked that tramps were not generally in the habit of keeping back copies of newspapers. The Chief Constable said that the various hairs sticking to the body parts had been collected and scrutinised with the aid of a magnifying glass. They were of several colours and thicknesses, including some that could be whiskers. This naturally raised the suspicion that the murderer might be a barber, and the premises of a number of local barbers were searched but no evidence was found on which to base an arrest. However, the case has gained a place in the history of crime as it was the first case in which dogs were used to find key evidence. A man from Preston offered the services of two dogs, which were taken to two local barbers' shops. Although the dogs found nothing at the first, when they were let loose in the second shop, which was in Moss Street, very close to where Emily Holland had lived, the dogs immediately scented something. First of all they became excited by the 'slopstone' where the barber, William Fish, washed his implements. Then the dogs ran upstairs and barked furiously in front of the fireplace. When the police officers felt up the chimney they found the burnt skull and arms of the child. There was also a portion of fabric that matched the dress that Emily had been wearing when she disappeared. They found a pile of old newspapers from which the editions that had been used to wrap up the body parts were missing.

Fish was arrested and, although he initially protested his innocence, the next day he confessed to the murder. It was said that he had cut the little girl's throat with his razor in the upstairs room and then gone downstairs and shaved customers with the same blade. He was hanged at Kirkdale Gaol in Liverpool on Monday 14 August 1876. He blamed his 'bad end' on 'breaking off Sunday school and keeping bad company'. Shortly before he went to the gallows, he implored his fellow prisoners to 'avoid those cheap bad journals on which I spent all my spare time'.[251]

The postscript to the Fish case was all about one of the two dogs that had found Emily's remains. This dog, Morgan, belonged to an oil merchant in Preston, a Mr Parkinson, and was an excellent animal that would fetch items to order over unfeasible distances. But when Morgan began to grow fierce and to bite people for no reason, Mr Parkinson gave him back to George Spencer, an ex-gamekeeper, from whom he had got him in the first place, so that he could be retrained. This was achieved, but Spencer then told Parkinson that a Mr Smith, a druggist, wanted to borrow Morgan for a few days, to which Parkinson agreed. At this point Morgan was passed around from one person to another (all of whom had something important for him to do) until it was almost impossible for Parkinson to retrieve him. Eventually, Spencer went to Broughton, near Preston, to fetch the dog back but went on the lash on the way back and ended up leaving him with the landlord of the York Castle Inn, a Mr Bailey, who wanted to take Morgan shooting for a few days. Bailey lent the dog to Peter Taylor, a housepainter, and it was Taylor who offered the dog's services to the police in the hunt for Emily's remains.

Weeks had passed, but all of this was unbeknown to Parkinson, who believed the dog was still with Spencer. However, when Parkinson read in the newspapers of the dog's famous success, he wanted him back. A Mr Chegg had, it was claimed, offered him £750 for the dog (an enormous sum, equivalent to around £75,000 today). Meanwhile, Taylor had been showing the dog to admirers for profit, before finally returning him to the pub landlord, Mr Bailey. Bailey also began to charge people for a look at the dog and when Parkinson went to retrieve him, he fobbed him off with various excuses. Finally, at the end of April 1876, Parkinson turned up at the York Castle (which was in Adelphi Street, Preston) with ten 'heavies'. Morgan was being exhibited in an upstairs room when Parkinson burst in and took the animal back. On the way out, Mrs Bailey, the landlord's wife, tried to prevent Parkinson from taking the dog but it was successfully removed.

Several generous offers were made for Morgan, including a two-week stint at a music hall in Camden, London, for a fee of £400, plus expenses, but Mr Parkinson turned everyone down. He told the newspapers that he would exhibit the dog in the provinces with the aim of raising funds for Emily Holland's family and also for poor Mrs Fish, who had been left destitute. It was very unusual for charity to be extended to a murderer's family in this way.

The *Preston Chronicle* called the rape, murder and mutilation of Emily Holland 'the most dreadful crime ever recorded'. It went on, 'This is saying a good deal, and yet, we are afraid, it is only too true . . . We venture to say that nothing so shocking as this stains the annals of any country, whether savage or civilised.'[252] In the same week that the Preston paper published their editorial, however, the *Newcastle Chronicle* published a piece that drew direct comparisons between the Fish case and the murder of Sarah Melvin, ten years earlier:

Traditions and Mysteries of the North
No. 132 – THE CARR'S HILL TRAGEDY

What appear to be the worst crimes have almost invariably their parallels. The monstrous deed committed by William Fish at Blackburn would seem to overtop the height of human wickedness; but it only serves to recall the memory of an event quite as terrible which took place in the North of England just ten years ago.

At the end of 1865 and the beginning of the following year, Carr's Hill, near the Felling, became notorious as the scene of several crimes, the perpetrators of which were never detected. Stack-firing was not nearly so common a form of crime as it had been a number of years previously; nevertheless, several stack fires took place in farm-yards near the Felling, and there was no difficulty in proving that they were the work of an incendiary. The farm-yard of Mr Matthew Laws was twice fired in three days, and the stack-yard at Claxton Farm was fired exactly a week afterwards; yet the daring criminal who was guilty of such wanton destruction left no clue behind him, and was never traced.

But the place became notorious for other things besides the burning of corn and hay stacks. In May, 1866, five men were sentenced to long terms of imprisonment at the Durham Assizes for rapes on women in the same neighbourhood.* Nor was this the worst. On the 7th of the same month† a little girl, named Ann Brown, was brutally violated and left insensible in the neighbourhood of a quarry at Carr's Hill. The perpetrator of the abominable act was never discovered, but the circumstances may receive some elucidation from the facts we are about to relate.

On the night of the 13th of April, 1866, as a man named Bourne and his wife were passing the corner of a road between Carr's Hill and High Felling, their attention was arrested by something which it was difficult to recognise in the dim twilight. They stooped down and found that this strange bundle was the dead body of a little girl. The tender and placid remains were quite cold; the weak young arms were folded crosswise, and tied with a cord; a piece of the same cord was drawn tightly round the throat and compressed into the flesh; and there was blood on the head and about the clothes. It was evident that a murder of a most foul and unnatural kind had been committed, and Mr and Mrs Bourne lost no time in communicating with the police. There was not much difficulty in identifying the body of the child. It was found that, some hour and a half before the discovery, a little girl named Sarah Melvin, five years old, had been seen on the road, and had been directed on her way home. She was the

---

* This is a reference to the Mary Ann Thirlwell rape case (see Chapter 2).
† In fact it was the 5th.

daughter of a woman who sold crockery, and she had just been to her father's house, the two married people living separately. Unfortunately, she had loitered on the way, or had been lost. At any rate, there was her dead body, brutally ill-used, and bearing evidence of the perpetration of a horrible crime.

The whole facts of the case are too loathsome to be detailed with any minuteness. A post-mortem examination made by Dr Barkus of Gateshead showed that the lower part of the poor child's body had been cut or torn open with some blunt instrument, and that she had first been stunned by a blow on the head, and then strangled with a cord. The affair caused immense excitement in the district, and the greatest anxiety was shown for the apprehension of the murderer. Superintendent Elliott, now Chief Constable of Gateshead, followed up the faint clues in his hands with all that keenness and ardour which has distinguished his official career; but three months passed over, and the mystery seemed to be as far from solution as ever.

A few weeks after the perpetration of the murder, a young man named Cuthbert Rodham Carr was taken before the Gateshead magistrates on a charge of threatening the life of a youth named Curry. He lived at 'Carr's [Villa]', the place which had given the name to Carr's Hill, and he bore a very questionable character in the neighbourhood. Superintendent Elliott said that Carr was the terror of the neighbourhood, and hinted his suspicion that he was the person who had been guilty of the hitherto unpunished crime. But though Mr Elliott had very strong suspicions against Carr, he seems to have had no proofs to proceed upon. Carr was discharged on this occasion, and no further steps seem to have been taken to identify him with the murderer of Sarah Melvin.

But the intense excitement which had prevailed on the

subject was destined to be allayed in a remarkable manner. On the 27th of June, Cuthbert Rodham Carr again presented himself to Superintendent Elliott, and made such a confession as left no doubt that he was the murderer. Perhaps a more singular confession is not to be found in the records of criminality. It was taken down in Carr's own words, just as he uttered them without prompting, and careless of the effect they might produce. To exhibit the curious character of the man's mind and the cold-blooded and callous manner which distinguished his conduct in the commission of the crime, we will quote a few sentences from his horrible confession. 'On Friday afternoon,' said he, 'the 13th of April – that is just the time – I saw the little girl coming up the road . . . I took hold of her first and carried her away. She was over-frightened to cry – never spoke a word. I took her into the stable and up yon ladder at the far end, like. She then said, "Mother, mother!" I just choked her then. Before she was choked I laid her down . . . She was choked after that. I laid her underneath the hay to keep her warm. I can tell you the time when I think on. It was half-past six o'clock. I got one piece of string about a yard long. I split the twine in two – did not cut it. You know I just split it with a pull. I tied the twine on her neck first. The neck had a lump* in it. If I can mind right, she was dead long before it . . . I never had a knife. She was torn by my fingers . . . There was a lot of blood come and I burned the hay that it came on to. I choked her until she was insensible. Her heart was beating. She was breathing by gasps, and died about ten minutes after that.'

---

* 'Lump' should be 'loop'; this is an old transcription error that has been carried over from the writer's source material for the piece.

What strikes a reader as most singular in this confession, after the appalling facts which it relates, is the horrible vividness of the sensations of the murderer. Every slight circumstance seems to have scorched into his brain. The lump in the throat, the beating of the heart, the light infantine gasps – these might have been expected to impress him; but he forgot nothing, from the moment of carrying the little girl away until the moment he threw her over a wall into the road where she was found. And yet there is no doubt that this man was insane. The human mind is so constructed, indeed, that it is to be doubted whether a man could commit such crimes and remain perfectly sane. It seems reasonable and probable that he would go mad out of pure horror at his own brutality. But Carr was insane, not merely after the crime, but all through.

He was brought up at the Gateshead Police Court on the 29th of June, and it was easily perceived that he was a person of weak intellect. When he was placed in the dock, his father stepped forward and kissed him, and even some feeling of pity and commiseration mingled with the sentiment of horror and repulsion which swept over the persons in the court. Of course, Carr was committed for trial. At the Assizes he would persist in pleading guilty. 'I will plead guilty and take the consequences,' he said. To plead not guilty would, he thought, be a sin against his conscience. As he resisted all the persuasions of his counsel, the only thing that could be done was to take evidence as to his sanity, and in the end he was confined during Her Majesty's pleasure. From that time Carr has been an inmate of Broadmoor Asylum, but even there he has been distinguished for the violence of his nature. He has, we are informed, escaped on several occasions, but has always been recaptured. He is still living, though it is to be hoped that his memory was frail enough to forget the miserable crime of ten years ago.[253]

The article is an accurate and really quite reasonable reiteration of the Sarah Melvin case, commendable in its marshalling of the facts and the way it brings in the stackyard fires and the attack on Ann Brown (which were only discussed together in a single editorial article, in the *Caledonian Mercury*,[254] written very presciently right at the start of the Melvin case, before the inquest into Sarah's death had even been convened). The unnamed author of the later piece had evidently referred to the *Mercury*'s thinkpiece, as it follows the same sequence of events and also repeats the error in the date of the Ann Brown attack).

Cuthbert, now 28 years old, somehow got wind of this article in which his own crimes were compared to the murder in Blackburn. Given how important accuracy was to him, he was no doubt highly anxious to check how he had been portrayed and to make sure that the facts in the case had been faithfully relayed. There was surely also an element of egotism at play: to show off that he was the subject of a big piece in the most important of the Newcastle newspapers a whole ten years after his crime. Perhaps there was a degree of pride that he was still notorious – and some concern that the new outrages of this William Fish in Blackburn might eclipse his own. Once, his ego had been nourished by his place at the heart of the Carr kingdom: not only did his name coincide with the name of his house, his hill and his village, but his swift-footed familiarity with his hilltop territory had ensured his dominion there. Deprived of those external validators of his self and his pride, his self-absorption was exacerbated in the asylum.

Cuthbert's desire to read the article intensified and he worked himself up to the highest pitch of longing. His considerable will now focused on trying to force his family up in Gateshead to send him the article. It became the cause of a serious rift with them.

16

'My Unfortunate Son'

In the notes about Cuthbert in the patient case book, in his escape attempts, his violence and other efforts to resist succumbing to the treatment regime, we see revealing glimpses of his role as a spanner in the Broadmoor works. This was the persona he made for himself inside the asylum bubble, but he also maintained relationships with people in the outside world, including his family. In his archived file, the majority of the twenty-seven items are letters from Cuthbert's father. These are not letters to Cuthbert himself – no doubt there were very many of those as well, but they have not been found. Rather, these are letters written to the asylum authorities (usually to the superintendent), asking them to intercede on Cuthbert Sr's behalf when communication with his son became particularly challenging.

It would have been understandable if Cuthbert's family had disowned him once he had been taken away from Carr's Hill and locked up in a lunatic asylum. The shame brought on the rest of the family by his terrible crimes would surely have given them reason enough to cast him off, so that they could salvage their own reputations.

The letters in Cuthbert's Broadmoor file show this assumption to be quite wrong.

Yet it's clear that Cuthbert's difficult relationship with his father – the defining characteristic of his personality – continued from within Broadmoor's walls. As early as January 1867, when he first arrived at the asylum, there was a note in the patient case book:

18th January

His letters to his father display great and apparently ground-less animosity. He accuses his father of poisoning the minds of the officials of the asylum against him. The fact being that his father has appeared desirous of doing anything which could contribute to his comfort, sending him books etc.

It is impossible to know whether there were in fact any grounds for Cuthbert to dislike him so intensely: once again, one wonders whether Cuthbert Sr had abused or bullied his son in any way. All the evidence we have tends to suggest, rather convincingly, that Cuthbert's father was kindly and to bear out this note. It could be that Cuthbert Sr's only 'crime' was to have apprenticed Cuthbert to the glassworks.

It's possible to catch a sense of the dynamic between them through the letters in the file (fleshed out by one or two significant notes in the patient case book). This dynamic seems to have changed over time: whereas the adolescent Cuthbert had been either persuaded or coerced into embarking on the apprenticeship at the Carr's Hill glassworks and had found it intolerable, this slightly older Cuthbert, a confessed rapist and murderer, was somehow able to draw on reserves of willpower and stubbornness to force his father onto the back foot – it chimed with the Cuthbert who bargained with his father in the dock at the aborted trial, refusing to plead not guilty unless his father and brother apologised to him over the apprenticeship.

Cuthbert Sr's letters to the Broadmoor authorities beg for intervention and support in his efforts to make things right with his son. The impression is that, despite being hundreds of miles away in a secure institution, it is Cuthbert who has the upper hand and who is able to manipulate his father, keeping their relationship on a knife-edge of emotional blackmail.

At the time of the first letter in the file, which is dated 30 September 1876, Cuthbert was refusing to write to his father. The reason was his father's 'refusal' to send Cuthbert the article about himself from the *Chronicle* which he was so desperate to read. In fact Cuthbert's father had sent Cuthbert the article but the Broadmoor staff had intercepted it as they felt it was not 'desirable' for Cuthbert to see it. Unaware of the asylum's hand in things, Cuthbert was not only refusing to correspond with his father but had applied a further turn of the screw by telling his sister that if his father didn't comply with certain conditions he would refuse to see him if he visited Broadmoor (such visits were permitted, if prearranged with the staff).

This is the letter to Superintendent William Orange in full. It is written in loose handwriting with a pen that delivers a little too much ink with every fresh stroke of the nib, the small, regular blots taking on the appearance of tiny leeches wriggling across the page:

> Carr's Hill
> Gateshead on Tyne
> 30th Sept 1876
>
> Sir,
> I am sorry to trouble you, knowing how onerous must be your
> duties; but under present circumstances, I can see no other way

out of a difficulty that has arisen between me and my unfortunate son, Cuthbert Carr, causing him to cease writing to me as
he had been doing. Enclosed with a letter of his dated 3rd May
last was a piece of paper containing the following:

'Postscript. Please send me the Newcastle Weekly Chronicle
of April 29th merely that I may be cognisant of certain currents
of opinion; but you know that I am not liable to be influenced
by erroneous opinions, political or otherwise. C. R. Carr.'* I
concurred in the propriety of the intimation given in red ink as
above; but I have, in subsequent letters I have sent him, avoided
giving the reason, and he blames me for not sending it, and now
refuses to correspond with me. Since he ceased writing to me,
he has written letters to one of his sisters; but in the last letter
to her, dated 27th ult.,† he states that if certain preposterous
conditions, most of which I hardly understand, be not complied
with, he will cease for ever to correspond with any of his family.
I had intended to come to Broadmoor a few months ago; but in
consequence of my not sending him the newspaper, he wrote that
he did not wish to see me. Some person at Broadmoor must have
informed him about the paper containing the article on himself.
Under the melancholy circumstances, it is some consolation for us
to receive letters from him occasionally; and I think if he could
be certified that I was not to blame for not sending the paper,
he would be satisfied. I shall therefore feel exceedingly grateful

---

* Across this transcribed postscript, Cuthbert Sr has also inscribed a message in red ink,
written at right-angles: 'This is not desirable. The paper asked for contains an account
of the writer's crime and trial.' These words had been superimposed on Cuthbert's by a
member of the asylum staff when they checked Cuthbert's letter of 3 May before forwarding it to his father. Now Cuthbert Sr is reminding the asylum of the position they
had taken back in May.

† 'ult' comes from the Latin *ultimo mense* and means 'last month'.

if you would kindly, in such ways as you may deem best, put him wright [sic] in this point, either by informing him that it was contrary to your regulations for such a paper to be sent, or in some other way.

Apologising for the trouble I am giving you,

I am respectfully,

Sir,

Your humble servant,

Cuthᵗ Carr[255]

In his next letter to Dr Orange, dated three months later, Cuthbert's father is still fussing about the article:

Carr's Hill

Gateshead on Tyne

30th December 1876

Sir,

I duly received your letter of the 12th inst., and beg respectfully to thank you for the trouble you have kindly taken with a view to soften the feelings of my unfortunate son. When my attention had been directed by a friend to the article in the Newcastle Weekly Chronicle of the 29th April last, I procured a copy and cut the article out, but I had mislaid it amongst other papers. Having now turned [unclear] upon it, I have taken the liberty to enclose it herewith. I shall feel obliged if you will tell him that we are well, and that we send our love to him and I should likewise, after Cuthbert shall have perused the article, like to have it returned as we cannot procure another copy.

With sentiments of esteem and gratitude
I am,
Sir,
Your greatly obliged
humble servant
Cuth[t] Carr[256]

As we don't have Dr Orange's side of the correspondence at this point, we don't have the full picture, though we can infer from Mr Carr's letter that Dr Orange was not unsympathetic to his plea and had perhaps tried to persuade Cuthbert not to take such a rigid stance *vis à vis* his father. It was unfortunate that Mr Carr had now laid hands on the article, some months after Cuthbert had first tried to obtain it. It would have been better to let matters lie and not to send the cutting down to Broadmoor at all. Presumably the asylum staff did not pass it on to Cuthbert (why would they have thought it was any more suitable for him to read now than three months earlier?). Cuthbert was still refusing to communicate with his family and his father was increasingly desperate to mend the situation. Christmas had just passed, no doubt with something of a pall cast over it.

In depriving himself of news and affection from his family, Cuthbert had armed himself with another 'formidable weapon'. It was highly effective as a means by which to force his father to do his bidding.

The campaign continued. In the new year Mr Carr sent another brief letter to Dr Orange which reads, in part:

> Carr's Hill
> Gateshead upon Tyne
> 25th January 1877

> ... I beg to express my warmest thanks for the trouble you have taken in trying to soften the asperity of his feelings towards me,

and I hope that he will resume epistolary correspondence with us as formerly. As to the party whom he wishes me to see, I know nothing about them in particular, and I never in my life had a conversation with them.

I am,

Sir

[*etc*][257]

Once again, the subject is Dr Orange's efforts to 'soften' Cuthbert. A rock-solid refusal to shift was Cuthbert's most effective strategy, it would seem, and probably one he had learned as a small child. This letter contains a further reference to the 'preposterous conditions' alluded to in Mr Carr's letter of 30 September 1876. Cuthbert wanted his father to see somebody – one or more people – for a particular purpose. This was so difficult for Mr Carr to contemplate that he could only allude to it obliquely, without naming names – though, as we shall see, he did eventually reveal what Cuthbert was asking him to do, when the stakes became particularly high. It was a stand-off between father and son, with Cuthbert seemingly having the upper hand. For now, Mr Carr's only strategy is a rather disingenuous dismissal of the 'party' as people he doesn't know. He is in denial.

Further letters came from Mr Carr begging Dr Orange to intercede with Cuthbert. Cuthbert was using his position of silent strength to force his father to make other concessions. Mr Carr sent Cuthbert his indenture document from the glassworks – as we know, the apprenticeship was heavily freighted with significance for Cuthbert, so to possess the papers that represented it must have had great meaning for him, perhaps giving him a sense of power or of control over his own destiny. It seemed to matter to Mr Carr as well and he wrote anxiously to Dr Orange to tell him that he had sent Cuthbert 'the Indenture which he has long wished for. I did not wish to part with the Indenture, but I hope now he will be conciliated.'[258]

The two Cuthbert Rodham Carrs, father and son, were locked in a dance of power – the younger Cuthbert leading, his father following, step for step. Yet it is also evident that Mr Carr continued to love Cuthbert unconditionally. He tried constantly to mend rifts and reopen communications with his son. In his letters – the only way we have of knowing him directly – he comes across well. His writing style, although a little pedantic, is probably less fussy than the standard epistolary style of the time. And he doesn't ingratiate himself too cringingly with Dr Orange but is relatively straightforward in asking for his help. On balance, what insights we can glean from these letters tend to suggest that Cuthbert's antagonism towards his father may have been more a symptom of his mental illness than an entirely rational response to abuse (though, of course, abusers are also often expert dissemblers).

In August 1878, when Cuthbert was 30, his father wrote to Dr Orange to broach a major new issue. Such was its importance that Mr Carr had travelled down to the asylum from Carr's Hill in order to talk to the Superintendent about it in person. It seems very unfortunate that Dr Orange was unavailable to see him – and that the asylum also failed to send him the letter they had promised.

15 Aug 1878

Sir,

On 13th June last I came to Broadmoor with the special object of wishing to see you on the subject of my unfortunate son Cuthbert Rodham Carr, but was informed that you had left the asylum that day. I had a short interview with Dr Isaac [the Assistant Medical Officer], to whom I communicated the purpose of my visit and he informed me that I would hear from Broadmoor in the course of about a week. Not having received a letter, I respectfully beg to state to you what I am wishful to ascertain.

For several years my family and myself have had the intention of emigrating to some British Colony, provided Cuthbert could be allowed to go with us, on our giving an undertaking to take care of him, and now, provided this can be done, I shall endeavour to make arrangements to go away to Canada, with a view to culti-vate the land. I know it is a very delicate question and I hope you will excuse me for the liberty I am taking. I and every member of my family yearn to have him along with us, and I fervently hope that we may not be disappointed.

I am respectfully,
Sir,
Your most obedient
Humble servant,
Cuthbert Carr [259]

One might have assumed that the family wished to emigrate in order to make a fresh start, with the slate of their troubles wiped clean. One might also have assumed that their fresh start would not include the cause of all their woes, Cuthbert Jr. Yet, far from this being the case, it is absolutely clear from this letter that Mr Carr wanted nothing more than to be allowed to take Cuthbert with them wherever they might go.

Although Cuthbert was being kept in Broadmoor 'at Her Majesty's pleasure', that is to say indefinitely, there was nonetheless the possibility for such 'pleasure men' to be discharged if the right circumstances could be achieved. The Superintendent might make a formal request to the Home Office for a particular patient to be discharged if they had 'recovered their health' and no longer showed any signs of insanity; the other chief requirement for discharge was absolute certainty that the patient would be able to continue to live quietly and simply, kept safe in the charge of responsible family members or friends. The ex-patient must not only be provided with somewhere to live but also an industrious and steadying routine.[260]

In Cuthbert's case, it might seem that the latter part of the criteria for release would be very adequately fulfilled by a new life in Canada 'cultivating the land' in the bosom of his family. Yet Dr Orange was not convinced. In this instance, the Superintendent has drafted his reply on the back of Mr Carr's letter, so we discover that Dr Orange was not minded to allow Cuthbert to be released into the custody of his family. He wrote to Cuthbert's father: 'I cannot hold out much hope at present of your son being allowed to leave this asylum. He does not appear to be inclined to be guided by you. I should be glad to know whether you think that you would be able to exercise any control over him.'

Mr Carr's answer, while seeking to persuade him that he could control Cuthbert, rather brilliantly demonstrates that he could not:

Carr's Hill

Gateshead on Tyne

4th September 1878

Sir,

With reference to your letter of the 19th inst. in reply to mine of the 15th [August 1878] asking whether I would be able to exercise control over my son Cuthbert R. Carr, I beg respectfully to state that I think it could be done if I could previously satisfy him on certain absurd matters which he has for some time been insisting upon. I may state that his opposition to me arose out of the circumstances of an article in the Newcastle Weekly Chronicle which some person at the Asylum must have told him about . . . The principle [sic] obstacle to a reconciliation between him and me, according to his way of writing, appears to be my not offering some sort of apology to the Melvins; but as he has said in some of his letters that he would not insist on this being done immediately, provided I would undertake to do it ultimately, I think I might comply with this condition [by] agreeing to make some sort of apology shortly before leaving this neighbourhood.

I think if he knew what I and our family wish to do, he would be glad to go with us to share [*unclear – possibly 'start'*] in the work of cultivating land.

I feel confident that if his present obstinacy could be overcome by my complying with his own conditions as to the apology there would be no further difficulty.

I have not so far in any letter that I have sent him told him of our project to emigrate; and I think if you would kindly undertake the trouble to move [*unclear*] it to him it might be better than for me to do so. I thank you fervently for your kindness . . .

The exercise of clearing and cultivating land in the midst of his family would be agreeable to his feelings and would tend to his improvement.

[*Yours, etc*][261]

These, then, are the 'preposterous conditions' that Cuthbert has laid down as the 'price' for his resuming communication with his father and the rest of his family: Mr Carr must 'apologise' to Mr and Mrs Melvin for the murder of their child. Although, ostensibly, Cuthbert is asking his father to apologise on his behalf, the underlying psychology adds a further dimension: Cuthbert is trying to hand over the blame for the murder to his father. Thus he would absolve himself of any guilt and make his father, at least symbolically, responsible for the child's death. Such is Mr Carr's desperation to win Cuthbert's approval again that he is willing to make this powerful gesture, even though it clearly causes him deep embarrassment (and perhaps, subconsciously, guilt). Perhaps if he waits until just before the family disappears abroad, he will be able to bring himself to do it, he suggests.

Once again, Mr Carr asks Dr Orange to speak on his behalf, in effect to tell Cuthbert the news that he himself is too afraid to announce – for the implication is that, even if Cuthbert is not discharged to go with them, the family intend to emigrate anyway, with Cuthbert left behind in the old country. Surely Cuthbert's father could not believe that complying with Cuthbert's conditions was going to convince Dr Orange that he was fully in control of his manipulative son?

Written in pencil at the end of the above letter is Dr Orange's draft reply:

Nov 11th 1878

In reply, etc . . .
I do not think you would be successful in your attempt to exercise due control over him. You will see by the enclosed that he refuses to hold any further correspondence with his brother.[262]

The 'enclosed' was presumably a letter from Cuthbert's youngest sibling, John William, then aged 21, being returned unopened.

Swift was the response from Mr Carr. The following letter, although undated by him, is stamped 3 December 1878 by the asylum.

Sir,
I duly received your letter of 11th ult., and enclosure, and was grieved at the nature of the communication. It is a pity that my son Cuthbert had not read the last letters, because, I think, they

might have removed some of the objections that he had got in his mind. Along with some musical books which Cuthbert had written for, his brother John W had sent him a valuable book on music which we had in our possession. Cuthbert in his letter to me praised the book but expressed his intention not to keep it, on the ground that he would not deprive his brother of so valuable a book, and requested him to send stamps to enable the book to be returned to us. Sufficient stamps were sent, with an intimation that the book ought to be registered at the post office, but we have not up to the present time received the book, and have never been told if it had been sent. I should feel obliged, Sir, if you would kindly make enquiry on this matter and let me know. Cuthbert had likewise written for some book designated 'Mother Shipton's Prophecies',* stating, I presume on the authority of some person in the asylum, a Bookseller at Bradford where the same was to be got. Thirty stamps were sent to the Bookseller, but we were never told whether he had received this book. As far as I can infer from some of Cuthbert's latest letters, those were amongst the most prominent of his requests, and we instantly took steps to have them gratified. Possibly he may have been offended alas at his sisters not writing to him sooner. I am sorry to give you so much trouble, but under the circumstances, having

---

* Mother Shipton (real name, Ursula Southeil, c.1488–1561) was a self-styled prophetess born in Knaresborough, Yorkshire. In 1862 Charles Hindley published a new edition of what purported to be her rhyming prophecies, later admitting that he had written them himself. It may have been this edition that Cuthbert was after, the doomladen riddles perhaps appealing to the paranoid conspiracy theorist in him. A note in the patient case book (BRO: D/H14/D1/1/1/2) suggests that Cuthbert's obsession with the non-arrival of his copy of *Mother Shipton's Prophecies* may have been eating away at him. It reads in part: 'Is eccentric, whimsical and insane in his ideas . . . His mind is greatly exercised about trifles – such for instance as the precise number of postal deliveries a letter ought to take in coming from Yorkshire to him.'

no other way of ascertaining facts, I shall feel exceedingly obliged if you will make enquiry in these points I have mentioned, and if you will try to ascertain what other particular thing Cuthbert would have done, so that his feelings towards his family may be softened.

I am,

Sir,

Your greatly obliged humble servant

Cuthbert Carr[263]

This is the letter of a defeated man. Apart from saying that he is 'grieved', Mr Carr leaves all mention of Cuthbert's possible discharge, the apology to the Melvins, the emigration untouched and, instead, retreats into the minutiae of books and stamps. Tellingly, this is the last letter written to the asylum authorities by Mr Carr during Cuthbert's time there. A handwritten note in a corner of the front page says, 'To be put up with papers of C. Carr'. I suspect that means it went unanswered. Perhaps Dr Orange, busy medical superintendent of the national asylum for the criminally insane, lost patience, finally, with Mr Carr's requests for trifling (as well as more significant) favours.

Cuthbert Rodham Carr Sr and four of his children left Carr's Villa in February or March 1879. We don't know whether Mr Carr apologised to the Melvins for their daughter's death before the family left Gateshead. It seems very likely he did not. What could he have said that would not have seemed insincere or meaningless? Above all, it would have been the class division between the two families that probably put paid to any attempt on the Carrs' part to atone for Cuthbert's rape and murder of the Melvins' little girl.

While the Carrs had the opportunity to emigrate, the Melvins stayed in Carr's Hill for the rest of their lives. Whatever the reasons for their separation in 1866 had been, after the murder Michael and Mary lived together in Clark's Houses on Split Crow Lane. All their children had left home, but James Beveridge, a grandson, lived with them for a while. He worked as a blacksmith, so had perhaps established himself on a firmer footing than his grandparents ever managed. Michael died before Mary and she spent her last few years at No. 17 Coldwell Street with her daughter Mary Ann and her family. There are no further reports of Michael having been in trouble with the law after 1866, so perhaps his daughter's death and all that followed from it served to chasten him. In May 1872, along with four other women, Mary was sentenced to a week's imprisonment for stealing coal from Pelaw Main colliery, near Carr's Hill, the minimal sentence suggesting that the magistrates looked fairly benignly on poor women desperate for a bit of coal for their fires.[264]

The Carr family made landfall on Canadian soil on 21 March 1879 and made their way to a tiny town called Jordan (later renamed Richmond and, later still, Plumas), in Manitoba, Canada. Mr Carr was 69 when he left England, quite an age to be making a new start. Jane was 37, Sarah 29, Elizabeth 24 and John 22. One of Cuthbert's siblings, Richard, didn't travel to Canada – he and his wife emigrated to Chicago. Mr Carr's other daughter, Ann, had died of tuberculosis and bronchitis in January 1868, aged 22.

Jordan had been founded by English settlers just seven years earlier. It was a farming community with simple wooden houses set within the straight-edged boundaries of just one of the hundreds of square plots into which the vast prairie had been divided. But the land was cheap and reasonably fertile. As they gazed across the endless horizons of Manitoba, the family must have missed the rocky outcrops of Gateshead Fell and they had that in common with their Cuthbert. Did he seem any further away, now that they had crossed a great ocean? Or had they already lost him when he was taken away to Broadmoor?

17

'Value – Nominal'

A letter dated 17 March 1879 was copied out in the patient case book. It was addressed to the Home Secretary, the Hon. Sir Adolphus Liddell:

> The humble petition from Broadmoor Criminal Lunatic Asylum of Cuthbert Rodham Carr sheweth, that Mr Liddel [*sic*], the permanent Under Home Secretary, having signified to Dr. Orange your refusal to comply with your petitioner's prayer for him to be sent to Canada, your petitioner's present request is that he should be, at sometime or other, liberated in England, leaving it to his own discretion as to where he should take up his habitation. That it is your petitioner's further request that 'sometime or other' aforesaid should be interpreted to mean the present time, and no other. That your petitioner being possessed of more self-control than anyone else in the world, is desirous that the usual guarantees should in his case be dispensed with, depending upon your

petitioner's own guarantee. And that your petitioner is anxiously
awaiting for an answer in the affirmative.

[signed] Cuthbert Rodham Carr.[265]

The petition is scaffolded with rhetorical language that all but hides
the simple message, 'Let me out!' It almost strikes a humorous note,
clarifying that 'sometime or other' actually means 'right now'. Cuthbert seems to have grasped that self-control was the key quality any
potential asylum-leaver would need to have in spades. He uses childish
hyperbole to insist that he has more of it than 'anyone else in the world'
(and no doubt in the whole universe); on the basis of his supreme self-
discipline he even wants a special dispensation to be made for him that
he shouldn't have to find people to guarantee his good conduct, perhaps
because he knows that no such guarantees of his behaviour from other
people will ever be forthcoming. It is a touching little attempt to finesse
the system but one that also reveals Cuthbert's arrogance. That he should
have even thought this worth a try! It was a hopeless cause. Cuthbert no
doubt continued to burn with the intense, corrosive frustration of the
powerless. There is no evidence of any response at all to this petition,
and in all likelihood it was never even sent.

When Cuthbert wrote it, his family would have been at sea on their
way to the New World. After they emigrated, Cuthbert remained in
Broadmoor, almost certainly receiving fewer letters and probably no
visitors at all. He studied German from books and perhaps attempted to
practise his conversational skills with Wilhelm Stolzer, a German patient,
though Stolzer's madness was characterised by muteness and incoherent
noises.[266] Cuthbert also played the flute and read books. As we know, he
was not coerced into doing any work that would have contributed to the
asylum community. Perhaps his aversion to work was lifelong, following
the trauma of his early try-outs at the glass factory and as a bricklayer.

Active psychotherapeutic treatment was not part of the asylum regime either and, from the limited evidence available, it seems unlikely that Cuthbert's mental state was fundamentally improved in any way at Broadmoor. In truth he became more severely disturbed in the later decades of his time there.

On 21 March 1885, when Cuthbert had just turned 37, the following note was made in the patient case book (six years after the last entry about him): 'Says there are 5 murderers in the block (patients) who he thinks are disguised and that he is afraid they will kill him.' This was par for the course: Cuthbert's deep paranoia is all too familiar, although most if not all of the patients in Broadmoor were indeed murderers, so one might take the view that this was a perfectly rational concern. What is clear is that Cuthbert had not yet found peace of mind.

Then, just over two months later, a further intriguing entry was made: 'In seclusion at his own request – sits all day, even in winter, without shoes and stockings – talks connectedly on ordinary subjects, but with a consequential sententious air.' Cuthbert's pomposity seems to have increased in the asylum. Perhaps it came about from living among so many other disturbed individuals; certain styles of communication might develop because they were more effective than others. And he was better educated than most of the others too, which might lead to a certain sense of superiority.

The note went on, 'His numerous extravagant delusions find vent more readily in the long letters which he frequently writes than in conversation – in a letter of this date, to a gentleman in Gateshead, he says, "Although I am undoubtedly the lawful heir of the present King of Bavaria". In good bodily health.'

Cuthbert's physical health may have passed muster, but there seems to have been a step change in his mental state. He had not been recorded as entertaining this kind of delusion about his own identity before this point. His belief that he was heir to King Ludwig II of Bavaria, himself notorious for being mad, has something gloriously flamboyant about it.* Was there a specific cause of this new derangement? From this point onwards, the patient notes regularly say that Cuthbert's physical health is 'good'; it seems very likely that this was being watched more closely in the expectation that it would not be 'good' for much longer. Cuthbert's steep mental decline was a fanfare heralding the final onslaught of a dreadful disease – and one with which the asylum staff were only too familiar.

Towards the end of the same month, on 20 June, there is a further note:† 'Some days ago told the M[edical] O[fficer] that he knew that his discharge had been sent here by the Home Secretary, and was now lying in the Superintendent's office – and demanded that it should be acted on. Wrote to Superintendent to same effect, saying that he knew from [having] "read in the lineaments of the Chief Attendant's face" that his discharge had arrived.'

Needless to say, no notice of discharge was forthcoming from the Home Secretary. It would be unthinkable for someone exhibiting such clear symptoms of mental illness as Cuthbert now was to be released

---

* Ludwig II of Bavaria was renowned for his extravagant spending (on the fabulous Neuschwanstein Castle, amongst other follies) and would be declared insane the following year – though the declaration had strong political overtones and may not have been made in good faith: as a result of being declared unfit to rule, Ludwig's uncle, Luitpold, a man who was much more willing to cooperate with ambitious Prussia, became regent. Cuthbert would only have a year to wait to see if he would inherit the throne of Bavaria as Ludwig would die in highly suspicious circumstances in June 1886, very shortly after he had been declared insane.

† The change in the rate at which entries were being made in the case book is notable: a new phase of Cuthbert's life seems to have begun – or, of course, it could just be that asylum staff had made a change of practice. One should be wary of drawing conclusions. As the patient case book is not yet open to the public, entries about a particular patient have to be transcribed by Record Office staff on request and it is not possible to survey the whole book in order to gain a wider context.

from secure care. Desperation and delusion wound themselves ever more tightly around him; the pace at which he was drawing away from reality seemed to be accelerating – and yet, ironically, his grasp of German *realpolitik* was rather impressive.

On 3 September 1885 an entry noted that the day before Cuthbert had written 'to a friend in Gateshead, "I am determined to insist on obtaining possession of the throne of Bavaria . . . which my elder brother, Ludwig or Lewis*, has forfeited by oppressing his subjects . . . Prince Bismar[c]k has known who I am many years . . . I will invite you to Germany on the occasion of my wedding at Munich . . . If, last June, for the purpose of preventing a sanguinary and internecine war in South Africa, and for doing good otherwise, I adroitly, without making any fuss, effected a change of Government in Britain, then it is also feasible for me to effect a change of Government in Bavaria . . ."'

There is much more detail here about Cuthbert's delusion regarding the Bavarian royal family. He seems to have identified with Otto, Ludwig II's younger brother. Bismarck was the pre-eminent Prussian statesman who had unified Germany and who held the most powerful political position in the new German empire. It was certainly true that Bismarck knew who Otto was, as he made sure he could not exercise any power once he succeeded his brother Ludwig on the Bavarian throne. Otto was more incontrovertibly mad than Ludwig; Cuthbert's identification with him is a good fit. Otto was born just two months after Cuthbert, in April 1848. Both he and Ludwig had difficult childhoods; relations with their parents were strained. The career set out for Otto was as a soldier on active service in the many wars waged by the German states and, where Cuthbert was traumatised by his experi-

---

* 'Lewis' is simply the English version of the name Ludwig.

ences of the male world of work, Otto suffered from the trauma of the battlefield, developing classic signs of post-traumatic stress disorder, including insomnia, anxiety and depression. It has been suggested that Otto developed schizophrenia and, far from marrying in Munich, as Cuthbert fantasised, he never married, nor was he capable of effecting a change of government in Bavaria. Although he might have wanted to do so (being opposed to Bismarck's rise to power), he was controlled so heavy-handedly that he had no opportunity to instigate anything. To Cuthbert, a keen reader of the newspapers, Otto must have seemed his German doppelgänger.

A note in the case book made on 19 October 1885 said that Cuthbert had written again to the same friend, 'giving a very minute account of unnatural offences and barbaric acts perpetrated on the person of a female to whom he often alludes in his letters, and stating that the knowledge of these acts had been revealed to him in a supernatural way within the last three or four days. The document is put with his papers. Health continues good. Still in voluntary seclusion in Block 1.'

This letter, then, was not sent but intercepted and placed on file, presumably because it was too obscene to be countenanced. It is no longer in Cuthbert's archived file, unfortunately. Cuthbert is very disturbed here. He seems to be hearing voices that tell him about terrible things done to women – these 'unnatural offences and barbaric acts' would be sexual fantasies of his own that he perhaps strove to project onto some external agent. They may have frightened as well as excited him. A clue as to the object of his violent fantasies may perhaps be gleaned from the next entry in the book (made six months later, on 3 April 1886):

Had a long conversation last night with the M[edical] O[fficer] to whom he gave a written demand to show cause why he is not allowed to 'write and speak to my lawful wife, Lady Alwina

Valleria'. He professes an intimate knowledge of the appearance and abilities of this person, says she has appeared to him here recently (which is not the case), accuses the doctors here of clandestine correspondence with her, and of 'ulterior motives' in preventing his correspondence with her – asserts stoutly his absolute right to maintain an intercourse with her, but refuses to state the grounds of his right. His mind is full of the most extraordinary delusions, and he evidently believes that he possesses supernatural powers, but he is patient regarding these subjects, and declines to converse much upon them. Health good.

Alwina Valleria was not a titled Lady but a well-known opera singer. Photos of her show a rather plain, unsmiling woman with neat dark hair. Taken in isolation, it's rather difficult to know why Cuthbert fixated on her. She seems to have been at the centre of a maelstrom of disturbed and highly anxious feelings. We don't know for certain that Alwina Valleria was the person upon whom Cuthbert wished to commit 'barbaric acts' but it seems likely. And there is further evidence from another source to support this.

I have been able to identify Cuthbert's 'friend' in Gateshead, to whom he wrote these letters. At first I thought the friend was perhaps one of those who gave him their support during the Joseph Curry affair and testified to his good character in court. This was not the case.

Not all of Cuthbert's letters were intercepted. There is a record of the reaction of at least one person who received letters from him at this period and this person was almost certainly the 'friend' mentioned in the case book, because he records the very same quotation from one of Cuthbert's letters as was written down in the case book. He was William Edwin Adams, who at the time was the editor of the

Newcastle Weekly Chronicle.* It was the *Chronicle* that had published the account of the William Fish murder in 1876, with its mention of Cuthbert, about which he became so obsessive, but Cuthbert's letters to the editor only began in 1885 (we can't call this a 'correspondence' as it seems unlikely Adams sent any letters in reply). In 1903, Adams published his two-volume *Memoirs of a Social Atom*. Included was a chapter entitled 'Eccentric and Crazy People'. By far the most 'crazy' of those mentioned by Adams as having plagued him with letters was Cuthbert:

> But a genuine madman was numbered among the correspondents of 1885. There had occurred about twenty years before a horrible murder in the North of England. The victim was a little girl, and the crime was of such a character that nobody but a lunatic could have committed it. The murderer was sentenced to be confined in the criminal asylum at Broadmoor. Thence he wrote a series of astonishing letters. 'I am undoubtedly,' he declared, 'the lawful heir of the present King of Bavaria.' But he had received 'warnings from Providence of the rancorous opposition of Windsor Castle.' In consequence of this opposition, 'I have decided upon deposing the present Queen Alexandria Victoria d'Este Guelph, dispossessing her and the rest of the Guelphs of all their riches, except so much as will enable them to live in comfort without luxury.' Then he asserted that two of the leading ladies of the operatic stage at that time – Madame Marie Roze and Madame Alwina Valleria – were sisters. For the latter the poor lunatic designed a high distinction. 'I have resolved,' he wrote, 'to get myself and my betrothed wife, Emily Jaques of Osmotherley,

---

* Adams, a Radical, was editor of the *Chronicle* from 1864 until his retirement in 1900.

commonly known as Alwina Valleria, appointed conjoint and equal King and Queen of Great Britain and Ireland. Emily Jaques shall be wed to me under the same name as she had when we were betrothed; and the survivors of her former schoolmates and companions will be delighted beyond measure when they learn that the merry, gracious, and amiable little maiden, who in her puce mantle and frock used to diffuse joy and gladness in the upper part of High Felling, has become their Queen. Instead of bearing water-cans balanced on her head, she shall wear her own special tiara and sceptre; and instead of singing for the public in music halls, she shall sing for the private delectation of the most illustrious in the land.' A vast deal more of the same inconsequential maundering was written from Broadmoor in 1885 and 1886.[267]

This was a tremendously exciting discovery. Yes, Alwina Valleria pops up again: Cuthbert believed that she and another celebrity singer, Marie Roze, were sisters (they do look rather alike in photographs). But of much greater interest is the revelation that Cuthbert had conflated Valleria with a girl named Emily Jaques from Osmotherley. This is the only hint that Cuthbert was ever in love with anyone.

Emily was born in spring 1850 at Appleton Wiske near Osmotherley in what is now North Yorkshire. Her mother, Elizabeth Poynter, was from Osmotherley and married Robert Jaques in 1835. There were several children, of whom Emily was the youngest. Robert was a licensed apothecary and surgeon and if all had been well the family should have been quite comfortably off. But when Emily was 11 the 1861 census recorded that her father was in the Union Workhouse in Northallerton whilst Emily and two of her siblings, Robert Henry and Mary Ann, were living with an aunt and uncle in Leeds (probably their mother's sister and brother-in-law). Of their mother there is little trace – it is possible she may have died as early as 1851, not long after Emily was born. Poor Mr Jaques died in the workhouse a few years later, dropping dead from heart disease 'whilst sitting on a chair'.[268] Who knows what calamities set him on the path to penury and an early death? Emily's brother Robert Henry prospered in spite of the difficult circumstances of his childhood and became the proprietor, with his son, of Jaques & Jaques, a fashionable draper's shop in Darlington. Emily's sister Mary Ann married another pharmaceutical man and also seems to have led a steady adult life. Of Emily there is no further trace (and she most likely got married), unless she is the Emily Jaques, a 'middle-aged woman', who was fined 2s 6d for knocking apples down from a farmer's trees in Chester-le-Street in 1881[269] – Chester-le-Street is closer to the Felling than Osmotherley.

The passage about Emily from Cuthbert's letters to William Adams paints a vivid picture drawn from memories that Cuthbert had held on to and treasured through all the years since his childhood, and his freedom, had ended so abruptly. We know that Cuthbert did have sex at least once as a teenager – indeed, it was the source of many woes. Apart from that, it's impossible to know how sexually active he was and whether he had only wretched couplings with prostitutes (or, worse, only ever coerced women into sex) or whether there is the possibility that he had an affectionate friendship with this Emily, the affection perhaps even returned. Maybe she was just one of the young women that Cuthbert watched from his various vantage points on Carr's Hill, yet another girl who was scared of the 'mad boy'. Or, setting aside all sentimentality, could Emily have been someone who had sex for money, even the woman who infected Cuthbert with gonorrhoea? So much speculation, so few solid answers.

Since the age of 18, Cuthbert had been locked up in the company of disturbed men, guarded by other men, seeing women, if at all, only over the walls of the airing court or in the distance. But sexual desire was still pulsing strongly within him. His fantasies about Alwina Valleria were pornographic, violent: had his feelings towards women always been dangerous or had they only become so in Broadmoor? By contrast Cuthbert's description of Emily is so very charming and seems so heartfelt that it's hard not to be persuaded that this is a memory of something untainted. Was Cuthbert actually betrothed to Emily or is this part of the fantasy? Perhaps they were childhood sweethearts who promised to marry when they were grown-up – she was two years younger than Cuthbert (a typical age gap between married men and their wives over a very long period of history). It may be that, when her family fell apart, Emily was sent to the north-east to be a domestic servant (a common fate of dispossessed girls in the nineteenth century) and that's why Cuthbert remembered her carrying water-cans on her head. Given the horrific turn that Cuthbert's life took when he was still an adolescent, his memory of 'the merry, gracious, and amiable little maiden . . . in her puce mantle and frock' is moving, a hint of a more innocent path his life could have taken.

At the beginning of 1888, just two weeks into the new year, a member of the asylum staff recorded that Cuthbert 'complains of dyspepsia and loss of appetite. Mentally unchanged.' There was a new frequency to the medical notes and the emphasis was suddenly on food and Cuthbert's ability to digest it. On 6 February he was 'refusing food – ordered whiskey – is most fanciful regarding diet, asking for sweets and very indigestible things.' Is there an implication that patients' requests for particular foods were fulfilled if possible? Certainly one doesn't get the sense that meals were slapped down in front of patients on a 'take it or leave it' basis. But Cuthbert's digestive system was struggling. On 4 March:

'Takes very little food – losing flesh – gets wine and bismouths and soda powders – vomits frequently. Removed today to Block 3 Infirmary. Has several times assured the Med. Officer that he had not many hours to live, though no signs of such speedy dissolution were apparent.'

It sounds as though something was seriously wrong with Cuthbert and he was all too aware of it. Soon the rate of his physical decline began to accelerate. On 10 March: 'Continues to lose strength – stomach will retain very little food – motions passed in bed at times.' Two days later, an entry in the case book noted:

> Yesterday he began to lose his voice, and towards evening became unable to speak. Today, when seen by the Superintendent, was unable to speak to him. Can with difficulty be induced to take any nourishment or stimulants – up to the time his voice failed he continued to insist that only such articles as he asked for – fruit, sweets, and the like – would do him any good. This evening he indicated to the writer to come close up to his bed side, indicating that he wished to speak to him – when within reach, struck him on the nose and the leg – owing to his weakness the blows were very light.

This was the last gesture of defiance of Cuthbert's recalcitrant spirit. He never gave up on his efforts to break the system. But the system outlasted him.

On 14 March this note was written: 'Soon after 8 am today he became restless, passed a motion in bed at 8.40 and fainted while being cleaned. About 8.45 he was convulsed – there was cyclospasm, slightly affecting right side, conjugate deviation to the right, and pupils greatly dilated. The spasm passed off, and he died quietly at 8.55 am . . . in presence of Attendant McKay.'

Cuthbert was 40 years old and had spent more than half his short life in the asylum when he died.

Several documents in Cuthbert's official file record his death and the names of the people who were present. Deaths in the asylum, especially of younger people, must have caused anxiety lest anyone call foul play. As soon as death hove into view, the language used by the asylum became much more formal and technical – 'cyclospasm' (contraction of a muscle in the eye), 'conjugate deviation' (both eyes rolling up or to the side) – no doubt to protect themselves should there be any accusations of malpractice.

All patients who died in Broadmoor were routinely autopsied and given the formality of an inquest; Cuthbert was no exception. Each year the autopsy reports of all patients who had died during the previous twelve months were printed in the official annual report (fourteen patients in total died in 1888). Thus we know the following facts about Cuthbert, which neatly close off his life.[270]

The information is set out in a table of ten columns across a double-page spread at the end of the report. The first column contains only Cuthbert's patient number, 388, identifying him even in death. In the next column, only the initials C.R.C. are given, rather than his full name, in a small nod towards discretion, together with his height ('5ft. 8½ in.'), sex, age and the date that he was admitted to the asylum.

The third column gives the briefest of case histories: 'Glassworker. Arraigned at Durham Assizes on 6th December 1866 for wilful murder of a little girl whom he had violated. Found insane and unfit to plead. Admitted from Durham County Gaol.'

It is so strange that he is labelled a 'glassworker' even in death, when that was the very last thing he wanted to be.

In the next column his particular madness is diagnosed as 'Chronic mania with delusions'. This reflects Cuthbert's mental state in the last years of his life, rather than the 'partial imbecility' with which he was labelled at the time of the murder.

Cuthbert's 'bodily health' was recorded as 'good up to within a few months of his death'.

The autopsy was carried out twenty-eight hours after Cuthbert's death. First the brain was dissected: 'Scalp thin ... Over right fronto-parietal and left frontal regions there were portions of extravasated blood spread over in a membranous form with small cysts ... Along the under surface of the hemispheres was a film of extravasated blood interspersed with numerous small flat clots the size of millet seed to a small pea ...'

The 'extravasated' blood and small clots were the actual cause of Cuthbert's death. There is no explicit mention of a disease such as syphilis having been the underlying cause of death, but the formal cause of death given at the inquest, 'Meningeal haemorrhage with inflammation', is entirely consistent with tertiary syphilis. It seems clear that when Cuthbert got the 'bad disorder' at Berry Edge he picked up not only gonorrhoea but also syphilis. One manifestation of the late stages of this illness is neurosyphilis, when the disease attacks the central nervous system. As well as causing meningitis, there will often be psychiatric symptoms, including marked personality changes such as grandiose delusions, mania, hostility and apathy, which would account for Cuthbert's descent into paranoia and fantasy. This final, terrible stage of the disease is known as 'paresis' and in the mid-nineteenth century it was incurable. Until an effective treatment for syphilis was developed in the early twentieth century (Salvarsan, a compound of arsenic), the asylums of Europe were increasingly filled with men and women suffering from the psychiatric symptoms of tertiary syphilis. No doubt Cuthbert's disease was readily diagnosed by the asylum staff but it was not formally named in the record of his death. The stigma surrounding syphilis was powerful.

Next to be dissected were the heart and lungs: 'Both lungs congested at the base. Pericardium contained an ounce of yellow clear fluid. Heart walls very firm.' The stomach and other abdominal organs: 'Mucous membrane of stomach bile-stained . . . Liver pale, firm, and fatty. Gall-bladder distended and contained about thirty small gallstones . . . Both kidneys much contracted, tough, and fibrous . . .'

At the end of the report, the weights of various organs, in ounces, were given, starting with the parts of the brain:

Right hemisphere	25 ¼
Left "	25 ¼
Cerebellum	5 ½
Pons and medulla	¾
Total encephalon	57
Right lung	27 ½
Left "	22
Heart	18
Liver	58 ¼
Spleen	9 ¼
Right kidney	3 ½
Left "	2 ¾

Cuthbert was finally reduced to a pile of body parts on a weighing scale.

There was not much else left to remember him by either. Cuthbert's father was informed of his death by letter on the day after he passed away, but of course it took some time for the news to reach him in Canada. In less than three weeks, Mr Carr had received the letter and replied to Dr Orange. He wanted all Cuthbert's possessions to be returned to him as keepsakes:

Richmond,
Manitoba,
British North America
2nd April 1888

Sir,

I beg to acknowledge the receipt of your letter of 15th ult. informing me that my dearly beloved but unfortunate son Cuthbert Rodham Carr was dead. I wish to have his Books, Manuscripts and whatever belonged to him sent to me to the above address.

. . .

I shall also feel obliged if you will inform me how long my dear son lay in his last illness.

I am,

Sir,

[*etc*][271]

The next item in Cuthbert's Broadmoor file is another letter from his father, sent three months later, when evidently a meagre parcel of belongings had arrived from Broadmoor. Mr Carr was roused to asperity by grief and frustration:

Richmond,
Manitoba,
British North America
6th July 1888

Sir,

I received from Mr Phelps, the Steward of the asylum, a parcel of letters and manuscripts belonging to my late son and I have sent him a dollar of the Canadian Dominion in payment of the postage. He says, 'As regards his books he desired before his death that they should be handed over to the chaplain for the general use of his fellow patients in the asylum, and this request of his was at once carried out.' The first letter I received, from your secretary, informing me of his decease, stated that he died of 'brain fever', and by consequence I cannot understand how at that time he could make such a request whilst he would be in a state of unconsciousness. In my last letter to the asylum I requested to be informed how long he lay in his last illness, but this request has not been answered. I still wish to know how long he lay on his deathbed, and what in the opinion of the medical gentlemen had been the immediate cause of the brain fever. Mr Phelps says in reference to the books: 'There were none of any value amongst them,' but this could not strictly be the case, and amongst others there was a German–English and English–German dictionary. I presume this and other German books cannot be of any use to the other patients. An Indenture containing an agreement for him to learn the business of glass-making might have been returned to me.

Respectfully submitted,

Cuth[t] Carr[272]

At such a great distance from the asylum, Mr Carr evidently felt powerless to engage with the staff there or to ensure that he was not fobbed off with half-truths. It does seem rather convenient that Cuthbert should have bequeathed all his books to the benefit of the fellow patients about whom he showed little feeling other than paranoia. No doubt they had more pressing calls on their time than sorting out the effects of dead lunatics. Still, Mr Carr's letter did bring results. A handwritten note to Charles Phelps, the asylum steward, dated 24 July 1888, says: 'Mr Phelps, All the effects of C. Carr might be sent to the father.' This suggests that there were indeed items belonging to Cuthbert that had still not been sent.

Then, on the back of the letter, Dr Orange's reply is drafted in pencil:

15 Aug 1888

Ackn receipt of letter & dollar.

He died of inflammation of the brain but he had been ill for Ten weeks before his death. At the time that he made the request to have his books given for the general use of the Asylum he was in his normal state of consciousness and this did not fail him until within a few days of his death – The immediate cause of death was the effusion of a thin layer of blood over the surface of his brain – We have not the least desire to interfere with your very natural wish to have possession of his few effects and if you will send instructions as to their transmission & pay for the same, the whole of his chattels will be forwarded to you as soon as we hear from you. The weight of the parcel is ¾ cwt.

I must express my regret that you shd have had any trouble in this matter.

I am yr obedient . . .

[*initialled by Dr Orange*]

At least Dr Orange's account of Cuthbert's final illness is truthful (if perhaps incomplete) and matches the progression of his symptoms as recorded in the patient case book.

Now began a dreary process of transatlantic shipments, with receipts and bills of lading all carefully filed. A small piece of yellow paper contains the following list, in poor handwriting:

Carr's Books etc
55 Books
21 Annuals
46 Periodicals
1 flute
3 prs hose [273]

This was the final consignment of Cuthbert's belongings to Canada for which the carrier's receipt read simply: 'secondhand books, old flute & 3 prs hose. Value–nominal'.[274]

The very last item in Cuthbert's file is a final, sad letter from Cuthbert's father to Mr Phelps. He was unhappy that some of Cuthbert's German books had not been included in the last parcel he had received from Broadmoor: 'I should particularly like to have these books and my dear son's translations of the same, on which he undoubtedly would beguile [*unclear*] many tedious hours.'[275]

Mr Phelps' draft reply, scribbled on the letter, says: 'I am quite satisfied that all books, papers and other articles belonging to your son were transmitted to you in the box forwarded in November last.' There is a hint of exasperation in Mr Phelps' note and this did bring an end to the to and fro.

When Cuthbert died in Broadmoor at the age of 40, it seems unlikely that he was much mourned by the staff. It was one less prickly, paranoid lunatic for them to deal with – and no doubt a new lunatic would soon arrive to take his place. That year, 1888, water closets with an 'automatic flush' were introduced at Broadmoor. The Superintendent's annual report noted that they gave 'every satisfaction'. That was probably the most memorable thing that happened in the asylum that year.

Cuthbert's father died the following year, aged 80. The *Manitoba*

Daily Free Press mourned the loss of 'one of Westbourne County's most respected residents ... His hospitable habits and kindness of heart will long be remembered.'[276] Eighty was a good age to have reached, especially given the challenge he had faced of making a new life in the harsh climate of Canada in his eighth decade. It would be sentimental to believe that his death followed swiftly on from that of his son for any reason other than old age, but there is something both touching and pitiful in his efforts to gather in the sad items that were all that were left of his 'unfortunate son'.

18

'The Land of Windmills'

In July 1843, just a few months after the trial of Daniel M'Naghten had established the rules by which an individual might be found not guilty of a crime because they were deemed insane, a young man named William Obins Tillard set off into the Hertfordshire countryside from Hertford, where he lived. He was 20 years old.

Like Cuthbert Carr, William had been labelled as 'of weak intellect' since his childhood but had not been thought insane. Being pronounced 'insane' was as much a question of behaviour management than of any sort of objective judgement. Up until now William's behaviour had been very carefully managed by his father, who was a clergyman and magistrate in Huntingdonshire. In 1841 William had been sent to live with the Reverend Henry Skrimshire, rector of St Andrew's church in Hertford, where he was constantly attended by a 'keeper', Samuel Allen. William's family paid the Revd Skrimshire for this valuable service.

On Tuesday 11 July, while Samuel Allen was eating his lunch, William took his chance and sneaked out of the house, setting off at a run in the direction of Brickendon. This was not the first time he had slipped his chains – three years earlier, when he was 16 and still living at home, he had run away so that he could attend a bell-ringing; he had a particular fondness for the sound of church bells. On that occasion he had been found eight miles away ordering supper in a pub, even though he had no money. That was the first time that William had been unmanageable and it was felt that a 'mischievous irritability'[277] was becoming his dominant personality trait as he headed towards adulthood, leading to his being sent to the Skrimshire household to be more carefully overseen.

Samuel Allen, William's keeper, was fortunate that day, because on the previous evening William had hidden a sharp knife in the lavatory. He had had plans, at one point, to cut Samuel's throat with it,[278] but now that the chance had been presented to him, he took the knife and made a bid for freedom instead. William ran steadily south for around three miles, eventually coming to a halt at Dixon's Farm in the isolated hamlet of Monk's Green.

A farmhand named Thomas Bangs was working by a barn near the road that led to Hoddesdon. William seems to have become confused at this point, as he started to run round in circles; each time he came round to Bangs he asked him which was the way to Hoddesdon. Nearby was a cottage where another of Mr Dixon's farmhands lived. At the time there was only an elderly lady at home, minding her two grandchildren. Bangs saw William Tillard run in and out of the cottage more than once. Suddenly the older of the two children, a little girl, ran out of the cottage, crying, 'They are murdering George.' Bangs rushed into the house and found the younger child, George Pallett, aged 4, on the ground in a pool of blood and William calmly putting his knife away. Tillard had grabbed George, laid him across his knee and drawn the knife across the back of his calves, making two deep wounds. When

Bangs yelled, 'For God's sake, what are you after?' William replied, 'I have done the deed I wanted.' George Pallett appeared to be in shock.[279] He was relatively lucky, though: according to one report, William had also intended to cut his throat but, because he had struggled, George had fallen forwards onto his face and William slashed the back of his legs instead.[280]

The little girl who had been with George was screaming and this brought Farmer Dixon and other men running. They subdued William and then Mr Dixon rushed George to a doctor in Hertford who dressed his wounds. The arteries had not been severed and George was expected to make a full recovery from his ordeal. Mr Dixon also alerted the police and an Inspector Dunn went down to the farm to arrest William. As soon as he saw the policeman, William said, 'I know what you've come for; I've cut its legs nearly off.' He demanded to be tried at the assizes (which were due to take place the following week) and said that his crime was premeditated. He had made up his mind to murder someone the night before, he said, and it was 'a clear case of *malice prepensé*'.[281] William argued doggedly with the police officers that it would not be necessary to prove in court that he intended to kill anyone in particular, and that it was quite sufficient to show that he intended to kill somebody. But when the Revd Skrimshire came to the police station, William was released on bail (which he wouldn't have been, had he been charged with a potentially capital case) and taken back to the care of Samuel Allen, complaining loudly of injustice.

The next day the magistrates were sitting and George Pallett's father came to press charges against William Tillard. When one of the magistrates said to him that he could of course press charges if he wished to but that it was obvious Tillard was an idiot and that he would clearly be found insane at any trial, Mr Pallett agreed not to proceed. He said he only wanted William to be placed somewhere where he couldn't hurt anybody else; he didn't want to hurt the young man.

What had motivated William Tillard to attack a small child so viciously? He had an obsession with windmills, complemented by a strong aversion to watermills. He longed for nothing more than to see windmills, to live in a windmill (to which end he had even discussed the price of a windmill with a millwright);[282] most of all he longed to be tied to the sails of a windmill so that he too could go round in the air. He talked about windmills incessantly and had ultimately hatched his plan to commit a murder so that the judge would have him transported 'to the land of windmills'.[283]

But the issue of William Tillard's sanity was rendered more critical (according to the standards of the day) by the fact that when he reached the age of 21 the following year, he was due to come into upwards of £15,000, thanks to a bequest from his father's wealthy brother James. A man must be able to handle such funds responsibly and if he wasn't capable of doing so then a formal declaration would have to be made. Even though William Tillard had made repeated declarations of his intention to commit murder and had attacked a small child, it wasn't until money was at stake that the law came fully into play.

On Saturday 2 September 1843 a Commission *de lunatico inquirendo* was opened at the Cadogan Hotel, Sloane Street, Chelsea, before one of the Commissioners in Lunacy, together with a special jury of sixteen freeholders, chiefly magistrates. The commission would decide whether William was fit to receive his inheritance. William's legal representative before the panel was Mr Montagu Chambers.

After William had attacked George Pallett, he had been sent to Mr Sutherland's private lunatic asylum, Blacklands House in Chelsea, London. From there he had been writing letters to his sister who lived in Nottingham. The panel heard that they were rather well written and spelt pretty well, but contained such sentences as, 'I shall be happy when I can come and see the windmills, or be owner of some. Dr Bright said I ought to have some windmills – let me come and see, or be apprenticed to some windmill. No objects here I care about, neither common sails or patents, so don't keep me away from the windmills. I am sorry for what I have done [alluding to cutting the child's legs]. Let your William come and be among the windmills. Don't rob me of them, they look so pretty. I would sooner live in one than be where there are neither smockmills or windmills.'[284]

When William had first moved to the Revd Skrimshire's house in Hertford (where there were no windmills) he had asked his sister if he could go and stay with her instead as he had been told that there were plenty of windmills in Nottingham. When she replied that she couldn't have him to live with her just then, he had declared that he would stab her.[285]

William was not in the room at the start of the commission, but at a certain point Mr Chambers went out, returning shortly afterwards with the alleged lunatic. 'He was a slight-made young man, his coun- tenance exhibiting not the slightest symptoms of ferocity; to the whole of the evidence he appeared to pay great attention, and occasionally instructed his counsel, by whose side he was seated, but at various parts of the statements he smiled idiotically.'[286] The London Standard remarked on 'the peculiar formation of his head, together with the idiotic laugh into which he repeatedly broke out'.[287] As we saw in the cases of both Cuthbert Carr and Henry Gabbites, there were certain traits which always seemed to be discernible in young men of 'weak intellect', foremost among them the phrenological marker of the mis- shapen head and the ever-present idiot smile.

Witnesses, including William's father, were called to give testimony about the roots of his mental-health problems. It seemed that, just as with Cuthbert, these could be traced back to early childhood:

> the young gentleman's misfortunes might be dated as far back as three years of age, previous to which he had been twice attacked violently with croup and once with bilious fever; these diseases required violent remedies, such as copious bleedings and depletion, which had checked the growth of the brain and prevented the development of the faculties, and he was found different from other children; he could not speak so soon, and was now altogether imbecile, notwithstanding that the greatest care had been taken of him ... His memory was rather good, he could learn some things, but it was with the greatest difficulty that he acquired a knowledge of figures.[288]

The question of whether or not he had a head for figures was very important, in the circumstances, and the commission looked into his ability to handle money in some detail. 'He was quite incapable of managing himself or his affairs. He had never had much money, but when he had any he would give it away to beggars, lose, or spend it foolishly.'[289]

With regard to his son's obsession with windmills, the Revd Tillard added that he would 'scarcely notice a windmill if still, his pleasure being to see the windmills go round.'[290]

Samuel Allen, William's keeper, was also called to testify: 'I was employed as keeper on the 2nd Feb 1841, and so continued until the removal of Mr W. Tillard to Dr Sutherland's on the 18th July [1843].' Samuel said that when William was living at home, where there must have been a windmill, he 'would look at a windmill in motion for hours together. When leaving his father's, he bowed repeatedly to the windmill, saying, "God bless you, I shall never see you any more." He disliked Hertford because there were only watermills, which he should like to blow up with gunpowder; and he wanted to go to the land of windmills.'[291]

The Revd H.F. Skrimshire also appeared and gave similar testimony to the other witnesses. He also mentioned William's passion for bell-ringing: 'He was always looking at his almanac for royal birthdays, in anticipation of hearing the bells ring.'[292]

Finally Dr Sutherland, in whose private asylum William was now ensconced, gave his medical opinion as to the state of the unfortunate young man's mind, which he believed was decidedly unsound.

The jury agreed that William Tillard was of unsound mind and they backdated the formal start date of his lunacy to 2 February 1841, when he had first been put into special care.[293] William never reached the land of windmills but lived out a long life in 'Northwoods', a private lunatic asylum at Winterbourne near Bristol. The money that he was not allowed to spend was almost certainly used to pay the asylum's fees.

William Tillard was clearly deeply eccentric and rather violent. A case had been made in the formal legal setting of the Lunacy Commission that he was insane and that his insanity had been caused, through no fault of his own, by childhood illnesses and the harsh treatments that had been necessary to save him from succumbing to them. As this model for the inception of madness was widely accepted, whether or not it was actually a valid explanation (it seems to have certain parallels with the misguided belief that autism could be 'caused' by the MMR jab, which took hold in the first decade of this century), it was a relatively simple task for psychologists to persuade juries (in court cases and also, as here, at lunacy commissions) that an individual was 'insane'. Where crimes had been committed by these individuals, they were then deemed not to be responsible for their acts and, in some instances, were spared from being hanged.

There were other theories about insanity and its causes as well, of course. In fact the study of madness grew exponentially in the late-eighteenth and the nineteenth centuries, the types of madness and the theories underpinning them multiplying faster than bacteria. As the interior spaces of the mind were explored and tentatively mapped, increased understanding of mental illness led to major reforms in the treatment of mentally ill people. In keeping with a strong impulse in Victorian society, responses to mental illness were characterised by an increasingly humane and empathetic approach (such as the 'moral treatment' regime at Broadmoor).

The presence of psychologists as expert witnesses in court cases was becoming more and more common and – given that support for capital punishment was in steep decline – if a doctor made a case for accepting an insanity plea, juries were agreeing with increasing frequency. To many lawyers, however, it began to seem that people who had committed terrible crimes were getting off the hook too easily; the pendulum was swinging too far towards leniency. The confrontation between the law and medicine in cases where insanity was a possible defence became increasingly problematic. William Tillard had clearly stated his intention to murder several people – why should he not be held accountable when he carried out his premeditated attack? Similarly, although Cuthbert Carr was said to be 'of weak intellect', his rape of Sarah Melvin was done for utterly selfish reasons and he then murdered her so that she would not be able to identify him. What was mad about that?

Drawing on the rather fluid taxonomy of madness that was a key part of the new psychiatry (attempting to classify mad people of every kind according to sets and sub-sets of 'idiots', 'imbeciles', 'lunatics' and so on), a number of legal minds tied themselves in knots in their efforts to impose 'sense' on the vexed question of the criminal responsibility of the insane. At one extreme was the position psychologists often took, that many crimes, in and of themselves, were proof of insanity: a rational person simply would not commit murder, for example (William Adams, the newspaper editor, had used this argument when he said that Cuthbert's crime 'was of such a character that nobody but a lunatic could have committed it'). This was a circular argument that deeply troubled some.

The newspapers took a lively role in the debate about madness and how it should be dealt with by the law. Everyone seemed aware not only of the near impossibility of pinning down the vagaries of the mind but of the inconclusive attempts of lawyers to do so. A long report in one paper described the law as 'sunk so deep in metaphysical subtleties'[294] as to have lost its way.

In 1853 the *Brighton Gazette* carried a detailed transcription of a magistrates' hearing held to decide whether a man named William Hill should be moved from the workhouse to a lunatic asylum. It seems clear that he bothered the other inmates of the workhouse but he could only be moved if formally declared insane. He had not done anything wrong apart from being 'highly excitable and dangerously irritable'.[295] A surgeon, Mr Seabrook, was brought in and closely questioned. His responses illustrate the problem perfectly:

Magistrate: 'He is excitable, but not insane, you think?'

Mr Seabrook: 'He is excitable, I am told. I have not seen him such; he was remarkably civil to me.'

Magistrate: 'He is not a monomaniac, not a lunatic in particular a point?'

Mr Seabrook: 'Not that I could find . . . One proof of his sanity is, that he is aware of his weakness of mind . . . He is imbecile, he is of weak intellect; I have not said he is of unsound mind . . . The term "unsoundness of mind" would run from a mad man up to a man who is not so bright as another.'

Permission to remove William Hill to an asylum was refused.

In an immensely long editorial article headed 'Legal Insanity', the *Fife Herald* tackled the issue head on.[296] The piece began airily enough:

A man whose intellectual powers are inferior to those of the average run of his fellow-men is vulgarly said 'to want twopence in the shilling'. And it must be admitted that, albeit the phrase is a vulgar, it is a very expressive one, and conveys a distinct idea of that mental state which it is intended to represent. And in this respect it has a great advantage over such expressions as 'mental imbecility', 'unsoundness of mind', 'insanity', 'mental alienation' etc, which are of so ambiguous a nature that they are not only understood by doctors to mean one thing, by lawyers another, and by the general body of the public a third, but even doctors themselves differ so widely as to their import that no trial, either civil or criminal, in which there arises a question as to the sanity of anyone, can take place without doctors of the highest respectability and position being found flatly contradicting one another upon oath as to whether the alleged lunatic is (what is called) insane or not.

The article went on to interrogate every aspect of the issue, using at one point the example of a man 'who believes he has a glass nose' and 'paints the calves of his legs pea-green'. Circling around and around points of the law – the M'Naghten Rules, inevitably – it eventually hones in on the ultimate conundrum:

Suppose a man to be what may be called morally insane – suppose him to be subject to no delusions, and to have a mind perfectly capable of distinguishing between right and wrong, but to have an intense and insane desire to commit murder, or some other crime, knowing all the time that it would be wrong of him to give way to the desire – ought such a one to be held responsible for his crimes? No, say the doctors. The lawyers, on the other hand, tell us that he is responsible, and therefore ought to be punished. And in this case law is in the right and medicine the wrong. For this species of 'Insanity' approaches so nearly to malevolence that it is difficult to see what distinction can be drawn between them. And if the doctors had their way in the matter, the result would inevitably be that murderers would invariably escape justice when it could not be proved what motive they had for committing the deed.

One of the problems posed by the new ways in which medical men were talking about diseases of the mind was that these diseases didn't have a physiological basis. Doctors might talk about a 'lesion of the will' as a way of explaining 'moral insanity' but that was a metaphor rather than indicative of any physical damage to the brain. For some judges (amongst other lawyers), this was too far-fetched for them to accept; they wanted facts, not fanciful ideas and mere opinions. Indeed, it was part of the problem that, unlike any other witnesses, who were obliged to stick to facts when they took the stand, expert witnesses, by contrast, were allowed to offer their opinions – and for some judges that in itself was problematic as it encroached on the jurors' right to form their own opinion as to the accused's guilt or innocence.

The concept of moral insanity had first been brought into an English courtroom during the trial of Edward Oxford, who had fired a shot from each of a pair of pistols at a young (and pregnant) Queen Victoria in June 1840. It was never proved with any certainty whether the guns had actually had bullets in them when they were fired but Oxford was charged with treason nonetheless. At his trial, four medical men, including the renowned John Conolly of Hanwell Lunatic Asylum, appeared for his defence and the idea was put forward that Oxford suffered from moral insanity. As historian Joel Peter Eigen has explained, 'those who suffered from this particular derangement suffered no errors in judgement, no confusion, no delirium. It was rather the "moral sentiments" that were deranged – how one ought to feel towards others, not what one *believed* [Eigen's italics] about others.'[297] The jury accepted the argument that Oxford was insane and he was sent to Bethlem Hospital, eventually ending up in Broadmoor, where his stay overlapped with that of Cuthbert Carr by almost a year (Oxford was discharged in November 1867).

When, eight years later, medical experts laid out a defence of moral insanity in the case of 12-year-old William Newton Allnutt, who had poisoned his grandfather with arsenic, the judge in the case, Baron Robert Rolfe, could not remain impartial. In his summing up he spoke in the strongest terms, saying that if juries did not dismiss the defence of moral insanity it would be 'disastrous for the rest of society'.[298] The idea that a person might know, intellectually, that it was wrong to kill someone and yet not be able to prevent themselves from carrying out a murder anyway undermined deep-rooted social values – and for 'expert witnesses' to try to convince juries that this was an acceptable defence was an affront to Rolfe and others. In this case the jury found Allnutt guilty and he was transported to Australia in 1851, dying of tuberculosis two years later, aged 18.

In 1856 at the trial of William Dove, accused of having poisoned his wife Harriet, three respected medical men gave evidence in support of an insanity plea for Dove. In fact the doctors in question were the same Dr Caleb Williams and Dr John Kitching who gave evidence for the defence in the case of Henry Gabbites, and Dr George Pyemont Smith, who had appeared for the prosecution in the Gabbites case.

In agreeing to act as expert witnesses for the defence, the three doctors had given themselves a challenging task. There was widespread understanding and acceptance of the idea that a person might act under an insane impulse to commit a crime that seemed otherwise out of character, but it was harder to persuade a jury that a sustained campaign of poisoning, with doses being administered over a fairly long period of time, might also be put down to madness. Indeed, under cross-examination, Dr Williams had to admit that he had never come across such a case before.[299] He characterised Dove's actions as 'an uncontrollable propensity to destroy, to give pain, or to take life . . . I think that a person, with such a propensity, committing murder, would not know that he was doing wrong.'[300]

The judge in the case, Baron George Bramwell, was having difficulty accepting this line of argument: 'If a man nourishes any passion until it becomes uncontrollable, that is moral insanity?' 'It is,' Williams replied.[301]

Although he had engaged politely with the three doctors when they were giving their opinions on the stand, in summing up the case Judge Bramwell famously railed,

Experts in madness! Mad doctors! Gentlemen, I will read you the evidence of these medical witnesses – these 'experts in madness' – And if you can make sane evidence out of what they say, do so; but I confess it's more than I can do . . . If the theory of these gentlemen were true of the prisoner, it would be equally true in the case of every criminal, and form a conclusive reason for liberating every person charged with crime.[302]

In this case, the jury seemed to agree with the judge and Dove was found guilty with little further ado.

This very brief survey of the battlefront between psychiatry and the law brings us to a more detailed look at John Hutton Balfour Browne's book, *The Medical Jurisprudence of Insanity* (first published in 1871 and ultimately hailed as a classic of medical jurisprudence).

Balfour Browne belonged to the 'common sense' school and certainly did not accept that mental illness was always exculpatory of crime. His instinct, as a lawyer, was that terrible crimes should be punished: to argue that a person had been subject to an 'irresistible compulsion' (the main thrust of moral insanity as a defence) and was therefore not responsible for their crime simply didn't stand up. What was the law for if not to ensure that such impulses to do wrong were resisted and to dole out punishments where they were not? Setting out the need for his book, he writes:

> The feelings of the community are at the present time all on the side of the humane treatment of our insane and criminals; and it is owing to this fact that the important question as to what the law ought to recognise as insanity ... has been lost sight of ... Medical men assert that it is theirs to say what insanity is, and lawyers assert that it is theirs to say what the law calls insanity ... So, between all the answering, the ear of the public has been quite full of noise and hubbub, but it has not received a satisfactory answer to the question.[303]

There is a further dimension to J.H. Balfour Browne's interest in the question of insanity: his father was the eminent alienist Dr William A.F. Browne – one of the pioneers of the humane treatment of the mentally ill – who had published *What Asylums Were, Are and*

Ought to be in 1837. In 1866 William Browne was also President of the Medico-Psychological Association (now the Royal College of Psychiatrists). Balfour Browne's older brother James Crichton Browne followed in his father's footsteps to become a highly regarded psychiatrist who influenced Charles Darwin, among others. So, in taking this rather antagonistic stand against 'medical men', Balfour Browne may well have been directly challenging his father (and also his brother). Certainly, when he wrote passages such as the following, he seems less than coldly objective:

> . . . in more recent times [the medical profession] has been somewhat incapacitated by the common sentiment of the time . . . The petting of lunatics and criminals was the game to play. Showy philanthropy was on the cards. A man who would say with Emerson that the insane and infirm were 'fit cases for a gun,' was looked upon as a brute. The man who gave a weekly dance and a halfpenny bun to the insane patients under his care, who never had recourse to restraint, and induced the lion mania to lie down in the same ward with the lamb imbecile, was looked upon as a true modern hero![304]

His reforming father was surely in Balfour Browne's sights there.

The chief problem Balfour Browne seeks to address is this: 'An act which in the case of a sane man would be a crime is committed, and the question arises as to whether the individual is sane or insane; whether, under the law as it at present stands, the person committing the crime is liable to suffer punishment for the act committed by him, or is he to be exempted on the ground of unsoundness of mind?'[305]

In what is undeniably a rather long-winded tract, Balfour Browne includes a great many criminal case histories in order to illustrate various points, and it's for this reason that his book is of particular interest. He went to town with his pitiless descriptions of 'idiots' and 'imbeciles', including the particular sub-class amongst whose number Cuthbert Carr had been placed by the medical establishment: 'There is another class [of imbecile], however, in which, together with very considerable capacity for the acquisition of knowledge, and for the retention of memories, there seems to be an entire absence of that power which is used for the determination of the moral qualities of acts.'[306] This description accords quite precisely with Robert Smith's analysis of Cuthbert's abilities – which he characterised as 'partial imbecility' – and it also comes close to defining moral insanity (which may bear some comparison to the concept of sociopathy in contemporary psychiatry).

The specific interest of Balfour Browne's book is that he uses Cuthbert's case to illustrate his belief that the insanity defence was being accepted far too liberally in English courts. First of all Balfour Browne touches on the case of William Tillard and his love of windmills, quoting *Guy's Principles of Forensic Medicine*, in which Tillard's crime was summed up as 'childishness of fancy, insufficiency of motive, absurdity of act, and ignorance of legal consequences . . . strikingly combined'. Balfour Browne's own view on the Tillard case is that 'it would seem to be wrong to hold the individual responsible for any act which was directly connected with his insane craving [for windmills], if it could be shown that that craving was so strong as to be unrestrainable.'[307] The idea of an 'unstoppable compulsion' was becoming well established in the courts and juries were growing more willing to accept it as the basis of an insanity defence. Even though it was no more physical than any other psychiatric concept, the language in which moral insanity was discussed tended towards visceral metaphors which seem to have persuaded juries that it was a physical ailment. However, they did not accept the argument in every instance, as we have already seen with the case of William Dove. In this instance Balfour Browne seems to accept Tillard's insanity as a legitimate defence.

Immediately following his thoughts on William Tillard, Balfour Browne introduces Cuthbert's case: 'It is much more difficult to see upon what principle the criminal Carr, whose case is given below, was exempted from punishment.'[308] This sentence was added to the second edition of the book, which expands considerably on the first. But, in both, Balfour Browne goes into Cuthbert's case in great detail. In between the publication of the first and second editions Balfour Browne had married Caroline Lush, the daughter of Justice Robert Lush, the judge in Cuthbert's case. So he is closely tied in to it. In fact the additions he makes in the second edition seem both to criticise Judge Lush and at the same time exonerate him from blame.

First of all Balfour Browne transcribes Cuthbert's confession word for word, including the second part where Cuthbert explained that his motive in attacking Sarah Melvin was to cure himself of gonorrhoea. Balfour Browne comments: 'Only too many circumstances corroborated this horrible story in every particular. The story in itself was indicative of considerable shrewdness, and all his conduct while he was awaiting his trial was a proof of the possession of considerable intellectual power. His personal appearance, however, was that of a typical imbecile, and some of his acts were so curious as to create a doubt as to his sanity.'[309] Here Balfour Browne adds a footnote to illustrate Cuthbert's intellect: 'Before the commission of the crime he had been engaged in compiling for his own amusement a dictionary of Anglo-Saxon words.'

This is the only place where this intriguing fact is ever mentioned. How did Balfour Browne know about it? The answer comes in the next paragraphs, where Balfour Browne quotes extensively from

'Some of the answers he gave to the medical men who examined him'.[310] Again, the material he quotes is not reproduced anywhere else at all. The key to the puzzle is Balfour Browne's older brother, James Crichton Browne. In 1866, when Cuthbert was undergoing psychiatric assessment, James Crichton Browne worked for a short stint on Tyneside, during which time he studied Cuthbert. It was Crichton Browne's 'minority report' that was mentioned by the prosecutor, Mr Meynell, at Cuthbert's abortive trial ('an examination by medical men from lunatic asylums and they are of different opinions') but the report itself was not made public at any time. Yet here it is, preceded by a long transcript of answers that Cuthbert gave to the men from the asylum as part of his assessment.

Not long after his spell on Tyneside, James Crichton Browne moved to the West Riding Asylum where he became medical superintendent and began to publish the influential *West Riding Asylum Reports*. The 1871 census return finds John Balfour Browne actually staying at the West Riding Asylum with his brother and it seems likely that during this or a similar visit James allowed John free access to his files about Cuthbert Carr, to help John in the writing of his book on insanity. Indeed, in the preface to his book, Balfour Browne acknowledges 'the kindness and assistance which he has received from Dr. Crichton Browne, of the West Riding Asylum'. In Cuthbert's case, this surely breached confidentiality and it is shameful that the material was reproduced while Cuthbert was a patient in Broadmoor. Cuthbert can't have been aware of the use that had been made of these confidential reports about him or he might well have been just as exercised as he was by the 1876 *Newcastle Chronicle* article, if not more so.

Balfour Browne's intention in reproducing all three of Cuthbert's statements is to present him as shrewd and clever: he may look like an imbecile but his powers of reasoning and his sheer callousness suggest

THE APPRENTICE OF SPLIT CROW LANE

otherwise. To crown his argument, Balfour Browne prints his brother James Crichton Browne's report on Cuthbert in full:

> I have to report that I have had two prolonged interviews with Cuthbert Rodham Carr, and I am of opinion –
>
> 1st. That he labours under mental weakness or defect, which displays itself in stolid indifference as to his future destiny, callousness of feeling, unreasonable obstinacy, and outbursts of violence upon real or imaginary occasions.
>
> 2nd. That this weakness or defect was probably congenital, and became more prominently developed as growth proceeded, and that it would be exaggerated by excitement, exhaustion, loss of sleep, intemperance, or great physical suffering.
>
> 3rd. That he is otherwise of fully average intelligence, apprehending everything that is said to him with clearness and precision, and replying with sense and aptitude.
>
> 4th. That he expresses himself with accuracy and facility, and deports himself with patience and placidity when under examination.
>
> 5th. That his powers of calculation and of memory are unusually acute, and that his acquirements are respectable for his position in life.
>
> 6th. That he is perfectly capable of distinguishing between right and wrong, and, indeed, does this with nice discrimination.
>
> 7th. That he is perfectly capable of foreseeing the consequences of any act which he may commit, and of regulating his conduct, under ordinary circumstances, with rational forethought.
>
> 8th. That he believes in the great truths of religion, but is confused as to the doctrine of rewards and punishments.

9th. That he labours under no delusions or hallucinations recognisable as such.

10th. That he exhibits no signs of labouring, ordinarily, under overpowering passions or morbid propensities.

11th. That his general appearance and manners are such as are usually associated with partial mental defect or eccentricity.[311]

If this report had been introduced into evidence at Cuthbert's trial, it is very possible that the jury would have been persuaded by it that he was not insane. The report could not be more explicit in stating that Cuthbert 'is perfectly capable of distinguishing between right and wrong' and of 'regulating his conduct . . . with rational forethought'. These capacities are the very bedrock of sanity, particularly in a legal context. As we have seen, the prosecution did raise the issue of this report's existence and the fact that it flatly contradicted the psychiatric reports commissioned by the defence. It was Judge Lush who ignored Mr Meynell and who seemed determined to have Cuthbert found insane. In the first edition of his book Balfour Browne's comment on this was as follows:

Yet Cuthbert Carr was held to be irresponsible. Certainly not upon any well-understood legal definitions of insanity. Indeed, almost at the same time that Cuthbert Carr was held incapable of pleading at Durham, Henry Gabbites was tried for murder at Leeds, and Mr. Justice Lush said, with reference to a test for the irresponsibility of insane persons, 'In all cases every man was presumed to be sane until the contrary was proved, and that to establish a defence on the ground of insanity it must be clearly proved that at the time of committing the act the party accused was labouring under such defect of reason or disease of mind as not to know the nature or quality of the act he was committing, or that, if he did know that, he did not know right from wrong.'

It was certainly not upon the principles laid down by Mr. Justice Lush that Cuthbert Carr escaped the punishment of his atrocious act. And we would be inclined to point to it as a case in which, through a want of appreciation of the true principles which ought to govern the admission of the plea of insanity or imbecility, justice has not been done.[312]

The 'principles laid down by Mr. Justice Lush' are effectively the M'Naghten Rules – in fact they are quoted verbatim from the official wording. Balfour Browne is not pulling his punches: he believes that Cuthbert's state of mind when he committed rape and murder had been shown to be such that he knew right from wrong, and so he should not have been declared insane. However, he does not point the finger of blame at a specific party.

In the second edition of the book, published after he had married Judge Lush's daughter, Balfour Browne rectified this, writing:

We cannot doubt that the accused [Carr] was a person of unsound mind, but we cannot doubt that, notwithstanding that unsoundness, he was a responsible being, and ought to have been punished for the crime he committed. We find it impossible to believe that he was found incapable of pleading upon any of the principles of the English law, and we cannot but regard the verdict as one of those indications of the pusillanimity of juries which are apt to disgrace that old and excellent institution.[313]

So the difference between the two editions is that Balfour Browne now pins the blame for what he sees as a miscarriage of justice on the 'pusillanimity of juries'. Whether or not Balfour Browne held his father-in-law responsible for this is unclear. And in fact he has further muddied the waters by saying that Cuthbert 'was a person of unsound mind'. As such, surely the law stated that he was not responsible for his actions? The arguments swirl around a vortex of ambiguity. The issues could never be pinned down with absolute objectivity. It would be fascinating to know whether Justice Lush and his son-in-law ever debated these questions in person, perhaps over Sunday lunch.

Unfathomable though its rights and wrongs might be, Cuthbert's case was now enshrined in the literature of medical jurisprudence. Could one come to the conclusion that Cuthbert was not 'out of his mind' when he raped and killed Sarah? He raped her in the hope of curing his sexual disease; he murdered her so that she wouldn't identify him; what's more, he planned a clever and quite complex sequence of events in order to divert suspicion from himself. In mitigation, though, one would have to decide whether his underlying mental illness meant that his judgement was fundamentally unsound and that he was therefore blameless in lacking a moral compass. On balance, it seems he was incapable of properly understanding the seriousness of his actions.

It is a terribly difficult call to make, particularly when condemning someone to hang; and it seems equally difficult to judge in turn those people who were required to judge Cuthbert.

19

'The Laughing-Stock of the Neighbourhood'

Eccentricity of conduct, singular and absurd habits, a propensity to perform the common actions of life in a different way from that usually practised, is a feature in many cases of moral insanity, but can hardly be said to constitute sufficient evidence of its existence. When, however, such phenomena are observed in connexion with a wayward and intractable temper, with a decay of social affections, an aversion to the nearest relatives and friends formerly beloved – in short, with a change in the moral character of the individual, the case becomes tolerably well marked. With some of the traits above described, it happens not unfrequently that extreme penury is combined, and the aggregate of peculiarities makes up a character which is generally the laughing-stock of the neighbourhood or of the whole circle of acquaintance by which the individual is surrounded.[314]

Prichard's 1837 description of moral insanity is a rather good fit with what we know of Cuthbert Carr, but at this distance in time we can't know all the factors that went towards making Cuthbert the person he was: the circumstances of his birth, the way his parents treated him, whether he was suffering from a particular mental-health disorder, whether he was ill-treated by people around him, whether he was punished for things he wasn't in control of. Can we reasonably ask why Cuthbert committed his crimes – beyond his own frighteningly prag-matic reasons? As well as thinking about Cuthbert as an individual, one can perhaps consider some broad social circumstances that might have had a bearing on him – and on others whose crimes are comparable.

Much of Balfour Browne's monumental book gropes towards reli-able definitions of sanity and insanity. For all his efforts to subdivide idiots from imbeciles and the demented from the manic, there is a pervasive sense that madness cannot be pinned down with absolute exactitude. Yet Balfour Browne claims to believe in the ability of the law to draw firm dividing lines between things which, in reality, shade into each other (such as guilt and innocence, or madness and sanity). Relativism lurks quite close to the surface, waiting to be called out. When the concept of moral insanity was defined – or perhaps 'con-ceived' is better – it brought relativist thinking about madness a little closer to being made explicit.

In his *Treatise on Insanity and Other Disorders Affecting the Mind* of 1837 J.C. Prichard had described moral insanity as 'a morbid per-version of the natural feelings, affections, inclinations, temper, habits, moral dispositions, and natural impulses, without any remarkable dis-order or defect of the intellect . . . and particularly without any insane illusion or hallucination.'[315] It was a very useful diagnosis, if one is cynical, because it allowed a person's sanity to be judged on the basis of their difference from the norm. Who was to say what was encom-passed by the idea of 'natural' feelings, 'natural' impulses? Such a way of thinking was wide open to crude societal judgements of what was acceptable. Calling the acceptable 'natural' has always been a powerful way to enforce such norms.

Lunacy was becoming more and more narrowly defined as 'a failure to conform to the increasingly rigid social and moral prescriptions of Victorian culture', as Sally Shuttleworth explains in her very interesting book, *Charlotte Brontë and Victorian Psychology*.[316] Balfour Browne himself expressed this very succinctly: 'a person who conducts himself in every respect like his neighbours is sane.'[317]

The idea of a 'normative' sanity was immensely potent, with ramifications in many dimensions of society. It's quite difficult to disentangle these as they are so densely interwoven but we will see that a person's 'insanity' could be inferred from a number of different failures to conform: to, say, gender expectations or economic expectations (these two, needless to say, were closely tied up with each other).

Victorian England was fixated on economic success. Never before had goods been manufactured in such great quantities, so many products exported and imported, so much profit made. It was Powerhouse Britain – how long could the 'miracle' continue? Perhaps for ever if the nation continued to hit the sweet spot (and, of course, ignoring those workers whose exploitation brought them less of the spoils). No wonder economics was such a potent metaphor: it was the dominant driver in society and was bound to be used to express ideas and ideals in other areas of life.

Nineteenth-century theories of mental health closely parallel nineteenth-century economic theories: as Sally Shuttleworth explains, 'the mind and body [were] regarded as an indivisible circulating system which, like the social economy, demand[ed] careful regulation: over-development in one area could lead to dearth in another, wealth could rapidly turn to waste.'[318] When Robert Smith 'profiled' Cuthbert, he pointed to overdevelopment in the boy's memory and imagination, with an implied deficit in other key areas. Ideally, all of the functions of the brain would develop equally, in admirable balance – a concept that can be traced back (as can so much of early psychiatry) to phrenology, where the ideal was equal development of all the 'separate organs' of the brain – twenty-seven in all – and no unsightly bumps to indicate overdevelopment in particular aspects. Dr Smith did not suggest which areas of Cuthbert's personality might have been diminished as a result of his excess of memory and imagination, but he would probably have included intellect and willpower: a lack of either (or, worse still, both) would predispose towards criminality. He said, 'I may state that it is a recognised fact that where Memory and Imagination are unduly developed or where they are not kept in check by other Intellectual faculties the unfortunate possessor is apt to be Eccentric and to become Insane.' Checks and balances are the watchwords of responsible economics.

Dr Smith further cautioned that Cuthbert's 'disease [was] liable to be increased by any disturbance of the cerebral circulation such as fear, intemperance, disease, exhausting discharges (seminal emissions).' The underlying idea is that 'overspending' is dangerous (of course the discharge of semen has long been referred to as 'spending').*

Dogma about gender roles was powerfully ramped up during the Victorian era. The ideal man became more masculine, the ideal woman more feminine. Body shapes were exaggerated by fashions to emphasise male and (particularly) female forms. It was not so necessary for the ideal man to be visibly delineated because he was rather defined by what he was *not*: in a series of binary pairs, a proper man was, for example, not a child, not a woman, not an animal and not mad. All of these qualities combine to a certain extent. For example, in *Victorian*

---

* Shakespeare's Parolles, for example, talks of 'spending his manly marrow' in *All's Well That Ends Well*.

Masculinities Herbert Sussman posits that, for the Victorians, 'the opposite of manliness is madness'.[319] And the mad man is frequently characterised as childish or animalistic or effeminate.[320]

The ideal man, for the Victorians, was perhaps the successful entrepreneur – to achieve perfection, he would also need to be a respected husband and father, a firm yet benevolent ruler of his own home and family, and an ambitious, high-achieving capitalist in the world outside the home. The binary of the private home and the public space beyond it is one to which we'll return.

Shuttleworth writes:

> While always crucial to the ideological formation of society, theories of gender division took on in the nineteenth century a near unprecedented power and importance, metonymically projecting and condensing the contradictions of wider social debate. The ideological separation of public and private, work and home, which underpinned the rise of the Victorian middle classes, was predicated upon a fundamental division between male and female spheres. Furthermore, economic ideologies of the free, independent agent, the self-controlled actor in charge of his own destiny, were supported and sustained by theories of gender division which contrasted male self-control with female subjection to the forces of the body.[321]

For young men in the nineteenth century, 'failure to show sufficient enterprise in the realm of commerce was judged sufficient evidence of insanity'.[322] Think now of Cuthbert Carr, who was apprenticed to be a glassworker at the age of 15 and found the male world of labour intolerable. He failed to 'leave' childhood, he failed to become a man, he failed to make his own way in the world. Although he experienced sexual desire (contracting gonorrhoea and syphilis in the process of finding an outlet for it), he seems never to have had a sexual relationship and by the age of 18 was segregated in a single-sex block of a lunatic asylum (of course it's possible that he may have had same-sex relationships there but such relationships would not have passed muster in terms of the Victorian masculine 'ideal'). The threat of uncontrolled sexuality, of which masturbation is a symbol, resonates here: doctors declared that emissions were explicitly dangerous for individuals like Cuthbert, the implication being that they were profligate, wasted expenditure outside the proper sphere of marriage and the marital home. (In Broadmoor his masturbation was prodigious.)

An inability to conform to these social expectations could place intolerable pressure on an individual, leading to mental breakdown. Whether or not these experiences literally 'sent Cuthbert mad', I believe these pressures on a boy with underlying mental-health issues would without doubt have exacerbated his condition.

The high importance, in the nineteenth century, of clearly delineating the border between the public and private realms led to the development of a schema for selfhood that similarly differentiated between concepts of 'inner' and 'outer'. A person had a public face and an inner persona; and, as psychoanalysis evolved, part of this inner persona – the subconscious – was understood to be incompletely accessible even to the individual himself. To be sane was to be able to control one's self.

Conceptions of madness such as moral insanity, monomania and partial imbecility (the diagnosis given to Cuthbert) all allowed for the idea that insanity might come and go, or only affect certain aspects of a person's life. Sally Shuttleworth writes:

> Madness is envisaged less as an inescapable physiological destiny, than as a partial state, to which anyone under stress is liable,

and which endures only so long as passion overturns reason . . .
all individuals (but particularly women) lived under the constant
threat of mental derangement . . . the only visible sign one could
cling to that one was not insane would be one's capacity to exert
self-control. Social conformity thus became an index of sanity;
the only measure available to the individual fearful of his or her
own normality would be a willing obedience to designated social
roles.[323]

In his short book, *On Man's Power Over Himself To Prevent or
Control Insanity* of 1843, John Barlow clearly subscribes to this view.
He talks of 'self-government' and seems to believe that almost any
individual is capable of exercising self-control to overcome 'mental
derangement'.[324] 'Man's nobler part' can triumph over 'all the ills of
the body'.[325] According to Barlow, 'a sound and moral education' is
sufficient to ward off most accesses of insanity.[326]

In earlier times, madness had been thought of as more of an absolute
– you were either raving mad or you weren't. As psychiatry became
so much more complex in the course of the late-eighteenth and then
through the nineteenth centuries, madness became relative, a question
of greater or lesser degree: to return to our initial idea of balance, the
difference between mental health and mental illness might hinge upon
'an excess or deficiency of elements integral to normal functioning.
Excessive activity in one sphere might engender physical or mental
breakdown; valuable qualities might turn into agents of pollution if
developed to too high a degree.'[327] At the same time, with the new
approaches to the treatment of mental illness ('moral treatment' in
short), it was believed that an individual might very well be restored to
balance in the asylum and be able to join society again. While this was
a very positive development, at the same time 'the borders separating

[madness] from sanity were being eroded,'[328] and that would have been unsettling to those on the 'healthy' side of the border: it would now be easier to cross in the opposite direction as well.

To sum up, failure to safeguard oneself against the stresses of 'modern life' might result in one's being overwhelmed by madness. In social terms, the fear of succumbing to derangement demanded ever more rigid self-control and conformity to social norms. Key to this, of course, was the requirement to observe gender roles at all times. Thus individuals were pulled in to a complex machine of social pressures and expectations which meshed with each other.

Cuthbert Carr's case allows us insights into the wider world of Victorian conformity and the way that ideas of sanity and insanity were shaped to create borders between those who conformed and those who didn't. Those who didn't had to be hived off from society and hidden away, as Cuthbert was.

As an adolescent Cuthbert could not manage social expectations of himself and tumbled into an abyss of anti-social behaviour. Already exhibiting signs of emotional disturbance, he found himself unable to endure the masculine world of work. As well as being ultra-masculine, work was also a very adult environment: children (as we would see them) soon became indistinguishable from adults once they were conditioned to work like adults. Childhood had to be prematurely left behind for Britain's army of child labourers. But for a boy like Cuthbert, whose damaged personality rendered him incapable of self-control, unable to 'grow up', unable to conform to the male stereotype, work was an unbearable torture. If he could not contribute financially to the family then his role within it would be fatally destabilised. The terrible sequence of social difficulties that led, ultimately, to murder was set in train.

20

'Lo, the Smoke of the Country Went up as the Smoke of a Furnace'[329]

Let's go back to the beginning of all this, to the stackyard fires that troubled so many farms around Newcastle and Gateshead in the autumn and winter of 1865.

The newspaper coverage of the fires was notably unsensational. The facts were reported straightforwardly and there was little in the way of speculation as to the possible motives behind the arson, beyond mention of strangers or vagrants having been spotted near the scene or else the possibility of careless sparks falling from pipes. Certainly the possibility that the fires were a response to harsh working conditions or low pay was not touched on at all. While it's possible that there was some sort of 'conspiracy of silence' regarding a political dimension among all the many local and regional newspapers that carried reports, that doesn't seem very likely.*

---

* Nationwide, the beginnings of unionisation amongst agricultural workers in the 1870s saw the dying away of firestarting as a way for despairing farmhands to punish their indifferent employers where it hurt most.

The fires seemed to be catching. No doubt the 'oxygen of publicity' in the newspapers helped to spread them. Farmers must have been terrified that their stacks would be next, as a bad stackyard fire could ruin a farm's business, especially if your insurance wasn't up to scratch. Before long the circumstances behind one or two of the fires were discovered and all the details published. These strengthen the idea of a rash of disaffected (and probably unconnected) opportunists who saw from newspaper reports how easy it would be both to wreak havoc and avoid being caught.

Two fires (three days apart) at Byerside Farm near Ebchester were started deliberately by Jane Thompson, an 18-year-old girl who worked for the farmer's wife. She confessed to having 'thrust a lighted stick into a corn stack while her master was at Newcastle and her mistress engaged in the house.'[330] And it seems possible that another of the fires – in nearby Lintz Ford – was either also started by Jane or by her brother, who worked there. At a hearing before magistrates Jane said that she didn't know why she had started the fires 'as her master and mistress had been very kind to her'.[331] Perhaps being a servant was motivation enough or perhaps she simply suffered from 'rooted malignity', which was the view of the judge in a similar case from 1844, when Sarah Jobson, a 14-year-old nursemaid, started a fire in her employer's stackyard in Hempstead, Essex, having said, a fortnight earlier, that she 'should like to see a good fire and her master's buildings all on fire.'[332] Jane Thompson escaped punishment because she confessed to the fires only after the farmer's wife had promised her she wouldn't be punished if she 'told the real truth'.[333] The promise was legally binding, much to the magistrates' frustration. One of them said, 'I suppose the devil put it into your head.'[334]

After six other fires had been reported around Newcastle within a week, from 28 September 1865 at least four fires plagued Thomas

Robson's farm at Barlow near Blaydon (causing more than £1,500 worth of damage – around £170,000 today). There was other criminal damage too – windows were smashed at night and outhouses vandalised. The Robsons' very way of life was under attack from persons unknown. On an inspection of the damage, a sharp-eyed policeman, Superintendent Jabez Squire, spotted that glass from a broken window in the farmhouse had fallen outwards rather than inwards, therefore it must have been smashed by someone inside the house. After questioning the family, he deduced that the arsonist plaguing Mr Robson was his 16-year-old daughter Mary. Mary was taken into custody and soon confessed to having started all the fires and everything else. Her motive was vengeful rage after she had been 'licked' (told off) by her mother.

When Mary (or 'the girl incendiary' as she was referred to in newspaper reports) appeared for committal proceedings in Gateshead, she was described as 'almost idiotic looking . . . she seemed to be half-asleep, appearing wholly regardless of the position into which her wickedness had brought her.'[335] She was sent for trial at Durham Winter Assizes (one year before Cuthbert would appear there), where she pleaded guilty. In sentencing her, the judge said, 'You have given no account of this very wicked conduct of yours, but that you had some cause, as you fancied, of complaint against your mother. It is a very serious offence; it shows clearly, to my mind, for some reason or other, you had not a proper notion of what is right and wrong.'[336] That sounds like the basis for a defence under the M'Naghten Rules, but no attempt was made to plead insanity. The judge was relatively lenient (probably because Mary was female) and sentenced her to be imprisoned for one month and then sent to the Sunderland Reformatory School for Girls for three years. As the school normally took girls aged between 12 and 14, they must have bent the rules for Mary. The damage Mary had wrought more or less ruined her father's livelihood as Mr Robson's insurers refused to make it good after the culprit was discovered.

These are the only two fire-raisers who were uncovered and brought before the law. So it is speculation to suggest that any of the other fires were also set by young people with a chip on their shoulder. However, the series was well established (the newspaper reports having given ample inspiration to mischief-makers with time on their hands) when fires started to be set around Carr's Hill. The first of these was at Mr Forster's farm near Windy Nook, the next village along from Carr's Hill. In all, seven fires were set within a two-mile radius of Carr's Villa between 28 September 1865 and 24 February 1866. At one or two of these fires a young man was glimpsed running away – surely this was Cuthbert, already the terror of the neighbourhood and now inspired to try his hand at firestarting?

Although, historically, rural arson was associated with worker disaffection, the prospect of starting a blaze could create an almost sexual charge. David Jones quotes Robert Dew, who was transported to Australia in 1845 for setting a fire at a farm in Walsham le Willows in Suffolk. Dew declared, 'It was the most beautifullest blaze I ever saw in my life, and I shall never forget it to the latest hour of my life.'[337]

Dr John Bucknill, the highly regarded superintendent of the Devon county lunatic asylum, believed that pyromania, or incendiarism, was 'a species of partial moral mania'.[338] In 1849 he said that people suffering from this form of insanity, which affected only their moral faculty, were prone to starting fires 'without any motive'. This chimes with Robert Smith's diagnosis of Cuthbert's particular form of madness. Today pyromania is understood to be an 'impulse control' disorder. Starting fires can relieve tension in the firestarter and give them a sense of power and agency when they may have little sense of either in their life. It is also now frequently cited as one of the early signs of sociopathy, part of a 'conduct disorder' in children that can develop into full-blown antisocial behaviour disorder in adolescence or early adulthood. Pyromania as a response to the great pressures and losses that Cuthbert endured and as a stepping stone to much more serious misdemeanours does not seem far-fetched.

On 7 December 1865 Matthew Laws, who farmed the land adjacent to Carr's Villa, died; there had been three fires at his farm. Five days later, Sarah Carr, Cuthbert's mother, died from bronchitis. Was stress a factor in both deaths? There was a hiatus in the fire-raising around the Carr's Hill district at this point. One might imagine that Cuthbert was very badly affected by the loss of his mother, coming after the death of his older brother and leaving him with one less ally (the most important one) to defend him against the perceived wrongs of his father. A couple of months later, the fires flared up again one last time. There were two fires in the vicinity of Carr's Hill for which Cuthbert might have been responsible. The last fire of all was started on Saturday 24 February, at a farm at Windy Nook.

Nine days later, 6-year-old Ann Brown was sexually attacked in a plantation of trees close to Carr's Villa. Cuthbert was the likely perpetrator of this rape, although he did not confess to it (nor to any of the fires) and was not formally named as a suspect. The firestarting, followed by the violation of one little girl, and then the rape and murder of another, have the escalating 'shape' of many criminals' activities, particularly at the beginning of their lives as criminals (he had also confessed to killing animals). While it would be reasonable to ask why he did not confess to the earlier crimes when he seemed so keen to confess to the murder, it is not the case that Cuthbert had a compulsion to confess to every wrong he committed: he went to Chief Constable Elliott and confessed to the murder because the level of accusations amongst local people was growing so great and he knew that he was the police's chief suspect as well. After the court case over the alleged assault on Joseph Curry, during which those who suspected Cuthbert of the murder had been further emboldened to speak up, I believe it was only a matter of time before he would have been arrested anyway. Or, rather, that is what Cuthbert believed, and he was probably correct.

In July 1866, directly beneath the report in one newspaper of Cuthbert's confession, there was a piece about another terrible child murder.[339] Nineteen-year-old James Longhurst had grabbed 7-year-old Jane Sax as she was walking along a field path on the outskirts of Shere, near Guildford in Surrey. Longhurst held a gate open for Jane to go through but as she went past him, Jane later recounted, 'he took hold of me and squeezed me, and laid me down on the path and lay on the top of me for a short time. He then picked me up and took me into a wheat field amongst the wheat, when he threw me down again and put his hand up my clothes. I cried out and the prisoner tried to choke me. When he was holding open the gate I saw a knife in his hand. Whilst I was in the wheat field he cut me with the knife.'[340]

The cut that Longhurst inflicted on Jane was very severe, almost severing her windpipe. She was taken to hospital in Guildford but when it became clear that she was not going to survive the attack, a magistrate and a clerk went to her bedside, accompanied by James Longhurst (who had been arrested with blood on his hands shortly after the assault) and Jane bravely gave her account of what had happened. She identified Longhurst as 'the boy who did it'. She died that same afternoon.

A farm labourer, Longhurst had been convicted of arson two years earlier, making for an interesting parallel with Cuthbert Carr, if Cuthbert was indeed a fire-raiser. Subsequently Longhurst had also been convicted of larceny and sentenced to fourteen days in prison. When he grabbed Jane Sax, she was a random victim and his motive seems to have been sexual. It was when he failed in his attempt to violate her that he attacked her with one of his knives (four were found on him when he was arrested). Although an attempt was made to defend Longhurst using a plea of insanity, it was rejected and he was hanged in April 1867. On the day of his execution, which was to be carried out by the infamous hangman William Calcraft (infamous partly for his incompetence and insistence on using the particularly cruel 'short-drop' method of hanging), when it came time for Longhurst's arms to be pinioned to his sides, he began to struggle violently, injuring one or two of the four or five warders who were trying to hold him down. He struggled again at the bottom of the steps leading up to the scaffold and had to be dragged up them by force. Fortunately for him, his was not one of the hangings where Calcraft had miscalculated the length of the rope, so he died quickly rather than it taking several minutes for him to be strangled to death.[341]

Longhurst's murder of Jane Sax may have planted the idea of child murder in the mind of another disturbed young man. In August 1867, a few months after James Longhurst had been hanged, yet another sexually motivated child murder was committed. It took place only thirty miles from Shere, at Alton in Hampshire, and the similarities between the two cases were sufficiently strong to suggest that the second was a 'copycat' crime.

On a sweltering Saturday afternoon, three little girls were playing in the water meadows near their homes when Frederick Baker, a respectable young man (he was 29 and worked as a solicitor's clerk in Alton) came up to them. He gave two of the girls, Lizzie Adams and Minnie Warner, some pennies to go away and he then led the third child, Lizzie's older sister Fanny, aged 8, away into the hop gardens nearby. Within an hour Baker had sexually assaulted Fanny and not only killed her but also mutilated her body horribly, scattering the parts over the hop gardens and the fields beyond. He placed Fanny's head on a pole with the eyes removed. He eviscerated her torso and scattered those inner organs about as well. It is hard to imagine the sickening reality of this, both for Fanny's family and for the people who went to help in the search for her. One man, Harry Allen, found Fanny's heart on the evening that she disappeared and then her lungs the next morning. Another man found a single foot. One of the child's eyes was found by a policeman in the nearby river, the other was on the bank.

As Fanny's mother and aunt had both encountered Frederick Baker in the course of the day and Minnie Warner had already pointed him out as the man who had given the girls money, Baker was arrested at the solicitor's office where he worked on the evening of the same day (before all the parts of Fanny's body had been found). When the police superintendent went to arrest him, Baker was found to have damp socks and shoes, and the bottoms of his trouser legs were also wet. It was assumed that he had been trying to wash blood off them. A trace of blood was found on the cuff of his shirt. Baker was nonchalant and cooperative and went to the police station without demur. The next day Baker's keys were used to open his locked desk drawer at work and his diary was found. This contained a number of entries, including the note that it had been 'fine and hot' repeated on 164 different days; he also liked to record his twice-weekly attendances at church. A few months earlier, in May, Baker had recorded that a child had drowned in King's Mill pond at Alton; on the day of Fanny Adams' murder (the previous day) he had written: 'Killed a young girl. Fine and hot.'

The pre-eminent forensic pathologist, Alfred Swaine Taylor (who has already featured in this book), was given Frederick Baker's clothes from the day of the murder and his testing of the many stains on these proved them to be blood, without any apparent doubt. However, Dr

Taylor, under cross-examination, conceded that the blood might well have come from a nosebleed, from which Baker claimed to suffer (and one of the clerks at the solicitor's office testified that he remembered one occasion in the past when Baker's nose had bled). But when Baker was first taken into custody he had been asked about the blood on his shirt: he said that he couldn't account for it and went through the motions of looking for cuts and scratches on himself that might explain it (he didn't find any). He didn't make any claims about nosebleeds.

The defence lawyer in the case, Mr Carter, had a very challenging job. He took a two-pronged approach in which the prongs were mutually contradictory: he tried to argue, firstly, that the prosecution's case didn't stand up because so much of the evidence regarding Frederick Baker's movements on the day of the murder was contradictory. He was everywhere at once, according to all the various witnesses, and there was no time when he could have dismembered Fanny Adams' body, which was reckoned to have needed thirty minutes to an hour to complete. However, if it was thought that he *had* been responsible for the murder after all, then the defence was insanity: common sense dictated that anyone capable of committing such a crime must be mad. No proof of rape had been discovered (Baker had cut out the victim's vagina, impeding the forensic examination), so the defence counsel suggested that there had been no need to dismember the body. Why not simply dig a hole and bury it? The crime was that of a madman. Switching back to his first line of defence, Mr Carter even took issue with the entry in Frederick Baker's diary, arguing that the wording 'Killed a young girl' might just as well be understood as 'A young girl killed' and might not necessarily mean that Baker was responsible. This smacked of desperation. As did Mr Carter's contention that Baker regularly attended church and that to go from churchgoer to murderer was an unbelievable step.

Mr Carter, who seemed to be throwing everything he had at the case, then returned to the insanity plea. He brought up the concept of homicidal mania and said that Dr Taylor, the expert witness, had himself written that a man in the grip of homicidal mania might know that what he was doing was wrong and even know what the consequences of his act would be but still might not be responsible for his actions (because of the irresistible compulsion that characterised the mania). What's more, he said he could prove that there was madness in Baker's family, making it likely that he had inherited his insanity. Frederick's father was said to have been stopped from attacking someone whilst in the grip of a very similar mania. His cousin also had a homicidal tendency and had been in and out of asylums for twenty years.

Frederick's father, a tailor, then took the witness stand, with those nearby perhaps particularly watchful in case he was seized with mania again. He painted a pitiful picture of his son's childhood, dogged by headaches, nosebleeds, typhus fever and other illnesses. Frederick had not been able to go to school until he was 12. When he first started working as a clerk he complained bitterly about the work he had to do and would burst into tears when he came home for his lunch. Frederick had also been disappointed in love when his girlfriend broke things off with him in 1865 after they had been courting for a year. After that he had been suicidal and was prevented from killing himself on more than one occasion. Since then, he had tended to be in a low mood much of the time, as several other witnesses confirmed. In summing up, Mr Carter tried his utmost to persuade the jury that Baker was insane.

In rebuttal, the prosecutor, Mr Bere, said it had been proved that the entry in Baker's diary about 'killing a child' had been made during a window of time when no one else knew that Fanny was actually dead (her body had not yet been discovered) and so, however the wording was interpreted, it powerfully implicated Baker in her death. Finally, Mr Bere rubbished the argument for Baker's being insane, saying that the defence had produced no real evidence of madness (such as the opinions of medical experts who had observed him while in custody).

The judge, in his summing-up, went over the law as it applied to insanity very carefully and told the jurors that if they had any reasonable doubt about Baker's sanity, they should acquit him; otherwise, if convinced of both his guilt and his sanity, it was their duty to convict him. The jury took twenty minutes to find Baker guilty.

In pronouncing the death sentence on Frederick Baker, the judge spoke in the most sombre terms of Baker's crime and seemed to reach for words beyond the normal formalities: 'To say that I feel deeply that a man of your age and in your position should have been found guilty of so horrible an offence is to state what I really do feel, and I feel that it is a shock to our common humanity that such a crime should be perpetrated by a person of your age and condition. I beseech you to prepare yourself for your dread account. You must appear shortly before the Great Searcher of Hearts . . .'[342] After he had been sentenced, Baker wrote a confession in which he said that Fanny's crying had caused him to lose his temper and stab her. He was hanged on Christmas Eve 1867 in one of the last hangings to be carried out in public.*

J.H. Balfour Browne referred to Frederick Baker's case in his book on insanity and crime. Comparing Baker's being found sane to Cuthbert's successful insanity plea, he wrote, 'it seems to us impossible to distin-

---

* The slang phrase 'sweet Fanny Adams' derives from this case. In 1869 the Royal Navy introduced new rations of tinned mutton stew for sailors and these, proving unpopular, were likened to the chopped-up body parts of poor Fanny. The nickname stuck and eventually came to be used more widely to mean 'nothing special' or just nothing at all ('sweet FA'). The tins the stew came in were re-used as mess tins and these are still known as 'fannies' in Navy slang.

guish in any way between the mental condition of Cuthbert Carr and the man who in the same year was found guilty of a similar offence at Alton, and who was sentenced to death and executed.'[343] And he has a point. What seems to be demonstrated is only the lack of consistency in the judicial system of the time (or perhaps of any time): some would be spared punishment, some would be hanged or transported, and the seriousness of the crime or even one's true responsibility for it might not (could not) always be objectively evaluated. The class of both the perpetrator and the victim would always come into play, if only subconsciously. Cuthbert Carr came from a well-respected family and that stood him in good stead, whereas less value may have been placed on the loss of Sarah Melvin, coming as she did from a family of impoverished Irish hawkers. Frederick Baker was a clerk, the lowliest of 'respectable' positions and not much of a step up into the echelons of the middle classes. Money helped too. A key difference between Cuthbert's and Baker's trials was that Cuthbert's family had been able to arrange for medical men to assess his state of mind whereas Baker's had not. Justice was also at risk when the accused did not have proper representation. This was seized on in the case of George Clark, the Newcastle murderer whom Cuthbert later accused of an 'unnatural' assault. Clark refused counsel and had no money to pay a solicitor to collect evidence on his behalf. In court, it fell to Clark, 'a helpless lunatic, who had neither the means, inclination, nor capacity, to secure the indispensable legal machinery of a defence',[344] to defend himself. A doctor, George Robinson, wrote to the *Newcastle Daily Journal* to say he hoped 'we shall not again witness in England the spectacle of a . . . lunatic being left to prove his own insanity'.[345] Admittedly Frederick Baker did have legal representation, but Mr Carter certainly doesn't seem to have been the finest lawyer money could buy.

An individual's path through the legal system, and their ultimate destination – at the end of a rope, in an insane asylum or perhaps on the other side of the world – was the result of so many factors as to begin to seem more or less random.

As in so many areas of society, the nineteenth century saw immense progress in psychology and in the law as it pertained to psychological illness. While Victorian explorers were opening up the last great wildernesses on the planet, alienists were setting forth into the unknown interior of the human mind. And it did seem to be a true heart of darkness, more complex and contradictory than had been dreamt of, and becoming more so the further it was explored. Those left behind might try to follow progress via newspaper reports and scholarly tomes, but the dispatches from the frontiers of knowledge caused profound disquiet. Could these self-proclaimed experts be believed? And were their outlandish claims really to be taken as the basis for changes in the law, that bastion of solid rationality? The debate was fierce, outspoken, but essentially healthy. The psychiatrists mapped the mind little by little, adding contours and features to this strange landscape as they were tentatively surveyed. Their new knowledge informed a fundamentally liberal impetus towards better understanding of mental illness and more effective (and more humane) ways of treating it. Although nineteenth-century medical men were only at the 'Here be Dragons' stage in terms of psychiatric knowledge, the advances they made laid the foundations for subsequent steps forward. Today, we really only continue that voyage of exploration and the way is still beset with ferocious obstacles and challenges.

21

'Cries Unheard'[346]

Cuthbert Carr carried out a vicious sexual attack on a 5-year-old child and then murdered her to prevent her from identifying him. By the values of any period of history, his were appalling crimes that put him beyond the social pale. Yet in attempting to piece together his life, both before and after the murder, it has been impossible not to feel pity for him. In *Cries Unheard*, her book about the 'child murderer' Mary Bell, Gitta Sereny argues powerfully for compassion and understanding in the light of such terrible crimes as those committed by Cuthbert. No human being is 'born evil', simple and satisfying though it would be to believe this. Crimes committed are the product of pain inflicted on the individual by their circumstances and experiences, however difficult that may be for us to accept (particularly as it may seem to absolve perpetrators of blame when our instinct is to punish them).

In an effort to 'diagnose' Cuthbert, I delved deeper and deeper into the literature. The possibilities multiplied alarmingly. He could have had bipolar disorder, borderline personality disorder, delusional disorder, social anxiety disorder, schizotypal disorder – any number of problems with frightening symptoms and terrible prognoses for sufferers. I used a table from a psychiatry textbook[347] that cross-references a list of twelve personality disorders with thirty different personality traits, saying which traits are 'high', 'low' or 'not applicable' to each disorder. By mapping what I had gleaned about Cuthbert's personality onto this table, one disorder clearly emerged as most closely matching Cuthbert's traits: antisocial personality disorder, often also referred to as psychopathy or sociopathy.

When this emerged as the 'answer' to my matching exercise, it was as if the tumblers of a lock fell into place. The chief characteristic of a sociopath is a disregard for or violation of the rights of others. They have little conscience, a history of crime (often starting in childhood with seriously bad behaviour, including killing animals and firesetting) together with impulsive and aggressive behaviours such as fights or assaults. And when they hurt other people sociopaths often rationalise what they have done. Another marker for psychopathy is a failure to hold down a job.

Personality disorders often don't present themselves neatly, ticking all the boxes for one carefully defined set of symptoms. There are constellations of traits, clusters. My 'test' of Cuthbert revealed that he also showed some signs of narcissistic personality disorder and histrionic personality disorder. These both fall into 'Cluster B'* alongside antisocial personality disorder. Given the lack of insight during Cuthbert's lifetime into what are now recognised as personality disorders and the likely crudeness of any methods of dealing with someone with such a disorder, we may assume that Cuthbert's prognosis would

* Cluster B is one of several groupings of the currently defined personality disorders: Cluster A is labelled 'odd', B 'dramatic', C 'anxious' and then there are various ungrouped disorders. Cluster B includes antisocial, borderline, histrionic and narcissistic personality disorder.

have been exacerbated by, for example, lack of empathy, lack of any sort of therapy, lack of special education, not to mention bullying and perhaps even physical abuse (on the part of family members, teachers, employers, for example), born of frustration that Cuthbert could not do the things other boys could do. Childhood trauma, the death of a parent and any kind of abuse all add to the risk that psychosis (in which the mind breaks away from reality) will develop. There is a danger of too much supposition, but I think it is reasonable to imagine what life must have been like in the mid-nineteenth century for someone suffering from an as-yet-unknown neurological disorder, as it seems very likely Cuthbert must have done. In the simplest terms, it would have been profoundly alienating.

The death of Cuthbert's older brother, Matthew, in 1857 and the death of his mother in 1865 disturbed a boy who was already suffering from one or more mental disorders that gave rise to severely antisocial behaviour. He might have been on the autism spectrum; he might have been paranoid or schizoid as well. The causes probably lay in his childhood, perhaps even in his mother's womb: factors that can contribute to the development of psychopathology include the mother's health during pregnancy. Malnutrition, stress, infections such as chlamydia or toxoplasmosis in the mother can affect the development of the unborn child, sowing the seeds of later personality problems. Other factors might have come into play – a head wound in childhood, say a kick from a horse or a fall onto a stone floor, might have caused brain damage that contributed towards the development of a personality disorder. Harsh treatment of the boy – emotional neglect, or constantly shouting at him – could also have contributed to mental health problems. But the ideas about parenting that we value today only really began to take shape from the 1930s onwards. Before that, concepts of childhood were very different, perhaps particularly during the nineteenth century. Affection was often withheld 'for the child's own good' and children were expected to begin their working life as soon as possible (the more acute a family's financial needs, the sooner the children would have to start work). We might wonder that any child survived without succumbing to mental illness. There must surely have been many more people suffering from pathologies, all burning unseen in a world not yet able to treat them.

I believe Cuthbert was fearful of the world and incapable of understanding that random miseries such as Matthew's dying were simply random. Could it even be that he himself expected to die at the same age as his brother, so that when he reached 17 he felt he was tempting death and began acting increasingly recklessly? Bullied and tormented by other people, he would have learned to defend himself physically, becoming hypervigilant and wily. While there's no doubt that Cuthbert was a criminal, his crimes can be partly understood as extreme responses to circumstances that caused him acute mental suffering: the loss of his older brother and his mother, his being apprenticed to the glassworks when he associated his brother's apprenticeship with his death, and his falling victim to a sexually transmitted disease. There were huge social pressures on young people in Victorian England – to earn money, to take on adult roles at a young age, to conform to increasingly rigid social typing. Whatever class you were from, these pressures existed in one form or another.

There have been sexual attacks on women during every period of history and it might seem quite wrong to attempt to explain such terrible crimes as Cuthbert's as the result of social constraints. I don't seek to exonerate him for going far beyond the pale in his ignorant desperation to rid himself of gonorrhoea (and, as it turned out, syphilis too) and of course I accept that not all such acts are the result of circumstances, but at a distance of 150 years from him I feel something close to pity for a boy whose mental disability, whether it was autism or learning difficulties or schizophrenia or sociopathy, would probably have been diagnosed and treated (with whatever degree of success) if he were alive today. As it was, he met a frightening and hostile world as best he could and using what wits he had.

By the time the Carr family left Carr's Villa for Canada, Carr's Hill and the area around it were in steep economic decline (chiefly because the chemical industries of the Felling were relocating to Teesside further south). Three months after the family emigrated, in June 1879, the house was offered to the local Board of Guardians as a suitable site for the new workhouse they were planning to build, but the Guardians preferred a different location. As the area became less desirable and no longer appealed to well-to-do families in search of a spacious home, the house was eventually divided into two separate dwellings – a fate that befell so many substantial middle-class houses in northern England at the turn of the twentieth century (one half always seemed to make a much nicer home than the other, mainly depending on which one got the main stairs). The sand mill next to the Villa that had ground sandstone from the quarry and carried the sand to the glassworks in wheeled skips along a little track fell into disuse: tenants lived in the upper storey and kept a pig downstairs. The quarry itself became a refuse tip that smouldered permanently, filling the air with a fetid stink.

A few different families lived in the Villa's two halves. During and after World War I elderly Mr and Mrs Reece, originally from Cornwall, lived on one side with their grown-up daughter and her war-wounded husband. Another of the last families to live there were the Wheatleys. One of their children, Sylvia, was born in the Villa in July 1915. All these details of the last years of the house are from her 1978 account of her childhood there, which has also been very valuable in working out the lie of the land on Carr's Hill.[348]

During the depression of the 1920s Mr Wheatley was out of work and passed long hours with similarly unemployed friends playing billiards or cards or practising their party-piece songs. There was no electricity in the house, so games would continue by oil lamp or candle-light once it grew dark. Although it was no longer necessary to draw water from the well, the water that came out of the Wheatleys' single tap was peat-smelling and dried up in summer, drawn as it was from a nearby spring. The house still had an earth closet and cesspit and, apart from the tap, the nuts and bolts of life must have been much the same as when the Carrs lived there. There was not yet any public trans-port nearby so, just as in Cuthbert's day, it was a question of walking everywhere. Who knows, the torn-off heels of old boots, abandoned in the thick dust in the disused larder at the back of the house, may even have belonged to Cuthbert or his siblings. The 'imposing' iron gates, installed shortly after the murder, were still in situ.

Sylvia was a nervous child, the sort who frightened herself with made-up stories and always heard terrifying things in quite ordinary sounds. She conflated the old boot heels in the larder with the eels her father used to boast of catching as a boy, so that they took on a new frightening character. The branches of the pear tree scratching at her bedroom window scared her and she was convinced she could hear wolves howling up on Gateshead Fell. She writes of skirting round the back of Carr's Hill village to avoid a porch where a 'mad boy used to sit, ageless, school-less, ready to attack the timid like me'. That must have been just how it was when Cuthbert was a boy, with the local children using all the many paths crossing Carr's Hill to avoid the 'mad boy' if they could.

Sylvia had many fears, but 'one thing that never frightened me was Ghosts. Although I heard early on that a murder had been committed in our stable in times past . . . I was not afraid. I loved the stable, climbing up the stalls, into the hayloft under the belfry.' The boy next door, Nichol Davison, a few years older than Sylvia, 'would show me where the blood stains were and the young girl had died, but my peace of mind was quite unaffected.' In a pencilled note on her manuscript, Sylvia has added, 'This "Murder" was reputed to have been committed by a son of 'Cuddie Carr' who had owned Carr's Villa. A child was attacked by this slightly deranged youth, who hid her body in the Quarry. Date supposed to be about 1860.'

This last trace of Cuthbert Carr and Sarah Melvin is absolutely compelling. Here is the actual process of fact slipping into memory, then becoming story. The facts of the murder have been quite accurately passed down in the course of the preceding half-century or so but have lost their ability to disturb – even a nervous child such as Sylvia Wheatley. She puts the murder into 'irony' marks and says that it was only 'reputed' to have been committed. She prefers to believe that it was not committed, perhaps. Were there bloodstains in the hayloft? Surely not, for if there had been then they would have enabled Chief Constable Elliott and his men to solve the murder, rather than having to rely on the good luck of a confession.

Carr's Villa was eventually demolished in the early 1930s. The whole area was transformed when slums were cleared and great tracts of good-quality social housing built in an effort to ease Gateshead's chronic housing shortage. The house where Sarah was murdered is long gone and the place where it stood bears no trace of it now. The estates incorporate plenty of green spaces and Carr Hill (as it is known once again) is one such grassy expanse. You would never know that the landscape was once characterised by stone quarries and windmills – all is now long, rounded slopes and curving crescents of houses, although there are still the same clear views to the coast. In the 1960s a secondary school was built just behind the Gardeners' Arms. Where the Villa had been became the playing fields for the school but the school itself has also now been demolished and the fields are fenced off with spiked metal palings to keep people out. Yet even today the place retains its strong character of an almost secret place of shortcuts. Footpaths still loop around and across Carr Hill. They're the old paths and where they butt up against the security fencing it has simply been prised apart so that people can still criss-cross in the same way that Cuthbert found so useful. The paths are stronger than the barriers; they stand for the people that use them and the centuries-long use of the land as a throughway to somewhere else. Indeed, they are simply traces of people going to and from certain preferred points in the landscape. People make the paths, and if a path doesn't go where it usefully needs to go, then a new path will be trodden. These ways can't be erased and never will be as long as it suits people to use them.

On a visit to Carr Hill I stood just outside the metal fence, wondering if there was any point in my stepping through, just to stand on the unmarked grass on the other side. I'm not one for going where I'm not supposed to and I hesitated, but it felt important to stand on the spot where the murder happened – as near as I could estimate it. I bent down and went through the gap in the palings. I don't know whether I felt jittery because I was trespassing or because I was close to the locus of 'my' murder. I had only taken a few nervous steps when a man appeared on the far side of the field, no doubt having also crept through the fence. His dog was by his side, some sort of mastiff. Lacking a lead weight with which to see him off, I turned tail and ran all the way back to my car, parked on Split Crow Road (as it now is).

The Carr's Hill murder has never been written about before (or not since the *Newcastle Chronicle* ran their ten-year anniversary piece that so obsessed Cuthbert).

I came across it as I was doing some research into my own family.

My maiden name is Carr and it is quite easy to trace my father's side of the family to Heworth (the parish to which Carr's Hill belongs) in the 1860s. I admit to wanting quite badly to claim Cuthbert Carr as a family member – there is a weird 'glamour' to having a Victorian murderer in the family – but I haven't actually been able to confirm the connection, try as I might. Carr is an extremely common name in these parts, ranging from the aristocratic Carr-Ellisons to the very humble cartmen and forge workers who are fairly definitely my ancestors.

Whether or not I can claim any connection to the Carr family of Carr's Villa, the case has fascinated me: the awful coincidences that saw Sarah Melvin's own parents taken in for questioning over her murder; the local crime spree that I believe can be laid at Cuthbert Carr's door; the enigmatic figure of Cuthbert himself, a misfit, disturbed, readily labelled an 'imbecile' by the authorities but so articulate, so concerned to tell the truth and to make sure that his name was spelled correctly even if he might hang for it.

This, then, has been my attempt to bring the unknown Cuthbert Rodham Carr into view. Although he is only of interest to us insofar as he was a murderer, the sparse record of his life and the reasons for his unhappiness and its consequences have held my interest ever since I first came across him. Sadly, it has not been possible to create as full a picture of his victim, Sarah Melvin, as she was too young and too poor to be of much interest to anyone at the time. And isn't it almost always the case that murder victims are reduced to little more than names, while their killers are objects of fascination? Is Fanny Adams an exception to this, or is the fact that her name has come to mean 'fuck all' worse still?

As I've immersed myself in these events from the mid-nineteenth century, the sense of distance between then and now, which can easily be reinforced by differences in language, in the law, in society, has diminished little by little until I don't really feel any gap at all between those people affected by the murder and myself. The passing of time has a tendency to strip terrible events of their pain. Sometimes we treat 'historic' crimes with a kind of pantomime callousness as if there is no longer any need for compassion and we can simply revel in the gothic horror of it all. I understand that impulse and share in it too more often than not – there's an element of it in this book, I fully recognise. But, at the same time, I have felt touched by all the victims in the book, and there are very many of them.

It's pointless to wish that people in the past might have benefited from present-day knowledge – our understanding of mental-health issues, for example (which although by no means perfect is somewhat more advanced than it was in 1866): not just at the level of the medical profession but in terms of our tolerance of difference in very ordinary, everyday situations. We can only look back to see how very difficult things used to be for people who didn't 'fit in' and try to ensure that it continues to get easier for them, bit by bit.

While I was writing this book, a Polish man named Zbigniew Huminski, who was in Calais en route to the UK, snatched a 9-year-old girl, Chloe Ansel, from the playground outside her house. Within an hour and a half of being taken she was found dead in nearby woodland, having been sexually assaulted. Reading about this suddenly made Sarah Melvin's rape and murder seem much more real, as though the muffling layers of time and archaic language had been stripped away and the barbarity of the crime revealed – no less terrible than the rape and murder of a child today. I have developed a certain sympathy for Cuthbert Carr, but it would not be right to forget the true horror of what he did.

Incendiary

That one small boy with a face like pallid cheese
And burnt-out little eyes could make a blaze
As brazen, fierce and huge, as red and gold
And zany yellow as the one that spoiled
Three thousand guineas' worth of property
And crops at Godwin's Farm on Saturday
Is frightening – as fact and metaphor:
An ordinary match intended for
The lighting of a pipe or kitchen fire
Misused may set a whole menagerie
Of flame-fanged tigers roaring hungrily.
And frightening, too, that one small boy should set
The sky on fire and choke the stars to heat
Such skinny limbs and such a little heart
Which would have been content with one warm kiss
Had there been anyone to offer this.

Vernon Scannell [349]

Reference Notes

Foreword

1 https://serialpodcast.org/season-one

First Finders

2 TNA: DURH 18/1 Deposition of Joseph Bourne, 6 July 1866; *Newcastle Courant* of 20 April 1866 and other contemporary newspaper accounts

3 *Tyne Mercury*, 24 February 1824

4 TNA: DURH 18/1 Deposition of PC Alexander Kemp, 6 July 1866

5 *Caledonian Mercury*, 16 April 1866; TNA: DURH 18/1 Statement of Dr Benjamin Barkus at the inquest into the death of Sarah Melvin, 16 April 1866

One of the Most Wicked Counties in the Country

6 T144/1: Gateshead Borough Police Attestation Book, Tyne and Wear Archives

7   *Newcastle Courant*, 29 September 1865

8   Ibid.

9   *Newcastle Guardian and Tyne Mercury,* 23 September 1865

10 Ibid.

11 Ibid.

12 Letter quoted by David Jones, *Crime, protest, community and police in nineteenth-century Britain*, pp.41–2, Routledge & Kegan Paul, 1982

13 F.W.D. Manders, *A History of Gateshead*, p.299, Gateshead Corporation, 1973

14 *Newcastle Weekly Chronicle*, 30 September 1865

15 *Newcastle Courant*, 6 October 1865

16 *Newcastle Chronicle*, 7 October 1865

17 Ibid.

18 Ibid.

19 *Newcastle Guardian and Tyne Mercury*, 28 November 1863

20 Jones, *Crime, protest, community*, p.42

21 Ibid., p.47

22 *Newcastle Journal*, 16 October 1865

23 *Newcastle Journal*, 19 October 1865

24 *Newcastle Guardian and Tyne Mercury,* 21 October 1865

25 *Newcastle Weekly Chronicle*, 10 March 1866. See also *Newcastle Guardian and Tyne Mercury*, 10 March 1866

26 *Newcastle Courant*, 9 March 1866; *Glasgow Herald*, 9 March 1866; *Newcastle Guardian and Tyne Mercury*, 10 March 1866; *Caledonian Mercury*, 17 April 1866

27 *Newcastle Chronicle*, 30 March 1866

28 Ibid.

29 *The Times*, 26 April 1866

30 *Dundee Courier & Argus,* 17 April 1866

'Carefully Planned by an Enemy of the Human Race'

31   J.B. Priestley's terse description of Gateshead in *English Journey*, p.321, William Heinemann in association with Victor Gollancz, 1934

32   Jenny Uglow, *Nature's Engraver: A Life of Thomas Bewick*, p.333, Faber & Faber, 2006

33   Robert Surtees, 'The Parish of Gateshead' in *The History and Antiquities of the County Palatine of Durham, Volume 2: Chester Ward*, London, 1820

34   *Newcastle Courant*, 21 January 1786

35   Samuel Lewis, ed., *A Topographical Dictionary of England*, London, 1848

36   Joan M. Hewitt, *The Township of Heworth*, p.103, Portcullis Press, 1991

37   Manders, *Gateshead*, p.63

38   Hewitt, *Heworth*, p.89

39   Manders, *Gateshead*, p.52

40   Thomas Oliver, *A New Picture of Newcastle upon Tyne; or, an Historical and Descriptive View of the Town and County of Newcastle upon Tyne, Gateshead, and Environs, presenting a Luminous Guide to the Stranger on all subjects connected with General Information, Business, or Amusement*, pp.137–8, Newcastle upon Tyne, 1831

41   Manders, *Gateshead*, p.76

42   Ibid., p.19

43   *Yorkshire Evening Post*, 24 March 1934

44   http://www.dkrenton.co.uk/research/nehostility.htm

45   *Gateshead Observer*, 3 March 1866

'Then and There Lying Dead'

46 From the form of words at the beginning of the official record of an inquest, TNA: DURH 18/1

47 *Dundee Courier & Argus,* 17 April 1866

48 *Newcastle Courant,* 20 April 1866

49 *Newcastle Courant,* 15 July 1775

50 Manders, *Gateshead,* p.77

51 *Gateshead Observer,* 1 December 1838

52 *Newcastle Courant,* 20 April 1866

53 Alison Light, *Common People: The History of an English Family,* p.210, London: Penguin Books, 2014

54 G. Sims Woodhead, *Practical Pathology: A Manual for Students and Practitioners,* 2nd edition, p.3, Young J. Pentland, 1885

55 Alfred Swaine Taylor, *Elements of Medical Jurisprudence interspersed with a copious selection of instructive cases and analyses of opinions delivered at coroners' inquests,* p.v, Deacon, 1843

56 Ian A. Burney, *Bodies of Evidence: Medicine and the Politics of the English Inquest, 1830–1926,* p.81, Johns Hopkins University Press, 2000

57 Albert B. Deane, ed., *The Licensed Victualler's Official Annual, Legal Textbook, Diary and Almanack for the Year 1906,* p.211, London, 1907, quoted in Burney, *Bodies of Evidence,* p.86

58 PRO: HO45/9680/A47890E/1, 'Petition from the Mayor, Aldermen, and Burgesses of the County Borough of Sheffield', 23 September 1889, quoted in Burney, *Bodies of Evidence,* p.86

59 *Newcastle Courant,* 18 April 1866

60 *Kelso Chronicle,* 26 October 1849

61 *Newcastle Guardian and Tyne Mercury,* 8 August 1857

62 *Newcastle Courant,* 8 January 1858

63   Burney, *Bodies of Evidence*, pp.3–4

64   Kate Colquhoun, *Mr Briggs' Hat: A Sensational Account of Britain's First Railway Murder*, p.39, Little Brown, 2011

65   Communication from the Lord Chancellor's Office to the Home Office, 24 Nov 1889, PRO: HO45/9680/A47890E/2, quoted in Burney, *Bodies of Evidence*, p.92

66   Burney, *Bodies of Evidence*, p.92

67   PRO: HO45/9680/A47890E/1, quoted in Burney, *Bodies of Evidence*, p.92

68   TNA: DURH 18/1

69   *Newcastle Courant*, 20 April 1866

70   Ibid.

71   *Newcastle Courant*, 18 April 1866

72   Alfred Swaine Taylor, *The Principles and Practice of Medical Jurisprudence*, p.522, London, 1865

73   Ibid., p.520. The italics are in the original

74   *Newcastle Courant*, 20 April 1866

75   Ibid.

76   *Dundee Courier & Argus*, 17 April 1866

77   TNA: DURH 18/1

78   *Newcastle Courant*, 20 April 1866

79   Ibid.

80   TNA: DURH 18/1

81   All following quotations about the autopsy are from the *Newcastle Courant*, 20 April 1866

82   *Dundee Courier & Argus*, 17 April 1866

83   *London Evening Standard*, 2 July 1866

84   *Newcastle Courant*, 27 April 1866

85   This and all following quotations from the second session of the inquest are from the *Newcastle Courant*, 27 April 1866

86 *Newcastle Courant*, 27 April 1866

87 *Newcastle Weekly Chronicle*, 28 April 1866. All quotations from the four statements are from this source

88 *Newcastle Courant*, 27 April 1866

89 *The Times*, 26 April 1866

90 *Newcastle Courant*, 11 May 1866

91 TNA: DURH 18/1

92 *Newcastle Courant*, 11 May 1866

'The Particulars of the Present Revolting Case'

93 *Sheffield and Rotherham Independent*, 16 April 1866

94 *Dundee Courier & Argus*, 17 April 1866

95 Kim Stevenson, '"Crimes of Moral Outrage": Victorian Encryptions of Sexual Violence', in Judith Rowbotham and Kim Stevenson, eds, *Criminal Conversations: Victorian Crimes, Social Panic and Moral Outrage*, p.241, Ohio State University Press, 2005

96 Professor Kim Stevenson, personal communication, 10 May 2016

97 Stevenson, 'Crimes of Moral Outrage' in Rowbotham, *Criminal Conversations*, pp.232–46

98 *Leeds Mercury*, 16 April 1866

99 Ibid.

100 *Sheffield and Rotherham Independent*, 16 April 1866

101 *Caledonian Mercury*, 18 April 1866 and *Newcastle Courant*, 20 April 1866

102 *Leeds Mercury*, 28 April 1866

103 *Newcastle Courant*, 4 May 1866

104 Ibid.

105 *Newcastle Guardian and Tyne Mercury*, 5 January 1866

Edgeland

106 Details from the *Newcastle Guardian and Tyne Mercury*, 9 June 1866
107 BRO: D/H14/D1/4/1
108 *Newcastle Guardian and Tyne Mercury*, 9 June 1866
109 Ibid.
110 Details of the second hearing are from the *Gateshead Observer*, 16 June 1866
111 BRO: D/H14/D1/4/1
112 Deborah Cohen, *Family Secrets: The things we tried to hide*, pp.77–112, Viking, 2013
113 BRO: D/H14/D1/1/1/2

'All about the murder'

114 *Leeds Mercury*, 18 June 1866
115 *Newcastle Courant*, 22 June 1866
116 TNA: DURH 18/1 Deposition of PC Thomas Bryson, 6 July 1866
117 David Bentley, *English Criminal Justice in the Nineteenth Century*, pp.230–1, Continuum, 1998
118 TNA: DURH 18/1 Deposition of PC Thomas Bryson, 6 July 1866
119 All quotations from Cuthbert's confession are from TNA: DURH 18/1 Deposition of Chief Constable John Elliott, 6 July 1866
120 TNA: DURH 18/1 Deposition of Cuthbert Rodham Carr, 6 July 1866
121 *Dundee Courier & Argus*, 17 April 1866
122 Ibid.
123 Ibid.
124 Ibid.
125 *Newcastle Courant*, 20 April 1866
126 Ibid.

'Spoiled Entirely'

127 TNA: DURH 18/1 Deposition of Chief Constable John Elliott, 6 July 1866

128 *Dundee Courier & Argus*, 2 July 1866

129 *Carlisle Journal*, 3 July 1866

130 TNA: DURH 18/1 Deposition of Dr Benjamin Barkus, 6 July 1866

131 *Newcastle Courant*, 4 May 1866

132 *Newcastle Courant*, 11 May 1866

133 John Hutton Balfour Browne, *The Medical Jurisprudence of Insanity*, pp.74–5, J. & A. Churchill, 1871. Page references to this book are to the first edition (1871) unless otherwise stated. The text in the second edition (1875) is considerably expanded and the page numbering is quite altered

134 Ibid.

Sensation

135 *Newcastle Courant*, 29 June 1866

136 Ibid.

137 *Newcastle Guardian and Tyne Mercury*, 30 June 1866

138 *Caledonian Mercury*, 30 June 1866

139 Ibid.

140 *Carlisle Journal*, 6 July 1866

141 *Newcastle Guardian and Tyne Mercury*, 30 June 1866

142 *York Herald*, 30 June 1866

143 *London Evening Standard*, 2 July 1866

144 Judith Flanders, *The Invention of Murder: How the Victorians revelled in death and detection and created modern crime*, pp.280–6, Harper Press, 2011

145 TNA: DURH 18/1 Deposition of PC Thomas Bryson, 6 July 1866

146 *Carlisle Journal*, 6 July 1866

147 *London Evening Standard*, 2 July 1866

148 Ibid.

149 *https://www.oldbaileyonline.org/static/Trial-procedures.jsp*, accessed 23 July 2015

150 *Newcastle Journal*, 5 July 1866

151 Colquhoun, *Mr Briggs' Hat*, pp.84–5.

152 *Newcastle Courant*, 6 July 1866

153 TNA: DURH 18/1 Deposition of Mary Melvin, 6 July 1866

154 TNA: DURH 18/1 Deposition of Michael Melvin, 6 July 1866. See also *Newcastle Journal* of 5 July 1866

155 TNA: DURH 18/1 Deposition of Mary Melvin, 6 July 1866

156 TNA: DURH 18/1 Deposition of Alexander Kemp, 6 July 1866. Also *Newcastle Journal* of 5 July 1866

157 *Newcastle Journal*, 5 July 1866

158 *Newcastle Courant*, 20 April 1866

159 TNA: DURH 18/1 Deposition of Dr Benjamin Barkus, 6 July 1866

160 *Newcastle Courant*, 20 April 1866.

161 TNA: DURH 18/1 Deposition of Dr Benjamin Barkus, 6 July 1866

162 *Newcastle Courant*, 20 April 1866

163 TNA: DURH 18/1 Deposition of Dr Benjamin Barkus, 6 July 1866

164 *Newcastle Journal*, 5 July 1866

165 Ibid.

166 Alfred Swaine Taylor, *The Principles and Practice of Medical Jurisprudence*, p.516, London, 1865

167 TNA: DURH 18/1 Deposition of William Stephenson, 6 July 1866

168 *Newcastle Courant*, 6 July 1866

'We Use "Imbecile" in the Legal Sense'

169   Henry Herbert Goddard, *The Criminal Imbecile: An Analysis of Three Remarkable Murder Cases*, p.v, Macmillan, 1915

170   TNA: DURH 17/166

171   *York Herald*, 14 July 1866

172   TNA: DURH 18/1 Affidavit by George Brewis, 9 July 1866

173   *Newcastle Courant*, 13 July 1866

174   Ibid.

175   BRO: D/H14/D2/1/388/2

176   Balfour Browne, *Medical Jurisprudence*, p.29

177   Balfour Browne, *Medical Jurisprudence*, p.42

178   Balfour Browne, *Medical Jurisprudence*, pp.51–2

179   Franz Josef Gall, *On the Functions of the Brain and of Each of its Parts*, p.269, Marsh, Capen & Lyon, 1835

180   Balfour Browne, *Medical Jurisprudence*, p.47

181   BRO: D/H14/D1/1/1/2

182   *London Daily News*, 20 December 1858

183   Balfour Browne, *Medical Jurisprudence*, p.70

'Who Does it, Then? His madness . . .'

184   Shakespeare, *Hamlet*, V. ii.: '. . .What I have done / That might your nature, honour and exception / Roughly awake, I here proclaim was madness. / Was't Hamlet wrong'd Laertes? Never Hamlet: / If Hamlet from himself be ta'en away, / And when he's not himself does wrong Laertes, / Then Hamlet does it not, Hamlet denies it. / Who does it, then? His madness.'

185   *Newcastle Guardian and Tyne Mercury*, 18 December 1866

186   *Newcastle Courant*, 14 December 1866

187 Ibid.

188 *Newcastle Courant*, 14 December 1866

189 All details of the trial are taken from the *Newcastle Guardian and Tyne Mercury* of 18 December 1866

190 This account of Henry Gabbites' crime is taken from *The Times*, 22 November 1866, unless other references are specified

191 *Birmingham Daily Post*, 20 December 1866

192 *The Times*, 20 December 1866

193 Ibid. The italics are in the original

194 Ibid.

195 Ibid.

196 Ibid.

197 Ibid.

198 Ibid.

199 J.P. Eigen, *Witnessing Insanity: Madness and Mad-doctors in the English Court*, pp.72–9, Yale University Press, 1995

200 *Newcastle Courant*, 21 December 1866

201 *Birmingham Daily Post*, 20 December 1866

202 *Newcastle Courant*, 21 December 1866

203 *Australia, Death Index, 1787–1985* (online database), Ancestry.com

Patient No. 388

204 BRO: D/H14/D2/2/1/388/4

205 TNA: MH 94/19 Lunacy Patients Admission Registers

206 BRO: D/H14/D1/4/1 Patient description book, 1863–1877

207 BRO: D/H14/D2/1/388/1

208 *British Journal of Psychiatry*, Jul 1870, 16 (74), pp.311–2

209 Hansard 21.9.1841, col. 695, quoted in Andrew Roberts, *The*

     Lunacy Commission, its origin, emergence and character, section 4.4, www.studymore.org.uk, accessed 2 May 2016

210 *The Times*, 13 January 1865

211 Ibid.

212 BRO: D/H14/A1/2/1/1 Minute book for 1863–71: Minutes of the Broadmoor Council meeting held in May 1866

213 *The Times*, 13 January 1865

214 Ibid.

215 *Pall Mall Gazette*, 5 March 1877

216 BRO: D/H14/A1/2/1/1 Minute book for 1863–71: Minutes of the Broadmoor Council meeting held in January 1867

217 BRO: D/H14/A2/1/1/1 Superintendent's report for 1866, in Annual Reports of the Superintendent and Chaplain of Broadmoor Criminal Lunatic Asylum, printed by Eyre & Spottiswoode for HMSO

218 *The Times*, 13 January 1865

'Every Species of Mischief'

219 BRO: D/H14/D1/1/1/2 Case book: Males admitted 1865–1868. All following quotations from the case book in this chapter are from the same source.

220 *Newcastle Journal*, 28 February 1862

221 *Newcastle Journal*, 10 March 1862

222 Ibid.

223 Cohen, Patricia, Brown, Jocelyn and Smailes, Elizabeth, 'Child Abuse and Neglect and the Development of Mental Disorders in the General Population' in *Development and Psychopathology* 13 (4), pp.981–99 (2001)

224 *London Evening Standard*, 2 July 1866

225 *Caledonian Mercury*, 30 June 1866

226 BRO: D/H14/A2/1/3/1 Journal of Superintendent Dr John Meyer: entry for 25 June 1867

227 BRO: D/H14/A1/2/1/1 Minute book for 1863–71: Minutes of the Broadmoor Council meeting held on 26 July 1867

228 Mark Stevens, *Broadmoor Revealed: Victorian crime and the lunatic asylum*, pp.130–1, Pen & Sword, 2013

229 Ibid., pp.131–2

230 Ibid., p.136

231 BRO: D/H14/A2/1/3/1 Journal of Superintendent Dr John Meyer: entry for 6 May 1868

232 HCPP: 868-69 (244): 'Copy of a report made by the commissioners in lunacy on 14 October 1868 upon Broadmoor Criminal Lunatic Asylum' and 'Copy of letter from the council of supervision of Broadmoor Criminal Lunatic Asylum to the under secretary of state for the Home Department, dated 18 May 1869'

233 BRO: D/H14/A1/2/1/1 Minute book for 1863–71: Minutes of the Broadmoor Council meeting held on 8 June 1868

234 Stevens, *Broadmoor Revealed*, p.132 *passim* regarding Douglas

235 Ibid., pp.135–7

236 BRO: D/H14/A1/2/1/1 Broadmoor Council minute book for 1863–71

237 BRO: D/H14/A2/1/1/1 Superintendent's report for 1869, in Annual Reports of the Superintendent and Chaplain of Broadmoor Criminal Lunatic Asylum, printed by Eyre & Spottiswoode for HMSO

Refusenik

238 BRO: D/H14/D1/1/1/2 Patient case book: Males admitted 1865–1868. All quotations from the case book in this chapter are from this source

239 Robert I. Rotberg, ed., *Health and Disease in Human History*, p.100, MIT Press, 2000

240 *Western Daily Press*, 11 August 1868

241 *Pall Mall Gazette*, 15 December 1874

242 Stevens, *Broadmoor Revealed*, p.22

243 *Birmingham Daily Post*, 26 September 1893

244 Stevens, *Broadmoor Revealed*, p.22

245 *The Times*, 13 January 1865

246 BRO: D/H14/A1/2/1/2 Broadmoor Council minute book for 1871–1880

247 Ibid. Presumably Thomas Garland was not related to the Garland who confronted Cuthbert on the roof during his second escape attempt.

248 BRO: D/H14/D2/2/1/388/13

'The Most Dreadful Crime Ever Recorded'

249 *Blackburn Standard*, 1 April 1876

250 Ibid.

251 *Sheffield Daily Telegraph*, 19 August 1876

252 *Preston Chronicle*, 1 April 1876

253 *Newcastle Weekly Chronicle*, 29 April 1876

254 *Caledonian Mercury*, 17 April 1866

'My Unfortunate Son'

255 BRO: D/H14/D2/2/1/388/5

256 BRO: D/H14/D2/2/1/388/6

257 BRO: D/H14/D2/2/1/388/7

258 BRO: D/H14/D2/2/1/388/9

259 BRO: D/H14/D2/2/1/388/10

260 Stevens, *Broadmoor Revealed*, p.78

261 BRO: D/H14/D2/2/1/388/11

262 Ibid.

263 BRO: D/H14/D2/2/1/388/12

264 *Newcastle Guardian and Tyne Mercury*, 11 May 1872

'Value – Nominal'

265 BRO: D/H14/D1/1/1/2 Case book: Males admitted 1865–1868. All entries from the case book in this chapter are from this source.

266 Stevens, *Broadmoor Revealed*, p.69

267 W.E. Adams, *Memoirs of a Social Atom*, pp.524–5, Vol II, Hutchinson, 1903

268 *Yorkshire Gazette*, 27 August 1864

269 *Middlesbrough Daily Gazette*, 11 September 1884

270 BRO: D/H14/A2/1/1/12 Annual Reports of the Superintendent and Chaplain of Broadmoor Criminal Lunatic Asylum for 1866–1895, printed by Eyre & Spottiswoode for HMSO

271 BRO: D/H14/D2/2/1/388/16

272 BRO: D/H14/D2/2/1/388/17

273 BRO: D/H14/D2/2/1/388/25

274 BRO: D/H14/D2/2/1/388/26

275 BRO: D/H14/D2/2/1/388/27

276 *Manitoba Daily Free Press*, 2 August 1889

'The Land of Windmills'

277 *Hertford Mercury*, 9 September 1843

278 *London Standard*, 4 September 1843

279 *Leicestershire Mercury*, 22 July 1843

280 *Hertford Mercury*, Sat 15 July 1843

281 Ibid.

282 *Hertford Mercury*, 9 September 1843

283 *London Standard*, 4 September 1843

284 *Hertford Mercury*, 9 September 1843

285 Ibid.

286 Ibid.

287 *London Standard*, 4 September 1843

288 *Hertford Mercury*, 9 September 1843

289 Ibid.

290 Ibid.

291 Ibid.

292 Ibid.

293 *London Standard*, 4 September 1843

294 *Western Times*, 26 May 1849

295 All quotations from William Hill's case are from the *Brighton Gazette*, 3 March 1853.

296 *Fife Herald*, 18 February 1864

297 J.P. Eigen, '*Sense and sensibility*: fateful splitting in the Victorian insanity trial' in R.A. Melikan, ed., *The Trial in History, Volume II: Domestic and international trials, 1700–2000*, Manchester University Press, 2003

298 J.P. Eigen, *Unconscious Crime: Mental Absence and Criminal Responsibility in Victorian London*, p.114, Johns Hopkins University Press, 2003

299 Owen Davies, *Murder, Magic, Madness: The Victorian Trials of Dove and the Wizard*, p.114, Pearson Education, 2005

300 Ibid.

301 Ibid.

302 Judge George Bramwell, quoted in ibid., pp.116–7

303 Balfour Browne, *Medical Jurisprudence*, pp.3–4

304 Ibid., p.4

305 Ibid., p.2

306 Ibid., p.51

307 Ibid., p.71

308 Ibid., p.165 (2nd edition)

309 Ibid., p.74 (1st edition)

310 Ibid., p.74

311 Ibid., pp.75–6

312 Ibid., pp.76–7

313 Ibid., p.170–1 (2nd edition)

'The Laughing-Stock of the Neighbourhood'

314 J.C. Prichard, *A Treatise on Insanity and Other Disorders Affecting the Mind*, p.24, London, 1835

315 Ibid., p.16

316 Sally Shuttleworth, *Charlotte Brontë and Victorian Psychology*, p.49, Cambridge University Press, 1996

317 Balfour Browne, *Medical Jurisprudence*, p.38

318 Shuttleworth, *Brontë*, p.47

319 Herbert Sussman, *Victorian Masculinities: Manhood and Masculine Politics in Early Victorian Literature and Art*, p.48, Cambridge University Press, 1995

320 Valerie Pedlar, *'The Most Dreadful Visitation': Male madness in Victorian fiction*, Liverpool English Texts and Studies, no. 46, p.10, Liverpool University Press, 2006

321 Shuttleworth, *Brontë*, p.4

322 Ibid., p.50

323 Ibid., p.35

324 John Barlow, *On Man's Power Over Himself To Prevent or Control Insanity*, p.22–3, William Pickering, 1843

325 Ibid., p.23

326 Ibid., p.41

327 Shuttleworth, *Brontë*, p.12

328 Ibid., p.34

'Lo, the Smoke of the Country Went up as the Smoke of a Furnace'

329 Genesis 19: 28

330 *York Herald*, 7 October 1865

331 *Newcastle Guardian and Tyne Mercury*, 14 October 1865

332 *Chelmsford Chronicle*, 13 December 1844

333 *Newcastle Guardian and Tyne Mercury*, 14 October 1865

334 Ibid.

335 Ibid.

336 *Newcastle Journal*, 4 December 1865

337 Jones, *Crime, protest, community*, p.61

338 All quotations from Dr Bucknill are from *The Western Times*, 26 May 1849

339 *Lloyd's Weekly News*, 1 July 1866

340 *Liverpool Mercury*, 27 July 1866

341 *South London Chronicle*, 20 April 1867

342 *Hampshire Telegraph*, 7 December 1867

343 Balfour Browne, *Medical Jurisprudence*, p.77

344 *Newcastle Daily Journal*, 8 March 1862

345 Ibid.

'Cries Unheard'

346 Gitta Sereny, *Cries Unheard: The Story of Mary Bell*, Macmillan, 1998

347 Tasman, Allan, Kay, Jerald, et al., *Psychiatry* (third edition), John Wiley & Sons, 2011

348 Gateshead Central Library, 942.812 HEW

349 Vernon Scannell, *Collected Poems 1950–1993*, Faber & Faber, 2011

Bibliography

Abbreviations used in reference notes

BRO   Berkshire Record Office
HCCP House of Commons Parliamentary Papers
TNA   The National Archives

Primary sources

Berkshire Record Office (Broadmoor Archives)

D/H14/A1/2/1/1, 2 & 3	Minute book of the Council of Supervision of Broadmoor, Vols 1, 2 & 3
D/H14/A1/2/4/1 & 2	Chairman of the Council's letter books
D/H14/A2/1/1/1 to 12	Annual Reports of the Superintendent and Chaplain of Broadmoor Criminal Lunatic Asylum, printed by Eyre & Spottiswoode for HMSO.
D/H14/A2/1/3/1	Journal of Superintendent Dr John Meyer

D/H14/D1/4/1	Broadmoor patient description book, 1863– 1877
D/H14/D2/1/1/2	Broadmoor patient case book
D/H14/D2/1/3/1	Broadmoor patient case book
D/H14/D2/2/1/388	Case file of Cuthbert Rodham Carr

The National Archives

| DURH 17/166 | Palatinate of Durham: Clerk of the Crown; Indictments for 1866 |
| DURH 18/1 | Palatinate of Durham: Clerk of the Crown; Depositions for cases heard between 1843– 1876 |

Secondary sources

Adams, William Edwin, *Memoirs of a Social Atom*, 2 vols, London: Hutchinson & Co, 1903

Balfour Browne, John Hutton, *The Medical Jurisprudence of Insanity*, London: J. & A. Churchill, 1871

Barlow, Revd John, *On Man's Power Over Himself To Prevent or Control Insanity*, London: William Pickering, 1843

Bentley, David, *English Criminal Justice in the Nineteenth Century*, London: Continuum, 1998

Blank, Hanne, *Virgin: The Untouched History*, New York: Bloomsbury USA, 2007

Burney, Ian A., *Bodies of Evidence: Medicine and the Politics of the English Inquest, 1830–1926*, Baltimore: Johns Hopkins University Press, 2000

Carlton, I.C., *A Short History of Gateshead*, Gateshead: Gateshead Corporation, 1974

Cohen, Deborah, *Family Secrets: The things we tried to hide*, London: Viking, 2013

Colquhoun, Kate, *Mr Briggs' Hat: A Sensational Account of Britain's First Railway Murder*, London: Little Brown, 2011

Davies, Owen, *Murder, Magic, Madness: The Victorian Trials of Dove and the Wizard*, Harlow: Pearson Education, 2005

Eigen, Joel Peter, *Witnessing Insanity: Madness and Mad-doctors in the English Court*, New Haven and London: Yale University Press, 1995

Eigen, Joel Peter, *Unconscious Crime: Mental Absence and Criminal Responsibility in Victorian London*, Baltimore: Johns Hopkins University Press, 2003

Flanders, Judith, *The Invention of Murder: How the Victorians revelled in death and detection and created modern crime*, London: Harper Press, 2011

Goddard, Henry Herbert, *The Criminal Imbecile: An Analysis of Three Remarkable Murder Cases*, New York: The Macmillan Company, 1915

Hewitt, Joan M., *The Township of Heworth*, Gateshead: Portcullis Press, 1991

Jones, David, *Crime, protest, community and police in nineteenth-century Britain*, London: Routledge & Kegan Paul, 1982

Lewis, Samuel, ed., *A Topographical Dictionary of England*, London, 1848

Manders, F.W.D., *A History of Gateshead*, Gateshead: Gateshead Corporation, 1973

Melikan, R.A., ed., *The Trial in History, Volume II: Domestic and international trials, 1700–2000*, Manchester: Manchester University Press, 2003

Milne, Maurice, *The newspapers of Northumberland and Durham: a study of their progress during the 'Golden Age' of the provincial press*, Newcastle: Frank Graham, 1971

Oliver, Thomas, *A New Picture of Newcastle upon Tyne; or, an Historical and Descriptive View of the Town and County of Newcastle upon Tyne, Gateshead, and Environs, presenting a Luminous Guide to the Stranger on all subjects connected with General Information, Business, or Amusement*, Newcastle upon Tyne, 1831

Pedlar, Valerie, '*The Most Dreadful Visitation': Male madness in Victorian fiction*, Liverpool English Texts and Studies, no. 46, Liverpool: Liverpool University Press, 2006

Prichard, James Cowles, *A Treatise on Insanity and Other Disorders Affecting the Mind*, London: Sherwood, Gilbert and Piper, 1835

Priestley, J.B., *English Journey*, London: William Heinemann in association with Victor Gollancz, 1934

Roberts, Andrew, *The Lunacy Commission* <http://studymore.org.uk/01.htm> London: Middlesex University web, 1981

Rotberg, Robert I., ed., *Health and Disease in Human History*, Cambridge MA: MIT Press, 2000

Rowbotham, Judith and Stevenson, Kim, eds, *Behaving Badly: Social panic and moral outrage – Victorian and modern parallels*, Aldershot: Ashgate, 2003

Rowbotham, Judith and Stevenson, Kim, eds, *Criminal Conversations: Victorian Crimes, Social Panic and Moral Outrage*, Columbus, Ohio: Ohio State University Press, 2005

Sacco, Lynne, *Unspeakable: Father–Daughter incest in American History*, Baltimore: John Hopkins University Press, 2009

Sereny, Gitta, *Cries Unheard: The Story of Mary Bell*, London: Macmillan, 1998

Shuttleworth, Sally, *Charlotte Brontë and Victorian Psychology*, Cambridge: Cambridge University Press, 1996

Smith, Roger, *Trial by Medicine: Insanity and Responsibility in Victorian Trials*, Edinburgh: Edinburgh University Press, 1984

Stevens, Mark, *Broadmoor Revealed: Victorian crime and the lunatic asylum*, Barnsley: Pen & Sword, 2013

Sussman, Herbert, *Victorian Masculinities: Manhood and Masculine Politics in Early Victorian Literature and Art*, Cambridge: Cambridge University Press, 1995

Tasman, Allan, Kay, Jerald, et al., *Psychiatry* (Third Edition), John Wiley & Sons, 2011

Taylor, Alfred Swaine, *Elements of Medical Jurisprudence interspersed with a copious selection of instructive cases and analyses of opinions delivered at coroners' inquests*, London: Deacon, 1843

Taylor, Alfred Swaine, *Medical Jurisprudence*, London, 1845

Taylor, Alfred Swaine, *The Principles and Practice of Medical Jurisprudence*, London, 1865

Uglow, Jenny, *Nature's Engraver: A Life of Thomas Bewick*, London: Faber & Faber, 2006

Warren, Kenneth, *Chemical Foundations: The Alkali Industry in Britain to 1926*, Oxford: Oxford University Press, 1980

Watson, Katherine D., *Forensic Medicine in Western Society: A History*, London: Routledge, 2010

Woodhead, German Sims, *Practical Pathology: A Manual for Students and Practitioners*, 2nd edition, Edinburgh: Young J. Pentland, 1885

Index

Acknowledgements

Very many thanks for their kind help to staff at: Berkshire Record Office, especially Margaret Lord and the County Archivist, Mark Stevens; Durham Record Office; Durham University Special Collections, especially Sam Booth; Tyne and Wear Archives; Gateshead Central Library, especially Yvonne Kennedy; Newcastle Central Library; the National Archives.

I am also grateful to Newcastle Central Library, Gateshead Central Library and particularly the marvellous British Newspaper Archive (www.britishnewspaperarchive.co.uk) for access to historic newspapers; and to Berkshire Record Office and the West London Mental Health NHS Trust for access to the Broadmoor Archives.

Special thanks to Jon Riley and Rose Tomaszewska at Quercus. Rose, you are an incredible editor. And love to David, Charlie and Dora Housham.

R